Jeanette Swanson

Dissociative Children

Bridging the Inner and Outer Worlds

LYNDA SHIRAR

W. W. Norton & Company
New York   London

"Where is That Girl" reprinted by permission of the author, Corrine Ardoin.

Two entries from the newsletter *Come Together* reprinted with the permission of the publisher: "Integration" from Vol. 3, Issue 1, 1993, and "Feeling Different" from Vol. 3, Issue 2, 1993.

Table 2.1 reprinted with permission of *Dissociation* and Pamela A. Reagor.

Table 2.2 reprinted with the permission of Lexington Books, an imprint of Simon & Schuster Inc. from *Out of Darkness: Exploring Satanism and Ritual Abuse* by David K. Sakheim and Susan E. Devine. Copyright © 1992 by Lexington Books.

For information about permission to reproduce selections
from this book, write to
Permissions, W.W. Norton & Company, Inc.,
500 Fifth Avenue, New York, New York, 10110

Library of Congress Cataloging-in-Publication Data

Shirar, Lynda.
   Dissociative children : bridging the inner and outer worlds /
Lynda Shirar.
       p.   cm.
   A Norton professional book.
   Includes bibliographical references and index.
   ISBN 0-393-70213-8
   1. Dissociative disorders.   2. Personality disorders in children.
3. Child psychotherapy.   4. Dissociation (Psychology)   I. Title.
RJ506.P32S55   1996
618.92′89—dc20   95-32040   CIP

W.W. Norton & Company, Inc., 500 Fifth Avenue, New York, NY 10110
W.W. Norton & Company Ltd., 10 Coptic Street, London WC1A 1PU

1   2   3   4   5   6 7   8   9   0

This book is dedicated
to the children
whose stories live in this book
and whose courage to live, love, and laugh
affirm the human spirit.

CONTENTS

PREFACE

Dissociation is an old concept that is finding new relevance today. Children quite commonly use dissociative defenses — and most dissociative disorders start in childhood. My work as a counselor has confronted me with evidence of the worries and pain that many children endure in secret and of the need for dissociative defenses. A child's family is his or her world for many years; sometimes the trauma a child experiences in that world is inflicted unintentionally — but it is painful nonetheless. When trauma is severe and chronic, dissociation becomes more than a refuge. Survival may depend on being able to believe that "it isn't happening — not to me." But my clients have shown me that even as little children we fight to know what we hide from ourselves; we fight to feel — even when it is too painful to feel. We fight to become who we are, the "me" we were meant to be.

Writing this book was an outgrowth of getting to know the children who come to me for therapy. Their vulnerability, their strength, and their wisdom have left lasting impressions. The children and their families who are part of this book have been teachers, as well as clients, and have touched my heart. I want to share what I have learned from them.

I also want to encourage therapists to work with children, to respond to the challenges children give us — to see them, get to know them, believe them, and learn from them. Dissociative children, who of necessity escape inside themselves, can learn to readapt to the world. Given early intervention and a safe environment, they respond like seedlings to sunlight. Therapy becomes the footbridge the child uses, a path into feeling and knowing and finding oneself—and back out again to family—a bridge between the inner and outer worlds.

I am thankful for friends and colleagues who have supported me while I immersed myself in this project, and who have bolstered my spirits throughout. Heartfelt appreciation goes to Doris Bryant, for being there, and for believing in me always; to Judy Kessler, one of my first and best teachers; to Susan Munro, my editor, for both providing and prodding me with this opportunity; to Jean DeCosta and Julie Rider for their caring and thoughtful comments on the manuscript; to Karen Bernstein for humor and understanding when I needed them both; and to Vicki Graham-Costain and Carol Waldschmidt for wisdom kindly and gladly given, more than once.

The clinical examples that appear in this book are from a compilation of cases. To preserve the confidentiality of the children and their families, I have altered all identifying information, including names. Anecdotal material and artwork are provided with permission.

Where Is that Girl?

Where is the girl who they're calling?
Can she be found somewhere near?
Is she the one that came into this world
But has lost to her fear?

Oh, she might be me
  and I might be her
  but you'll never know
  if it's me or if it's she.

CORRINE ARDOIN

Chapter One

DISSOCIATION: WHAT IT IS AND HOW IT WORKS

> "What a curious feeling!" said Alice, "I must be shutting up like a telescope!" And so it was indeed: she was now only ten inches high, and her face brightened up at the thought that she was now the right size for going through the little door into that lovely garden. First, however, she waited for a few minutes to see if she was going to shrink any further: she felt a little nervous about this; "for it might end, you know," said Alice to herself, "in my going out altogether, like a candle. I wonder what I should be like then?"
>
> From *Alice's Adventures in Wonderland*

Dissociation is that wonderful ability to lose oneself in a daydream, to escape humdrum reality in fantasy or a good book. The dissociator can "make" herself different or "make" her surroundings change, just with the imagination. Dissociation is also the ability to make unpleasant thoughts and feelings go away inside somewhere so one can forget about them, at least temporarily. Under conditions of extreme duress, people may even put away whole experiences that might otherwise be too hard to bear.

To dissociate is to "sever the association of one thing from another" (Braun, 1984, p. 171, cited in Braun, 1986), to separate certain information from conscious awareness. Escapes can be very useful. But if dissociation becomes extreme, it can feel like the process itself gets out of control and "takes over," just as it did for Alice in Wonderland. Dissociation is not good or bad per se; it is

3

something that can be adaptive and helpful—or just the opposite (Donovan & McIntyre, 1990). And we all do it to varying degrees and abilities, especially during childhood.

NORMAL CHILDHOOD DISSOCIATION

Children and teenagers tend to dissociate more than adults (Putnam, 1993; Ross, Ryan, Anderson, Ross, & Hardy, 1989). Children use dissociation quite naturally in play and as a defense mechanism; both are developmentally normal. Age three to six in particular is known as a time of play and imagination (Briggs, 1970; Erikson, 1950); with the imagination one can bend reality, escape from it—or create a new one. A finger can become a toy gun and a broom a galloping horse. Children can "be" anything they want and make their playmates "be" something else too, as in "You be the hunter, and I'll be the bear."

From a view of the world that Piaget (1963) called "animistic," young children can find living, feeling qualities in inanimate objects such as teddy bears or cars or rocks; they can also project themselves and their thoughts and feelings onto such objects and then "have a conversation." Thus, a child finds it easy to talk about how "sad" the storybook house feels when no one lives there, or to experience the stuffed teddy bear as "asking" for sugar and cream at the tea party.

More than the adult capacity to visualize a mental image, or to hear a song in one's head, a child's imaginary capacities take on a quality closer to what would be called hallucination or delusion in an adult. The child interacts with objects as if those objects were moving, thinking, talking, and feeling on their own. In essence, the child is able to make the "not real" become real, and the real become not real. Even after children are old enough to know there is no tooth fairy or that houses don't really have feelings, they are still able to get into pretending quite easily.

Teenagers, too, indulge in fantasy and role-play, which is also developmentally appropriate. Teens "try on" different clothing, hairstyles, ways of talking, thinking, and behaving; and they often choose as their models not only their peers, but characters from television, movies, books, and video games. As Putnam (1991a) points out, "[a] central feature of such make-believe worlds is the redefinition of the child's or adolescent's identity and powers" (p. 524). The shy child who feels clumsy and homely can imagine himself a glamorous rock star or all-powerful cartoon hero.

Dissociation is also one of the first defensive coping methods children have available to them. Other more sophisticated defenses, such as rationalization, come with age and greater cognitive abilities (McElroy, 1992). As a defense, dissociation is very useful in that it allows the child to mentally "step around" scary information while in the process of encoding it, or storing it in memory, or retrieving other information from memory.

In the resulting altered state of consciousness, the scary information doesn't get cataloged and filed in conscious memory as it otherwise would (Ludwig, 1983). And when the child goes to remember it, that information isn't filed where it "should be," so the child may not be able to "find" it in memory—unless she can get back into that altered state. Young children commonly use dissociation to cope with difficult feelings, such as anxiety, guilt, or anger—especially if those feelings are strong and are implicitly or explicitly forbidden by adults (Bowman, Blix, & Coons, 1985).

For example, if Susie eats a candy when she has been told to wait until after dinner, anxiety strikes when Mother confronts her. Susie may say, "I didn't eat it!" even though Mother can see the chocolate on her face. While adults often view this kind of behavior as lying, in a young child the dissociation may be so complete that she may not remember wanting the candy, taking it, or tasting it. The dissociative response helps her disengage from the guilt she feels upon being confronted by Mother. She can truly believe that someone else—not herself—ate the missing candy. It's easy to see how dissociation can be helpful in warding off scary experiences, "bad" thoughts and feelings, body pain, and behaviors that might have negative consequences. With dissociation, the child doesn't have to know, feel, or experience.

These kinds of normal dissociative behaviors usually decrease with age. Dissociative experiences peak during the latency years around age 10, and steadily decline through teens and into adulthood (Putnam, 1993). Since dissociation is a common ability and defense strategy of childhood, it stands to reason that dissociative disorders might also have their beginnings in childhood. It is not yet clear just how dissociation changes developmentally with age, but we do know that dissociation can range from what is considered normal to what is unmistakably out of the ordinary, even in children (Braun, 1986; Malinosky-Rummell & Hoier, 1991; Putnam, 1991a, 1993).

THE DISSOCIATIVE CONTINUUM

Dissociation takes many forms, in both children and adults, and varies also in degree. Dissociative experiences exist on a continuum, from normal or minor dissociation to severe dissociative disorders (Braun, 1986, 1988; Putnam, 1991a, 1991b; Ross et al., 1992). The continuum of dissociation and its overlap with dissociative disorders is illustrated in Figure 1.1.

On the mild end of the dissociative scale are normal nondefensive dissociative behaviors. These include children's imaginary play, daydreaming, and the commuter's "highway hypnosis." Some people can become so absorbed in a book or a movie that they lose track of time. Other voluntary altered states of consciousness occur in mystical experiences and meditation; these, too, are considered normal. Ordinary dissociation also allows us to have "two tracks" going at once in our heads. Many routine tasks of daily living, such as brushing teeth and tying shoes, can be done on "auto pilot." These behaviors become relegated to a separate state of consciousness we call "automatic," and we don't have to give them undivided attention to get them done.

From this point on along the continuum, dissociative experiences are used more as a defense, rather than for play or efficiency. I include denial and repression next. While these two defenses are conceptually different from dissociation in some ways, the use of these terms in discussing dissociative processes is common. Braun (1988, p. 6) refers to repression as a "dissociative episode"; Hornstein (1994) notes that denial involves "isolating" an aspect of one's experience. Generically speaking, both denial and repression are ways of separating unpleasant thoughts, feelings, or experi-

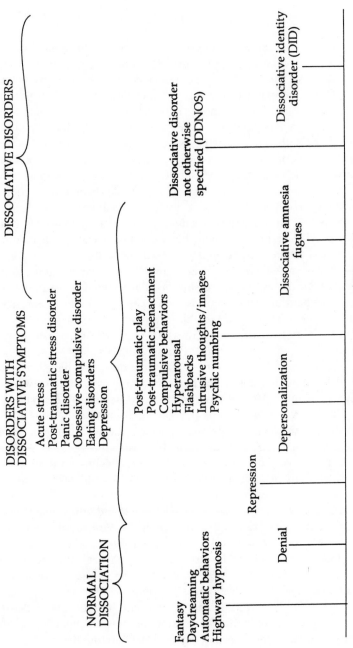

Figure 1.1 The Continuum of Dissociation.

ences from conscious awareness, a process which fits a more inclusive model of dissociation (Braun, 1988; Ludwig, 1983).

Denial is a fairly normal, temporary defense common to people who are undergoing a physical or emotional shock. The person who has lost a loved one states, "He can't be dead"; the person who has just tested positive for HIV says, "You must have made a mistake." With time, most people can drop protective denial and face the experience. But in other cases, people prolong denial as a way to block awareness or to put off taking personal responsibility for certain behaviors or feelings. For example, people with addictions may tell themselves, "I can stop drinking anytime," or "Smoking only one pack a day won't hurt." Denial can temporarily help with psychic or physical pain, but causes problems when it is allowed to become extreme or a major way of coping with anxiety.

Repression is a way to "press down" unwanted thoughts, feelings, or awarenesses. Repression "is a motivated forgetting that subtracts painful items from the data bank of available memories, moving them as it were into 'dead storage' . . . [but] the storehouse has its own rules . . . by which some items can break out again, disguised as symptoms" (Pruyser, 1981, pp. 144–145). Following successful repression, the person does not have to consciously know about scary or painful events, even while behaviorally reenacting aspects of those events unconsciously (Terr, 1994).

The farther one goes along the dissociative continuum, the more the dissociative response seems to engage the whole organism in altering the person's *experience* of life; from this point on, if the dissociative symptoms are persistent or severe enough, they may be considered dissociative disorders. Derealization and depersonalization are next. Derealization is a change in perception of the *external* world; objects may seem to shrink or expand, or change their shape. Depersonalization is a change in the perception or experience of the *self*; it may feel like being a robot or like "living in a dream." In adolescents depersonalization may be fairly common and transient (Putnam, 1991b). Perhaps this is because teens are changing physically, psychologically, and socially faster than they can keep up! Depersonalization can occur in drug abuse, sleep deprivation, schizophrenia, depression, near-death experiences, epilepsy, phobias, and migraine headaches (Putnam, 1985). People may also experience derealization or depersonalization when they have received a physical or emotional shock to the system, or when they feel extremely anxious. Again, dissociation acts as a defense.

Next on the continuum are dissociative amnesia and fugue states. By this point on the continuum, memory processes are highly involved in the dissociative experiences, and a person's sense of self-identity may become more disturbed also. Dissociative amnesia involves an inability to recall important things about oneself. It is different from an organically caused memory loss (Putnam, 1991b). Usually the amnesia is related to trauma or stress (American Psychiatric Association, 1994). Fugues are considered more severe, and involve sudden travel away from home or work, inability to remember some or all of the past, and confusion about self-identity (American Psychiatric Association, 1994). Again, dissociative fugue usually starts with the occurrence of a traumatic event or severe, overwhelming stress. Like amnesia, it allows the person to separate from awareness of the trauma.

At the extreme end of the dissociative continuum are dissociative disorder not otherwise specified (DDNOS) and dissociative identity disorder (DID). Both of these disorders commonly develop in response to overwhelming trauma. DDNOS is a classification for severe dissociation that does not meet the criteria for DID or any other single dissociative disorder. The requirements for dissociative identity disorder are: two or more distinct identities or personality states that recurrently take control of the person's behavior; inability to recall important personal information, which can't be explained by ordinary forgetfulness; and it is not due to a medical condition or to the use of drugs (American Psychiatric Association, 1994). In DID both memory and identity are affected, and unlike the previous disorders, dissociation at this level is more highly organized. Previously called multiple personality disorder (MPD), DID commonly begins in early childhood.

HOW PATHOLOGICAL DISSOCIATION DEVELOPS

"Pathological" is a term used to describe dissociation that begins as a defense but then creates problems for the child in other ways. When escaping from unpleasant thoughts, feelings, or experiences becomes a major priority in a child's life, dissociative symptoms begin to take some common behavioral forms: forgetting, "lying," stealing, acting out, destructive behaviors, etc. The dissociative aspect of these symptoms may be overlooked because of the glare of the behavior problems that are present. In cases where dissociative defenses fall short of dissociative *disorders*, the child's use of dissociation may still be contributing to his or her difficulties. Dissociative responses become a problem "when they prevent adaptive change" (Donovan & McIntyre, 1990, p. 64). I find that many children and adolescents *without a history of abuse* can get locked into dissociative defenses in an effort to cope with overwhelming stresses, expectations, losses, or fears in their lives. What looks like a very small problem to an adult can feel like trauma to a child. Figure 1.2, drawn by a child who had experienced a severe loss

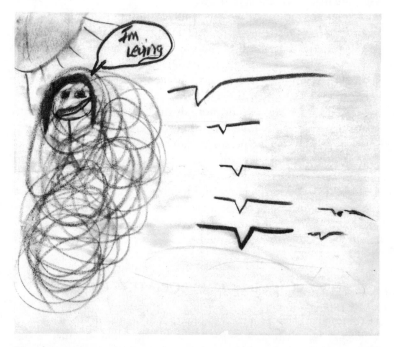

Figure 1.2 "I'm leaving," a child's concept of dissociating. Drawing by a boy, age 11.

years earlier, shows how he dissociated his own problem behaviors and difficult feelings.

The more habitual or chronic the use of dissociation as a defense, the more likely it is to impinge on the child's ability to function *nondefensively* in other ways. There are side effects of using dissociation day in and day out to cope with inner turmoil and traumatic environmental conditions; the energy spent on psychological survival may infringe on the child's ability to do other things in life. Self-defense may leave little room for paying attention at school, for learning socially accepted ways of interacting with other children, or for generally getting needs met that fall below those of survival.

Dissociation affects perception, thinking, feeling, behavior, and memory. Some children increase their use of dissociation as a defense until it becomes part of their personality style or behavioral style. Such children may show disorientation, trance-like behaviors, and disturbances in memory and in sense of self (Putnam, 1993). If the reasons for needing dissociative defenses are big enough, and happen often enough, or if the impact of trauma or loss is powerful enough, dissociative symptoms can become dissociative disorders.

Unfortunately, pathological dissociation may be a necessary tool for children who are trying to live through severe trauma and its aftereffects. Chronic abuse or the effects of any prolonged trauma may propel a child into using dissociation as a way of life. In many circumstances, dissociation is quite adaptive and helpful. Unless the abusive person is removed from the child, or the child from the traumatic environment, or until the trauma and loss are satisfactorily resolved within the child, he or she may need the protection dissociation provides.

The course of development for pathological dissociation and dissociative disorders has not yet been fully clarified, but several factors have been identified as playing major roles (Putnam, 1991a). Trauma and abuse are considered "dissociogenic" (Putnam, 1991b; Spiegel, 1991); sexual abuse is particularly so (Malinosky-Rummell & Hoier, 1991). Other factors that affect the development of a dissociative disorder are: infant behavioral states and attachment processes, biological changes related to trauma, state-dependent learning, and other familial factors.

Infant Behavioral States

Recent research on infants indicates that humans are not born with an integrated sense of "self," but rather with various discrete behavioral states of consciousness (Albini & Pease, 1989; Wolff, 1987 & 1989, as cited in Putnam, 1991a). Continuity in awareness of "who I am" develops over the first six to eight years of life (Albini & Pease, 1989; Putnam, 1991a).

> Studies have shown that infant behavior is composed of relatively predictable sequences of specific states that are anchored around sleep and mealtimes. . . . Switches between behavioral states are often triggered by environmental stimuli. . . . Regulation of behavioral state is an important developmental task which, at first, is largely the caretaker's responsibility, but is increasingly transferred to the maturing child. We see correlates of this increasing self-control process in increased attention span, increased resistance to environmental distractions and disruptions, increased ability to return to task following a disruption, and increased ability to appropriately match behavioral state to social context. (Putnam, 1991a, pp. 524–525)

Good parenting helps the infant to smooth out the transitions between separate behavioral states and begin to experience himself as a continuous being with a single identity. This might be related also to attachment cycles in infants and young children, which are part of a psychobiological process that harks back to instinctive survival in the animal world (Bowlby, 1969). The attachment cycle occurs over and over on a daily basis in an infant's life. It begins with a need (e.g., for food, sleep, physical comfort, closeness); as the need continues, physical discomfort increases, along with tension and anxiety. If the need still goes unmet, rage follows. When the parent or caregiver meets the baby's need (with a bottle, a clean diaper, holding, etc.), the need is gratified, the baby relaxes, and trust develops. The cycle is repeated when the next need arises (Rila, 1992).

The attachment process fits in easily with the infant's behavioral states. When the parents meet the child's need, they not only help smooth the rough edges between the various behavioral states of arousal, tension, rage, and gratification, but also build a bond of attachment and trust between baby and caregiver. Trust in the outside world becomes the foundation for self-trust and self-care as the child grows up. Disruptions in the attachment process have long-term effects. When a parent is absent, unresponsive, or abusive, the baby experiences "extremes of under- and overarousal that are physiologically disorganizing" (van der Kolk, 1988, p. 279). The child may then have difficulties managing his own intense emotions later in life, and be more vulnerable to other stressors as well.

Children whose early environment is unsafe may not receive the soothing and consistent parental responses that allow them to trust that the world is a generally safe and pleasurable place. It would be harder for them to learn to control and change their own behavioral states the way other children do. This could be the case in a home where there is parental neglect, physical violence, sexual abuse, prolonged separation, or even severe illness in child or parent. Maintaining the separateness of their various behavioral states could be beneficial to such children when their experiences are overwhelming (Albini & Pease, 1989). In fact, children could use their familiar normal dissociative skills "to escape from the trauma by specifically entering into dissociative states" (Putnam, 1989, p. 53).

A severely dissociative child may not have had the opportunity or adequate parenting to organize early behavioral states into a self-regulating whole personality; he may have no real sense of self (or "other"). When it begins in extremely young babies or toddlers, DID may originate not with a "coming apart" process, but with the maintenance of earlier arousal states that have not been integrated normally (Albini & Pease, 1989). The degree to which a child (later) continues to dissociate parts of himself may have to do with how much unity of "self" he was able to achieve before an overwhelming trauma occurred in his life (Albini & Pease, 1989). The "switching" from personality to personality in DID may signal changes in behavioral states (Putnam, 1991b).

Trauma, Dissociation and Biology
According to Ross (1992), "severe childhood trauma causes a long-lasting dysregulation at all levels of the organism including the

biological [level]" (p. 99). He notes the evidence that childhood sexual abuse is a major risk factor for development of other disorders that have biological components, such as substance abuse and depression. However, even situations and events that are nonabusive may be quite traumatizing to a child.

> "Psychic trauma" occurs when a sudden, unexpected, overwhelmingly intense emotional blow or a series of blows assaults the person from outside. Traumatic events are external, but, they quickly become incorporated into the mind. A person probably will not become fully traumatized unless he or she feels utterly helpless during the event or events. (Terr, 1990, p. 8)

The *helplessness* Terr mentions is an important factor in trauma. Because children are small and relatively powerless in their world, they are particularly vulnerable to trauma. Events such as loss of a family member, prolonged illness, serious accidents, unpredictable parental behavior, or a lifestyle of prolonged chaos can be traumatizing because they are completely outside a child's control.

Donovan and McIntyre (1990) cite van der Kolk and Greenberg's (1987) animal research on inescapable shock. It is not the electric shock per se that causes the most harm, but the experience of complete helplessness, of utter inescapability, that causes a "profound traumatic stress reaction" (p. 62). Inescapable trauma causes measurable chemical changes in the brain. Animals who had experienced inescapable trauma responded with behavioral helplessness and the same physiological changes later in situations where they *could* have escaped, or when the aversive stimulus was very mild. Donovan and McIntyre translate the animal data for humans:

> By virtue of the fact that infants, toddlers and children are literally dependent upon the care and goodwill of their caregivers for their very survival, the family itself can constitute an inescapable temporophysical space. . . . because there is no genuine real-world escape for the child. . . . The therapist who concludes that a child victim of family trauma was not exposed to inescapable

shock because he or she cannot identify specific instances of gross invasion of bodily space or confinement
abuse has failed to understand the experiential world of
the child.

   . . . [A]n abusive family is like an electrified cage:
overwhelming hurt and no escape. But the parallel holds
. . . where there was no parental abuse. The dependency of childhood and the child's place within the family itself constitute the inescapability—even when there
is no intentional proactive harm. Thus, children who
are traumatized by experience which is unintended but
still inescapable can be as affected as those who are hurt
by the most cruel of abusers. (1990, pp. 63, 64)

This is why even nonabused children often "feel abused" (Oaklander, 1988). Real dependency and the inequality of power between child and adult underlie every child's experience, even in the
most loving of families.

The *frequency* of trauma affects how it is stored in the mind and
how the child copes with it. Lenore Terr (1994) divides trauma
victims into Type I and Type II. Type I victims are children who
have experienced a single traumatic event; Type II victims have
been traumatized more than once or repeatedly over a period of
time. Victims of a single overwhelming traumatic event (such as
the Chowchilla children who were kidnapped on a school bus)
usually have crystal clear memories of that event. But victims of
repeated, chronic trauma, such as some who have experienced in-
cest or physical and emotional abuse, may not be able to recall the
events as clearly. They use more dissociative, distancing defenses.
Why? Terr (1990, 1994) theorizes that single events are unexpected and take the child by surprise before she has coping defenses
ready. But repeated abuses come to be expected, and the child
learns to marshal defenses in advance. One such defense is dissociation, with its ability to help the child "forget" or deny the event,
and disown the feelings and the pain, both during and after the
abuse.

Not surprisingly, studies show that abused children show more
dissociative symptoms than nonabused children (Deblinger, McLeer,

Atkins, Ralphe, & Foa, 1989; Malinosky-Rummell & Hoier, 1991). Already masters at being someone else or somewhere else in play, and already handy in using dissociation to defend against negative experiences, children fall back on this familiar process to cope with major trauma. Discovering that dissociation helps them "get away" inside their heads, chronically traumatized children turn to it again and again (Malinosky-Rummell & Hoier, 1991). Repeated use of dissociation then leads to generalization of dissociation as a coping mechanism (Putnam, 1993).

More than just an accessible mental defense, however, dissociation may have particular benefits for victims of traumatic situations. Dissociation involves an alteration in consciousness that affects perception, thinking, emotional expression, and neurophysiology (Ludwig, 1983; Terr, 1994; van der Kolk, 1994). The ability to achieve such alterations quickly may have survival value that is related to certain primitive reflex behaviors. In animals, "sham death" states and "frantic trial-and-error activity" may help them escape predators and other dangers (Ludwig, 1983). In humans, dissociation is protective in many ways, allowing: economy of effort by putting some behaviors "on automatic"; resolution of irreconcilable conflicts; escape from reality when reality is inescapable; separation of self from catastrophic experience; and removal of physical pain (Ludwig, 1983; Putnam, 1989, 1991b, 1993). These dissociative responses are rooted in biological changes that take place during and after trauma.

During trauma, autonomic arousal galvanizes the body into emergency readiness for fight, flight or freezing. During these episodes, the brain releases stress hormones that affect conscious memory (van der Kolk, 1988). Autonomic arousal also causes an increase in the brain's opioid response, which provides relief from pain. Analgesia and altered states have been found in both animals and people following situations of inescapable shock (van der Kolk, 1988). These physiological reactions help victims survive the trauma. "Freeze-numbing responses may serve the function of allowing organisms to not 'consciously experience' or to not remember situations of overwhelming stress" (van der Kolk, 1994, p. 257).

Dissociation of "explicit" or conscious memory of trauma fails to erase the "implicit" memory of the events (van der Kolk, 1988). Depending on the child's age at the time of trauma, memories may be stored in body sensations, movements, feelings, images, or sounds; the ability to encode and recall experiences verbally doesn't develop until 28 to 36 months (Terr, 1994). When trauma occurs before the child is old enough to remember it verbally, the child retains a *behavioral memory* of the trauma. Dreams, post-traumatic play, post-traumatic reenactment (repeating behaviorally with others what was done to the child), and trauma-specific fears are the legacy of trauma, whether the child remembers and expresses it verbally or nonverbally (Hollingsworth, 1986; Terr, 1990, 1994). It becomes apparent that dissociative states and dissociative behaviors like those described actually contain the evidence of the trauma itself; the body "remembers to forget" and gives away its secret in the process.

Trauma and Learning States
Behavioral memory of trauma and other classic post-traumatic symptoms are indicators that the child has experienced learning under traumatic conditions (Deblinger et al., 1989; Terr, 1990, 1991). Reexperiencing the trauma, avoidance, psychic numbing, depression and difficulty concentrating, hypervigilance and panic (autonomic arousal) are all *dissociative symptoms* in that they involve altered states of consciousness: changes in the child's thinking, feeling, and behaving states. Compartmentalization of experience, dissociative amnesia, and detachment are also post-traumatic responses that enable the child to say to himself, "it didn't happen to me" (Spiegel, 1991, p. 265). Thus, the PTSD child experiences both under- and over-remembering in various ways (Spiegel, 1991; van der Kolk, 1988).

State-dependent learning plays a part in this process of dissociative compartmentalization and recall. State-dependent learning refers to the ability to take in information, store it, and remember it under certain external and internal conditions. People remember information better in a similar external environment or in a similar internal (emotional) state as when they learned it (Bower, 1981; Putnam, 1991b). Information (events, feelings, sensations) taken in under certain conditions can be partitioned off inside by dissociation and "cataloged" under the emotions that were aroused during the event. The entire event (and the emotions) may then remain out of awareness until a situation similar to the original one occurs to "access the file."

This may be how triggering occurs in PTSD, as well as in DID. The current trigger approximates the original traumatic "learning" conditions in some way (e.g., by re-arousing the old internal emotional state), allowing the child access to the inner "file." Original responses (pictures of the event, thoughts, feelings, pain) then resurface (Putnam, 1993). The various personalities of DID may form and function in a similar way. In fact, DID may be seen as a severe form of PTSD. For complete compartmentalization to occur, trauma must be frequent and repetitive, with an element of unpredictability and inconsistency (Braun & Sachs, 1985). These are conditions guaranteed to produce high anxiety and feelings of helplessness. Chronic abuse both necessitates and reinforces repeated dissociations, "which when chained together by a shared affective state, develop into a personality with a unique identity and behavioral repertoire" (Braun & Sachs, p. 47). Separate personalities often contain or take care of "a related set " of conflicts and emotions (Wilbur, 1985, p. 27).

In DID the alter personalities may be containers for separate learning states in which very specific information was encoded and stored, and through which that old information can be retrieved or remembered (Putnam, 1991b). When environmental conditions trigger a DID child, she may switch to a certain personality that contains the information that matches the context (trigger) and then behaves and feels in ways that correspond to that environmental cue. In order to *remember* a traumatic experience that has been dissociated (taken in and stored in an altered state of consciousness), one must access the same emotional state (Spiegel, 1991; Terr, 1994). Triggering seems to access previous emotional states automatically.

Dysfunctional Families

Dissociation's saving grace is its ability to magically spirit the child away from pain, frightening thoughts or realities, or from overwhelming emotions. In short, when life itself is just too painful or too scary, dissociation comes to the rescue. What kind of a life might need such an escape *for survival*? A life of powerlessness, chronic anxiety, and secret knowledge that awful things are going to happen, again . . . and again . . . and again. "The need to escape pain . . . is one of the basic biologically rooted characteristics of the human organism" (Hicks, 1985). If the child cannot find any safe place in the real world, then he will, to the extent he is able, create a safe hiding place in the inner world.

For a detailed description of the family dynamics involved in growing up in a closed family system, see Bryant, Kessler, and Shirar (1992). The developing child is affected at each stage by the dynamics of her inescapable world. The mirroring she receives from parents, whether it is distorted or accurate, becomes the original information that tells her who she is (Briggs, 1970; Miller, 1981). The messages she is given about herself are often introjected or "taken in whole," becoming negative (or positive) self-talk that she carries around inside herself into adulthood. All these early experiences affect the child's sense of self. She views herself as good or bad, smart or stupid, capable or powerless, depending on what she has learned in her world. Because dysfunctional families are often closed systems, the child has few, if any, outside resources for correcting distorted self-images and making sense of confusing or hurtful experiences that may occur within that world. So, she must resort to what she knows intuitively—the inner escape.

In many severely dysfunctional families double-bind communication is common. Parents may almost literally require the child to be two people, e.g., a sexual partner and a child, a "good girl" who does things that feel "bad." Other double messages might be, "Do as I tell you; control yourself"; or "Home is the only safe place," when "home" is really a place where people get hurt. The child must also find a way to deal with her inner conflicts: her love, need, and dependency feelings toward adults who may be the cause of opposing feelings of pain, rage, and profound mistrust. Dissociation and compartmentalization may be efforts not only to meet paradoxical parental demands and beliefs, but also to contain inside the resulting conflicting "selves" in a way that minimizes the child's inner confusion and allows her to live with incongruity (Spiegel, 1986; Whitman & Munkel, 1991).

The capacity to dissociate to the extent children achieve it in dissociative disorders may be inborn or familial (Braun, 1986; Braun & Sachs, 1985). Kluft (1984, reported in Braun, 1985) found a dissociative disorder in one or both parents of 40% of child DID cases. It is also possible that dissociative skills may be passed down through the generations of a family even without a genetic component. This could occur by the process of overidentification between a child and a severely dissociative parent (Kluft, 1985a) or by any parent figure's conscious or unconscious conditioning and reinforcement of separate personalities in a child (Malenbaum & Russell, 1987).

Some authorities believe the major predisposing factor for development of DID is "inconsistent and unpredictable exposure to some form of traumatic abuse" (Braun & Sachs, 1985, p. 46). The alternation of affection and abuse, love and punishment, and the capricious, unpredictable, and often sadistic nature of the abuse make dissociation necessary as a defense (Braun, 1986). That DID can be traced back to severe childhood abuse is corroborated clinically in 90% of reported cases (Braun & Sachs, 1985; Putnam, Guroff, Silberman, Barban, & Post, 1986). Cases unrelated to abuse usually have a history of other trauma, such as death of a parent or sibling, traumatic accidents or illness, or other severe losses very early in life (see the case reported by Weiss, Sutton, & Utecht, 1985).

Child abuse is still a controversial topic. Society in general has tried to dissociate awareness of the extent to which child abuse occurs. Not long ago, disclosure of sexual abuse by children was interpreted merely as an indication of children's oedipal conflicts. For example, in one reported case of an eight-year-old girl who was known to have been molested by an uncle, the treating professionals spoke of environmental triggers arousing the girl's "incestuous desires" and of the "satisfaction [she] expressed in the gonorrhea" she contracted (Bornstein, 1946, pp. 235, 237). Today, children still encounter skepticism upon disclosure of abuse and misinterpretation of their coping responses. The truth is that few people are well enough acquainted with how children think and express themselves and how their communication style differs from that of adults to be able to perceive children's disclosures and coping behaviors accurately even in courtroom and investigative settings (Donovan & McIntyre, 1990, pp. 14–16).

The confusion that results from the child's own ambivalence about disclosing abuse, the disbelief she encounters from others, and implicit or explicit injunctions to keep the abuse a secret become part of the child abuse accommodation syndrome (Summit, 1983). Dissociative defenses that help her cope and distance inwardly from trauma make it difficult for the child herself to sustain a belief that the abuse happened. Research indicates that dissociation or repression of a conscious awareness of child abuse can extend into adulthood (Williams, 1992). Without understanding and support from adults, the child must keep on dissociating the original experience and any difficult feelings that may result.

CHILDHOOD DISSOCIATIVE DISORDERS

In *DSM-IV* terms, the childhood dissociative disorders essentially include dissociative identity disorder (DID) and dissociative disorder not otherwise specified (DDNOS). Many children, however, show dissociative symptoms outside of these disorders, from mild to severe (see Figure 1.1). Acute stress disorder and post-traumatic stress disorder (PTSD), in particular, include dissociative symptoms; some experts believe these stress-related diagnoses should be classified as dissociative disorders (Braun, 1988; Spiegel, 1991). Defensive numbing or detachment, poor concentration, dissociative amnesia, flashbacks, derealization and depersonalization may all occur in acute stress disorder and in PTSD. These and other trauma-related symptoms, such as increased arousal, intrusive thoughts or images, repetitive behaviors, and avoidance behaviors, all indicate altered states of mind that may appear in other diagnostic categories such as depression, eating disorders, panic disorder, and obsessive-compulsive disorder. Many of these disorders, which can occur in childhood, may also be related to defending against trauma (Ross, 1992; Sanders & Giolas, 1991; van der Kolk, 1994).

Dissociative disorder not otherwise specified is a disorder in which dissociation is clearly the predominant characteristic. DDNOS may include symptoms of derealization and depersonalization, dissociative amnesia, and trance states. It is used to describe some children who may have DID "in progress," sometimes called "incipient" DID (Fagan & McMahan, 1984), in which personality states are not fully developed and organized. DDNOS children tend to dissociate more globally and in a more unorganized fashion than DID children, and may appear to be more dysfunctional. They may behave strangely enough that their symptoms are mistaken for a CNS disorder, mental retardation, schizophrenia, or a severe developmental disorder such as autism (Donovan & McIntyre, 1990; Hornstein, 1994).

> George was three-and-a-half when his 23-year-old mother dropped dead of a stroke at home just nine days after giving birth two weeks prematurely to George's first and only sibling, Billy. . . . At the time of the initial evaluation, George was six years old, in a preschool class for three-year-olds, noninteractive, blissfully uninvolved and largely echolalic. . . . George didn't complain of feeling depersonalized (in fact, he didn't complain of anything); he just *was* depersonalized. (Donovan & McIntyre, 1990, pp. 60–61)

While in severe DDNOS children a sense of self (or other) may be quite underdeveloped, DID children learn to compartmentalize feelings and experiences in order to survive chronic abuse and *preserve* a sense of self. For some children the path to dissociative identity disorder includes a period of DDNOS; a more organized system of personalities may crystallize in the teen years with the impetus to resolve teenage developmental conflicts (Hornstein, 1994) and to formulate a self-identity (Erikson, 1950). However, even very young children may have clearly defined DID.

In children, since DID may be evolving or in progress, the symptoms may be less distinctive than in adults (Fagan & McMahon, 1984; Kluft, 1985a, 1985b). DID children show symptoms that may be misdiagnosed as conduct disorder, attention deficit hyperactivity disorder, learning disorders, seizure disorders, depression, or anxiety disorders (Putnam, 1993). Their symptoms may ebb and flow or switch on and off, as they change from one personality to the next, in a life that builds a pattern of only occasional continuity and a theme of confusing fluctuations.

There are other reasons dissociative identity disorder children, in particular, are missed. They may do well behaviorally, at least away from home, and may not be spotted by teachers or doctors; those who do come to the attention of child protective workers due to reported abuse may be moved around from home to home in the foster care system. While DID children may have easily recognizable behavioral problems, it may be difficult for any one set of caregivers to notice particularly dissociative symptoms (Bowman et al., 1985).

Children who are adaptive enough to develop DID are rarely obvious about it, unconsciously molding the inner personality system to look like other children. DID children may not realize until late elementary school level that they are "different," or that the voices they hear inside and the lost time and disorientation they experience periodically are anything out of the ordinary. By the time they are old enough to realize they are different in some way from others, they know that to survive in an unsafe environment they must keep their inner worlds a secret (Brick & Chu, 1991; Dell & Eisenhower, 1990).

Dissociative disorders, like the childhood trauma they are related to, have been kept waiting to receive proper attention in the field. Estimates are that DID occurs in about 1.2% of the general population (the same as for schizophrenia) and in as many as 25% of all abused children (Ross, 1991; Whitman & Munkel, 1991). However, dissociative identity disorder is still rarely diagnosed in childhood (Lewis, 1991). Partly this is because DID is more difficult to diagnose in children than in adults (Kluft, 1985a, 1985b). Also, professionals may not be as likely to systematically evaluate for childhood trauma and dissociative disorders as for other problems (La Porta, 1992; Peterson, 1990; Ross & Clark, 1992).

DISSOCIATION AS A FACTOR IN OTHER CHILDHOOD DISORDERS

Dissociation is a complex symptom that is found in many other disorders of childhood (Sanders & Giolas, 1991). Many dissociative disorder (DD) children are misdiagnosed, since the symptoms overlap or mimic those of other disorders (Hornstein & Tyson, 1991). Of course, children may have a DD concurrent with another diagnosis as well.

Children with oppositional disorders or conduct disorders may be using dissociative defenses (Putnam, 1991a; Sanders & Giolas, 1991). Children who dissociate frequently may have no memory of some of their (usually negative) behaviors, and vehemently deny doing things that others have seen them do (see Chapter Two). Arguing with adults, being spiteful or vindictive, and blaming others for their own mistakes are signs of oppositional disorder; however, the dissociative child who feels he is being punished for something he can't remember doing may have many of the same signs.

Deceitfulness and theft are considered to be indicators of conduct disorder. But the habitually dissociative child also gives the appearance of "lying" while denying a behavior he doesn't remember doing. Some of the other symptoms of conduct disorder, such as forcing sexual activity on others, cruelty to people and animals, and running away from home may in some cases qualify as behavioral memory of trauma and/or symptoms of post-traumatic stress: post-traumatic reenactment of abuse and attempts to avoid situations or stimuli that remind the child of abuse (Burgess, Hartman, & McCormack, 1987). In a child who is acting out sexually or being extremely aggressive, a dissociative aspect may not be immediately obvious. But studies of sexually abused children show that dissociative behavior is "highly correlated with sexual behavior problems, depression, aggression, delinquency, and cruelty" (Putnam, 1993, p. 43).

Teenage perpetrators who have been sexually abused themselves have learned by traumatic experience and post-traumatic replay to separate one set of feelings from another: to dissociate feelings of power and control from feelings of shame, terror, and vulnerablity that would normally help them empathize with their own victims (Burgess et al., 1987). Terr (1991) also notes that the rage of children who act out in aggressive or criminal behavior may be seen as post-traumatic reenactments of anger that form behavior patterns when repeated over time.

Attention deficit hyperactivity disorder (ADHD) is another diagnosis that may be confused with a dissociative disorder. And in some cases, both disorders may be concurrent. DID children may be seen as ADHD, since they often have trouble paying attention in school and miss out on information given in class when they switch from part to part. For the same reasons, dissociative children may be diagnosed with learning disabilities. Because of the dissociation, such children show changing patterns of knowledge, likes and dislikes, and skill levels (see Chapter Two).

> This is probably secondary to the state-dependent nature of memory retrieval in the dissociative disorders. In a dissociative state the child may not be able to retrieve and utilize information that was learned in a nondissociative state. These inconsistencies of performance are often misinterpreted. . . . (Putnam, 1993, p. 42)

ADHD indicators may also overlap with indicators of trauma and abuse. The symptom of hyperactivity itself, with or without attention deficit, has been found to correlate with physical abuse (Heffron, Martin, Welsh, Perry, & Moore, 1987); the presence of physical abuse in hyperactive children was found to be six to seven times greater than in the general population (p. 385).

Because dissociation is by definition a defense against anxiety, children who have panic disorders, PTSD, and other anxiety disorders are candidates for dissociative behaviors. Obsessive-compulsive disorder may include so much dissociation as to be considered a separate subgroup on the dissociative continuum (Ross & Anderson, 1988, cited in Sanders & Giolas, 1991). Eating disorders, which often begin in adolescence, may be related to an underlying dissociative disorder. Torem (1990) reports on many studies that show dissociation and unresolved trauma as significant factors in some cases of eating disorders.

Dissociative disorder children almost always show depression (Putnam, 1991a). Depression, like dissociation, is a common post-trauma symptom, and in some cases may be "driven primarily by trauma" (Ross, 1992, p. 100). There is evidence that self-destructive behaviors such as cutting and suicide attempts may be efforts to regulate overwhelming post-traumatic emotional states (van der Kolk, Perry, & Herman, 1991). Such behaviors appear not only in depression, but also in various personality disorders that may begin in the teen years. Children with depressive symptoms may need to be evaluated more closely for dissociation, especially where there is a history of trauma or abuse.

Substance abuse may be linked to dissociative defenses. Drug use may be a way to dissociate or detach from anxiety, tension, or the intrusive thoughts and feelings associated with post-traumatic reexperiencing. Drug use may also be a post-traumatic reenactment of behavior condoned and learned *during* traumatic experiences; drug and alcohol use may accompany sexual abuse, prostitution or pornographic exploitation, for example. Even the particular drug a child uses may be significant post-traumatically, in that it may be chosen to either decrease or heighten tension (Burgess et al., 1987).

Finally, dissociative symptoms are sometimes misinterpreted as evidence of psychosis. Dissociative identity disorder children may talk aloud to other parts and hear the voices of other personalities inside their heads. Visual hallucinations may also be present, especially in the form of nighttime imagery just before going to sleep or awakening. These symptoms in dissociative children do not indicate schizophrenia, however, and do not respond to medication that usually handles psychotic hallucinations effectively (Hornstein, 1994; Putnam, 1993).

Dissociation is a means to a state of being not-present with oneself and/or one's experience at any given moment. It is a common, but elegant defense that is available to the creative and resourceful child. Nonabused children may use it to cope with overwhelming stresses in their lives. And children who are faced with a world of incomprehensible trauma or loss use it to escape to an inner safe place.

Research in the area of dissociative symptoms and disorders in children needs to be a high priority; otherwise the painful compensations that children must make within themselves in order to cope with trauma and with their own dissociative symptoms will continue to wreak havoc in their lives into adulthood. While dissociation helps the child get through an overwhelming time, separating the self from the full-on immediate impact of the trauma, it eventually becomes a hindrance, preventing the child from processing the trauma and grief and from being able to put the events into perspective (Spiegel, 1991, p. 261).

The penalty of childhood trauma and the necessary dissociative coping become increasingly costly for the child growing up, even after the trauma itself has stopped. Any child who has dissociative symptoms, whether mild or severe, can benefit from identification and treatment of those symptoms. Given the opportunity, children can heal while they are still children.

Chapter Two

CHILDHOOD DISSOCIATIVE IDENTITY DISORDER (DID)

The distinctions between dissociative disorders as they apply to children may seem rather blurred. In the literature, the terms "dissociative disorder" and "dissociative identity disorder" are used interchangeably; symptoms of milder dissociative disorders are often not clearly defined. Some of this confusion may be due to the fact that the recognition of dissociative disorders is still fairly recent in the mental health field. Also, pathological dissociation is often more difficult to identify in children than in adults; the symptoms may be overlooked until they develop into a more severe disorder.

Childhood dissociative disorders include dissociative identity disorder (DID), formerly called multiple personality disorder, and dissociative disorder not otherwise specified (DDNOS). Depersonalization and dissociative amnesia are part of the symptomatology of DDNOS and DID. Dissociative episodes may also appear in other disorders, such as panic disorder, PTSD, or acute stress disorder. DDNOS is a diagnosis that can be used for children who have DID "in progress." Their symptoms are the same as those of DID, but their inner personalities may not be as fully formed and separated by amnestic barriers. DDNOS can also describe children whose dissociation is global, conspicuous, and unorganized; these children may look more disturbed than DID children and more dysfunctional. While massive dissociation makes the disturbance obvious, the dissociative disorder itself can be difficult to differentiate from childhood autism or schizophrenia (Hornstein, 1994).

Because severe DDNOS children may be less functional both at home and at school, these children are more likely to be found in hospital settings, residential treatment facilities, and county mental health day treatment programs.

In my private practice setting, the dissociative children I encounter are more adaptive. I see children in whom DID masquerades initially as another disorder, as noted in Chapter One. I have also found DID that is still evolving and, as such, could be called DDNOS. This chapter is a discussion of the symptoms of DID, since it is the most severe dissociative disorder likely to be found in children who come for treatment on an outpatient basis.

Dissociative identity disorder is not often immediately recognizable on a first visit with a child or with the parents. Although you may suspect DID as early as a first visit, particularly if the parents provide an initial history that includes many symptoms, you will most likely need several visits to diagnose conclusively. The following sketches illustrate the range of initial presentation.

Nine-year-old Jeremy edged into the playroom warily, quickly scanning the toys, shelves, pictures—all the parameters of my playroom—with his eyes. I was to find later that he always knew when any item, no matter how small, was moved to a new location, or when a new toy showed up in the room. A small-boned child with light brown hair and a sprinkling of freckles, he looked fragile and vulnerable. His adoptive mom and dad reported that he was having problems sleeping at night, getting up most nights to sleep in his parents' room. He often had nightmares. Jeremy did rather poorly in school, and had few friends, if any. He also had some strange fears—fear of authority figures and of accidents.

Jeremy was extremely anxious his first session, moving constantly about the playroom for some time. He painted a picture of a house and a person; each item was composed of three squarish globs of paint bordered and bound together by a paint stroke of another color. He talked very little.

*   ❊ ❊ ❊*

Merrie's foster parents came in to see me alone initially, to see what advice I could give them. Eight-year-old Merrie was having problems following the rules at home, but was also terrified that her parents would hit her when she disobeyed. On such occasions she went into panic attacks, shaking all over. On weekends she visited her natural mother. There was a history of some physical abuse by other relatives. Because of sexualized behavior toward the foster mother, the parents wondered if Merrie had also been sexually abused. A child psychiatrist who evaluated Merrie previously diagnosed her as having overanxious disorder and oppositional disorder, with no conclusive evidence of sexual abuse.

Merrie was a bouncy child with a round pixy face, sparkling eyes, and a fringe of bangs across her forehead. On her first visit she brought me a present. She entered the playroom and took immediate control, investigating every toy, every nook and cranny. However, she needed lots of permission and reassurance that it was OK to play with the toys, not just look. Her anxious flitting from item to item was thinly disguised by a constant stream of noisy chatter and laughter. She was willing to draw, play with any of the toys, whatever—as long as she could be the director about what to play.

She decided to play in the dollhouse. Whenever she accidentally toppled a tiny piece of dollhouse furniture, Merrie immediately exclaimed, "That wasn't my fault! I never get in trouble." I reassured her several times before she was able to bump things without worrying.

*   *   *

April, age 10, came in to see me following a visit from her grandparents, who had been caring for April for five years. The grandparents knew that April had been sexually abused in her original home, from which she had been removed at age four. April had had some therapy already, but her behavior problems and her fears seemed to be getting worse.

The grandparents reported that April lied a lot at home, denying both the lies and the misbehaviors with angry vehemence. At other times she dissolved into tears "for no reason." While she did well at school, and had friends there, at home she could be clingy or "babyish." She had an inordinate fear of the bathroom. The grandparents were exhausted trying to meet April's needs and deal with her changeable moods.

During her first visit to me, April was quiet and reserved, but smiled readily. She said she didn't want to come to therapy at all, but she was anxious to please her grandparents. She agreed to a game of UNO. I noticed April carefully kept back certain cards instead of playing them. "I don't want to be mean," she said. However, when I deliberately put out my best effort at winning, April decided to make it harder for me. We ended the game in a tie.

These three dissimilar children at first glance show signs of various childhood problems such as separation anxiety, overanxious disorder, post-traumatic stress, avoidant disorder, or oppositional/defiant disorder. The diagnosis of dissociative identity disorder was not immediately obvious, but came to light during subsequent sessions. Two of these three children had been previously seen for therapy or psychiatric evaluation, and the dissociative symptoms had been missed. It is not always easy to spot DID in children.

Among the three children, however, are some symptoms that indicate a reason to check further for the presence of trauma history or of a dissociative disorder:

1. All three children show fears that seem unusual or exaggerated for their age or their situation, e.g., fears of bathrooms, or of being punished.
2. Two have a history of physical or sexual abuse. All have experienced some loss, since all three children are no longer with a biological parent.
3. All three show very high anxiety levels, although each handles the anxiety differently. Jeremy talks little and is hyper-alert; Merrie flits around, takes control, and is excessively worried about blame; April takes care of the therapist, almost to the point of deliberately losing a card game.

DIAGNOSTIC TOOLS

Reagor, Kasten, and Morelli (1992) have published a Child/Adolescent Dissociative Checklist (see Table 2.1), which I have found to be very helpful in both screening out DID and determining it in

Table 2.1
Child/Adolescent Dissociative Checklist.
From Reagor, Kasten & Morelli, 1992.

Client Name _____

Age Described _____ Sex _____ Birthdate _____

Evaluator Name _____ Today's Date_____

Circle the answer which best describes at the time (within the last two years) you knew the most about him/her. Use also information from primary caregivers, teachers, counselors, social service workers, etc. Circle "?" if you are unsure, or if your client showed only suggestive signs; "Y" if signs are clear or strongly suggestive; or "N" if there are no signs of clinical significance.

Y   N   ?   1.   SEXUAL ABUSE: rape, attempted rape, or un-wanted sexual touching or fondling.

Y   N   ?   2.   PHYSICAL ABUSE: hitting, kicking, biting, beating, burning, hurting, with objects or weapons.

Y   N   ?   3.   EMOTIONAL ABUSE: tricking, harassing, abandoning, blaming, shunning, etc.

Y   N   ?   4.   SERIOUS ILLNESS/injury: may or may not be due to abuse.

Y   N   ?   5.   SERIOUS LOSS: may or may not be due to abuse.

Y   N   ?   6.   EXTREME INCONSISTENCIES IN ABILI-TIES, LIKES, DISLIKES: dramatic fluctuations in behavior/performance, unexpected changes in preferences for food/clothing/social relation-ships.

Y   N   ?   7.   DENIAL OF BEHAVIOR OBSERVED BY OTHERS: perceived as lying when confronted re: behavior witnessed by credible adults, often fierce sense of injustice if punished.

Table 2.1 (*Continued*)

Y   N   ?   8.   EXCESSIVE DAYDREAMING/SLEEPWALK-ING: trance-like behaviors, "spacey," extreme concentration/attention difficulties, sleep disturbances.

Y   N   ?   9.   PERPLEXING FORGETFULNESS: loss of time, unexpected test failure, confusion re: names of teachers, peers, inability to use or acknowledge prior experience, loss of familiarity with well-known objects.

Y   N   ?   10.   INTENSE ANGRY OUTBURSTS: often without apparent provocation, may involve unusual physical strength, brief or persistent, often followed by amnesia.

Y   N   ?   11.   PERIODIC INTENSE DEPRESSION: may include suicidal gestures/attempts, often without clear precipitation or focus, psychomotor slowing or agitation.

Y   N   ?   12.   REGRESSIVE EPISODES: often followed by amnesia, dramatic reductions in language or motor skills when exposed to trauma-related stimuli (e.g., frightened thumb-sucking at age twelve).

Y   N   ?   13.   IMAGINARY COMPANIONS (past age six): imaginary quality may be denied by client.

Y   N   ?   14.   AUDITORY HALLUCINATION-LIKE EXPERIENCE: friendly or unfriendly, content related to "imaginary companions" or to traumatic experience, voices arguing or commenting; usually inside the head.

Y   N   ?   15.   PHYSICAL COMPLAINTS/INJURIES OF VAGUE ORIGIN: may be self-inflicted, accidental, or abuse related; fluctuating degrees of discomfort expressed, often uncertain medical basis.

(*Continued*)

Table 2.1 (*Continued*)

Y   N   ?   16.   POOR LEARNING FROM EXPERIENCE: nor-
                  mal discipline/guidance/therapeutic measures
                  have little or no lasting effect, corrrective experi-
                  ence may be denied by client.

Y   N   ?   17.   FAMILY HISTORY OF MULTIPLE PERSON-
                  ALITY OR OTHER DISSOCIATIVE DISOR-
                  DER: may not have been formally diagnosed as
                  such.

TOTALS

— —   *Total score of 10 or more "y's" suggest a need for
                  thorough evaluation for multiple personality dis-
                  order.*

children. It is important to go over the checklist with the child's
(nonabusive) parent or current caregiver, or with someone who
sees the child nearly every day, such as a school teacher or regular
babysitter. While the child himself may not be aware of many of
the indicators, a reliable caregiver may be. A good history that
includes the points on the checklist is extremely helpful in making
the diagnosis.

The checklist indicators need to be taken altogether. Any one
"yes" answer does not in itself indicate the presence of severe dissociation or DID. However, ten or more "yes" answers call for further observation and evaluation for DID. Reagor et al.'s research
(1992) shows that a score of ten "yes" answers on the checklist
normally separates DID from other disorders, even those such as
PTSD that involve dissociative symptoms.

When using this checklist with parents, you will need to educate
them about what to look for and record. Sometimes I go over the
list twice with parents; first I scan it briefly, asking them to take
some time at home to note their observations. They report back
when we go through the checklist the second time during a subsequent meeting. Sometimes parents will check off a particular indi-

cator right away; about other behaviors, they may be astounded to note, after a week or two of observation, "I hadn't realized how often she does that."

Other behavior problem checklists for diagnosis are available as well, such as the ones devised by Kluft, by Putnam, and by Fagan and McMahon (Tyson, 1992). The Children's Perceptual Alteration Scale (CPAS), a measure of children's dissociation, can be helpful in separating normal and abnormal dissociation in children (Evers-Szostak & Sanders, 1992).

COMMON SIGNS AND SYMPTOMS

Here are some of the common signs of DID, based on the child/adolescent dissociation checklist.

1. History of abuse or traumatic experience. Without exception, every DID child I have seen has had a history of trauma. Most have experienced physical, sexual, and emotional abuse, as well as loss. A history of childhood abuse and/or trauma has been found to be a factor in 97% of DID cases (Putnam et al., 1986). Most documented cases of DID have a history of trauma beginning by the age of five (O'Regan, 1985). If a clear history of trauma is not revealed during the initial intake with the caregivers, clues are likely to appear rather rapidly with careful questioning of the adults or observation of the child's play themes in session.

Drawings, too, may show indicators of physical and or sexual abuse, since children project their own experiences onto the paper. The child's manner and approach to making a drawing are telling, as are the focal points and emotional content of the pictured objects or figures. Children's drawings may reveal, for example, preoccupation with sexual concerns or body parts, or extreme concern for self-protection; drawings may also offer insights into children's relationships with other people (Burgess & Hartman, 1993; Burns, 1982; Wohl & Kaufman, 1985). Figures 2.1 and 2.2 are drawings by children who had known histories of sexual and/or physical abuse.

2. Extreme inconsistencies in abilities and performance. The dissociative child may perform quite well in school one day and

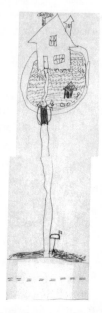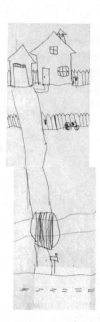

Figure 2.1 Two drawings by a girl, age 8, showing indicators of sexual abuse, male and female sexual symbols. Note the moat in the first drawing, sharply pointed fence in the second, and other barriers to the entrances of both houses.

miserably the next. He may score high on a test, and then be unable to remember how to do the same skill afterward. Or school performance may vary not so much from day to day as from month to month.

Jeremy's mother reported that in first grade Jeremy got A's in math. In second grade he seemed unable to grasp the concepts, although most of the work was a review of first grade math. At age nine, Jeremy often was unable to remember what day of the week it was, or how to tell time.

* * *

Monica's fourth grade teacher was confused. She had noticed that Monica failed to turn in homework nearly every day, and was

Figure 2.2 Kinetic-Family-Drawing by a boy, age 8. Shows everyone sitting at their own tables, separated, "watching TV." Child added himself to the picture at far left, only after the therapist's comment that he had not included himself. The child's extreme anxiety while drawing, and focal areas of the picture are risk indicators.

unable to concentrate on her work in class. "She's just gone," the teacher noted. However, Monica passed all her tests with flying colors. "I think Monica must have a very high I.Q.," she said, "but she won't pay attention."

Academic ability and performance may vary depending on which part or personality is "out" in the classroom and on the age and developmental ability of that personality. In such instances school personnel may suspect learning disabilities or attention deficit hyperactivity disorder (ADHD).

While some dissociative children may have bona fide learning problems, others show problems in attention or academic mastery due to a dissociative response to inner feelings of anxiety. In such cases, sudden changes in ability to concentrate in class or to take in the material may be directly related to being triggered. "Triggering" is a symptom of post-traumatic stress that occurs when a person who has experienced trauma in the past is exposed to something in the present that resembles the old trauma. When triggering happens, the person begins to feel, and sometimes to behave, just as he did when the original trauma occurred.

For example, if a child has been severely physically abused, he may be triggered when the teacher simply points to him, makes eye contact, and asks for the answer to a question. He may cope with the onslaught of anxiety triggered by his teacher's behavior by doing one of several dissociative tricks: "spacing out," distracting others around him (and himself in the process), or switching to another personality. Triggering can, of course, occur anywhere, at any time. If the child is being exposed to current trauma at home, or if old trauma has been severely triggered at home, the resulting change in behavior may last and be noticeable in the classroom as well.

Marked variations may also appear in the types of foods or clothes the child chooses. For example, a child who normally loves chocolate pudding and has for years may suddenly declare that she hates chocolate pudding and refuse to eat it, much to her parents' astonishment. Even the child's choice of friends may change along with her personalities, in a way that is different from the normal "you're in" or "you're out" of childhood friendships.

Merrie's foster parents noticed some peculiar inconsistencies in her choices of clothes. Just before going to visit her natural mother, Merrie looked through her closet for old, worn-out clothes to wear, rejecting the pretty new ones she usually liked. When she returned home, the changes in her clothing and behavior were even more striking. Merrie went from being very helpful, well-behaved, and wanting to clean house (what her foster mom called the "Pioneer Girl"), to suddenly being touchy and aloof and wanting to wear tight black leggings from her dance class.

* * *

Jeremy, typically a quiet boy with only one friend with whom he was comfortable, showed a major deviation from his usual social style one day. His regular classroom teacher was gone for a week, and the class had a substitute. During that time Jeremy began hanging out during free time with a "tough" kid to whom he had rarely spoken. His father noticed that Jeremy's behavior was different with the new boy; Jeremy walked with a swagger and spoke in "macho" tones to match. This personality came out at school for about a month after his regular teacher returned; then Jeremy reverted to his usual style of peer interaction at school. This "tough guy" part of Jeremy was a protector part; perhaps Jeremy had felt threatened or more anxious than usual with his regular teacher away. The tough personality made him feel safer.

3. *Tantrums or destructive behaviors.* Intense outbursts of rage, often without an immediately identifiable reason or provocation, are fairly common in dissociative children. The rages may be long or short, and the child may not remember them afterward. A parent will often call this a "mood change."

Monica's mother telephoned one night distraught. "She was doing so well, and we were having a really nice day; my sister was over to visit. Then, BAM! Her mood changed, and Monica was so angry. She threw a tantrum, and I couldn't even figure out what it was about. All of a sudden she was completely out of control. Even my sister noticed the change."

An angry dissociative child can show amazing physical strength for what one would expect given her age and size. A child may or may not remember what she did and said after the angry episode. The clinician should check to see whether she remembers the behavior she used, and whether she can actually talk about the feeling of anger or rage she experienced during recall of the incident. She may have dissociated the knowledge of what happened and what she did, or the feelings of anger, or the entire incident. For example, a child may not remember hitting her little brother, or she may remember the hitting but not the angry feeling; she may talk about the incident with no feeling at all, as if from an observer's point of view.

4. *Denial of behavior observed by others, especially behaviors considered negative.* After a "rage attack" like Monica's described

above, DID children, like other dissociative children, may deny what they just did, even if someone else was present to see it. This denial is often interpreted as lying by the adults who confront the child. The more dissociative the child, the less apt she is to own up to behaviors she knows are considered negative, especially if the behavior occurs at a stressful time. The child may feel very hurt and show hostile behavior when the adult punishes her for lying, loudly proclaiming that "it's not fair!"

And to the DID child, it may feel especially unfair—because there's a good chance that the child is not lying. An angry personality often comes out to protect the child or to get revenge without the permission or awareness of the "good" personalities who would never dare do such a thing. However, the angry part just as often disappears after the angry act, leaving the bewildered "good" child present to take the punishment.

Parents, teachers, and other caregivers may have a hard time changing their minds about the child being manipulative and lying, rather than dissociative. Often the parents don't bring a child in for treatment until their own coping methods and discipline skills have become depleted; the child is out of control and the parents are exhausted. Under those conditions it may be very difficult for a parent initially to give the child the benefit of the doubt.

Of course, the dissociative child may also use denial in a manipulative way. But denial needs to be reframed for the parent as a coping skill, as a way the child learned to get by during very traumatic circumstances. A parent should be given lots of permission and encouragement to be an observer rather than a judge regarding the dissociative child.

April's grandmother called me before she came in for her next session to say that April had been using bad language during a visit with her aunt and two young cousins. When April came to see me, I asked her about it. She lowered her head and stuck her chin out. "Aunt Bea told me I said 'fuck you.' But I didn't! I told her I didn't, but she doesn't believe me. She thinks I'm lying. But I don't know— why would Aunt Bea lie about me?"

In the following example, the DID child's denial personality disavows not only the "bad" behavior but goes on to deny the presence of other parts (although DID has already been acknowledged and validated by some personalities) and of any other "problems" in life.

One day Monica's mother brought her to session, stating there had been some trouble earlier in the day when Monica broke a door. Mother noted, "Her sister told me about it when I got home. [The sister] said Monica and her girlfriend were the only ones in the house when she got home, so it must have been them that did it." Monica was incensed. "Mom and sis are lying! They always blame me for things that happen!" I asked her if she could check inside to see if another part might know anything about the incident. Monica erupted again. "I don't have parts! I don't forget things, and I don't want to talk about it. You're blaming me! I'm really very happy, and I don't need to come here!" And with that, she stormed out of the playroom. The following day, Monica called me from home, no longer angry. "Guess what?" she said. "My friend remembered that the door got stuck when we tried to open it, and she said her and I did break it to get in. Now I remember."

For the dissociative child, the threat of blame and/or punishment creates such anxiety in and of itself that angry behavior must be disowned in order to cope. So the child may need more than one personality or part to cope with the entire episode: a part to be angry (this part risks showing a behavior or a feeling that is disapproved of); a part to be pleasing (this part often knows nothing about the angry behavior and seeks approval by good behavior); and one to cover for the dissociation ("now I remember"). The second and third roles may be filled by one part or more than one.

5. Excessive daytime "spacey" behaviors; sleep disturbances. As mentioned in Chaper One, extreme attention problems or concentration difficulties may be due to dissociation. It can appear to a classroom teacher, however, that the DID child is deliberately not paying attention, "doesn't care" about his schoolwork, or has attention deficit disorder. Trance-like behaviors and extreme spaciness can be the result of letting the mind go into "neutral," putting it on "idle." Attention problems in DID children may also be due to switching from part to part, especially if the child is stressed or being triggered by something in the environment.

Matthew's foster parents reported that Matthew, age seven, "spaced out" constantly at home and could not concentrate at school. He needed many reminders to finish any task. His foster mother noted that if she sent him to his room for a time-out, she found Matthew much later still there, just "sitting on the floor in the middle of his room with his mouth open — spacing." Sometimes he would be so unaware of her presence that he did not respond to his name immediately.

Some DID children show sleep disturbance, such as nightmares, constant nighttime awakening (see Jeremy's story at the beginning of this chapter), or sleepwalking. This can be an indication of the appearance of other personalities who are frightened or who are used to being awake and active at night, rather than during the daytime.

6. *Forgetting, especially forgetfulness that doesn't make sense.* Everyone is forgetful from time to time, and most of us even dissociate occasionally. On a continuum, normal dissociation includes highway hypnosis, daydreaming, or doing an everyday activity by rote. For instance, many of us have passed a freeway exit because we were preoccupied; and most of us turn off the stove automatically without thinking or remembering afterward whether we did or not.

"Perplexing" forgetfulness is the kind of forgetting that just doesn't make sense. For example, the child aces the test, but cannot remember how to do the same problems shortly thereafter. A ten-year-old forgets how to read the calendar, or how to get home from school, even though she walks the same route every day. Another child visits his grandmother on Saturday and Sunday, but by Tuesday forgets that he went or what he did at grandmother's house.

One day in session, I commented on a gift Monica had given to me. She replied, "What! Did I give you that?" She was unable to remember any of the three or four gifts she had given to me, even a pin she'd made for me. She tried to get the information by looking around the room, but couldn't recall.

* * *

Jeremy's mom often complains that he wants her to tell him what will happen ahead of time, so she explains as best she can the family agenda for today, tomorrow and the next day. However, Jeremy forgets what she has said and asks her over and over, saying, "You didn't tell me that."

Loss of time is another indicator of unusual forgetting. Hours, days, or weeks and months may go by, and the child behaves as if he were in the past, or seems to have no memory of the intervening time period.

Adam's mother noticed that he frequently lost his place in time. "He tells me something like it was just yesterday, even though it happened months ago. It's like today is back then and he's forgotten everything in between."

The therapist may be able to validate dissociative forgetting over a period of several sessions by asking the child to identify artwork she has done previously. I have found that the dissociative child may not remember certain drawings or paintings, depending on which personality drew a picture and which is trying to identify the picture.

Jeremy made a kinetic-family-drawing. I noticed that he showed a great deal of anxiety and ambivalence about drawing this picture at all. Two months later, we were looking through the artwork he had done. "I don't remember that one at all," Jeremy said.

* * *

Matthew came in and asked me to call him "Matt" today. He didn't remember telling me about some old abuse the previous week. We looked at old drawings he'd made two months ago. Matt frowned, "I did this one, but I don't remember that one or that one."

Sometimes the forgetting occurs within a very short time period, and the therapist will notice it within the same session. Children with fairly solid amnestic barriers between the personalities may not remember what they just said or what the therapist just said when they switch from part to part. In an early session with me, Merrie demonstrated switching from one part to another, with forgetting in between.

"What shall I paint?" Merrie asked.

"You can decide what you'd like to paint. Here's an apron to cover your dress."

Merrie looked at a painting hanging on the wall. "Oh, that's the one I did before," she exclaimed. As we opened paint containers, we talked about the story Merrie had told me about the painting now hanging on the wall. Suddenly Merrie interrupted, "Tell me again?"

"Tell you—about what?" I asked, confused.

Merrie was looking intently at the wall painting. "Hmm? . . . Oh! The girl in the painting is wearing what I'm wearing! I know that outfit!" She turned back to her current painting and paused. "Why am I wearing an apron?—Oh, yeah."

Several minutes later Merrie again pointed to the wall. "What is that painting about?" she repeated.

* * *

Jeremy and I made a visit to an ice cream shop one week during session as a special treat. At our next session he didn't remember the excursion. Jeremy was also surprised that the office manager had brought a doughnut for him that day, although she had promised it to him four days earlier after he returned from the ice cream store.

Continuing the session, we picked out puppets to represent parts. "The mouse will be the baby part," he said. Jeremy told me of some old abuse he had remembered since last time. He was a bit scared about it. Suddenly Jeremy picked up the mouse puppet and said, "This is me! I'm excited today, because [the office manager] just gave me a doughnut!" Jeremy had switched; this part (like the first one) knew nothing about the last visit and had not expected a doughnut today. But he also remembered nothing about the conversation we had just had about the surprise doughnut. He explained that last session "Regular Jeremy was here, not me." He didn't remember the mouse puppet, "the baby part," a few minutes earlier, nor did he remember feeling scared moments ago. "I don't know about that," he said.

For Jeremy the scared feelings expressed by one part were in themselves scary; switching to another part served as a distraction and a protection, since that part knew nothing about scared and scary feelings. At first glance, Jeremy appeared to have "forgotten" what happened both in session and four days earlier in the previous session; however, the parts who came had not experienced the ice cream adventure or the doughnut promise themselves, and were not in contact with parts of Jeremy who had.

7. *Intense episodes of depression.* The depression may include attempts at suicide or suicidal thoughts and gestures, sometimes without a clear precipitant. Some children show depression not with crying or verbalizations of feeling bad, but with psychomotor slowing—moving in slow motion—or the reverse, appearing to be "hyped up" or agitated. These children may bang their heads or hands on the wall or cut themselves. They may or may not remember doing so afterward, or may remember the behavior but be unaware of feeling emotionally sad or angry or feeling physical pain.

> Monica's mother found this note one day in her daughter's room:
>
> "Dear family, I'm not good enough for you. See you when I'm 19. Love, Monica."
>
> * * *

April tried to run away from home by skipping school with a friend. She was angry with herself later. April came in to see me the following day. She said, "I didn't mean to really run away, I just didn't want to go to daycare after school. I hate it there." She picked the skunk puppet to show me that she was a mad part today. This part told me she thinks about suicide, as well as running away. "I would wait until my grandparents were gone from *the house, and then I'd get a knife from the kitchen and stab my-self."* *

Depression and anxiety often turn up together. In a DID child the intensity of the depression and suddenness of onset reflect the discreteness of separate personalities. When the depressed/angry part is out, the child may act on depressed thoughts such as running away, hurting himself, or risky behaviors that can lead to self-harm.

8. Physical complaints or injuries of vague origin. Physical injuries may be self-inflicted, accidental, or caused by current abuse. As with any child in treatment, it is important to check out reports of physical pain or injury to rule out child abuse. If current abuse is not the case, other reasons for unexplained injuries may apply.

Depressed or suicidal thoughts can lead some dissociative children to self-injury by deliberate means—often with denial afterward of hurting themselves, or no memory of how the injury got there. Depression and anger can also lead to "accidental" self-injury by excessive risk-taking behaviors, such as jumping ledges on a bike or trying complicated physical maneuvers in play.

Adam's parents noticed that he sometimes injured himself outdoors while playing alone, and came in the house "looking like he thrashed himself." But Adam often seemed unable to say exactly how he got the injuries. In therapy, Adam told me about his "amazing crazy part" that could do risky stunts. His play also showed this part of him as willing to "commit suicide."

Sometimes dissociative children may be observably injured but express little discomfort. The dissociative child may be able to encapsulate the physical pain—just as he does certain emotions, knowledge, and behaviors—and put them away from himself where he doesn't have to experience them in the moment. Later, however, "body memory," like the other dissociated parts of mem-

---

*For ways to work with suicidal parts, see Chapter Six.

ory, may return with triggering or when the child is beginning to regain memory in therapy.

One day Jeremy's father reported that Jeremy had been run over by another child on a bicycle. Jeremy was knocked to the ground and had bleeding wounds on his legs, arms, hands, and face. His father marveled, "He didn't even cry."

Sometimes physical complaints may be related to past abuse. Checking may reveal that the child did not run into anything, fall, get pinched, or get in a fight. The stomachache, or back pain, or the pale bruise may instead indicate a body memory. In a child who walls off physical feelings as well as emotional feelings, body pain and old injuries from trauma can be triggered in the same way that environmental stimuli may trigger old feelings or memories of abuse. Essentially, the child is remembering with his body what happened to the body during the traumatic experience.

Jeremy often complained of headaches or stomachaches that seemed unrelated to activities of his day. Sometimes close inspection revealed that something had happened that reminded him (unconsciously) of old trauma. As Jeremy remembered more and more of the trauma that had happened to him, his body literally began to "remember" along with him, or just ahead of him. Jeremy came to therapy with physical symptoms that reflected the physical trauma he was remembering during sessions.

9. *Hearing voices.* Many children who have dissociated "big" feelings or whole parts of themselves may perceive thoughts arising from those feelings, parts, or personalities as "voices" inside their head. The child may have friendly or unfriendly voices (e.g., "He scares me"), mean or nice ones, etc. The child may report that two or more voices are arguing or fighting, or that one is telling him what to do (e.g., "Why did you do that? You're dumb." Or, "Don't tell me what to do!" Or, "Be careful!").

Sometimes the voices are related to imaginary experiences, like the kind that evolve from having an imaginary playmate; at other times the voices are related to traumatic experiences. Sometimes the voices are those of others involved in those traumatic experiences, e.g., other children or a perpetrator. Most often, the voices are those of other personalities — parts of the child.

In my early sessions with Jeremy, we talked about things that made him feel scared or nervous. Jeremy had a teacher who was very strict. She used a pointer stick up at the front of the room and would occasionally "whop" it on the blackboard for emphasis, which frightened Jeremy. In therapy, I asked him to draw a picture of the teacher, then to draw himself; he drew a view of himself from the back, watching the teacher as he sat at his desk. I asked him, "So when Mrs. H. is standing up there waving her pointer stick, what do you say to yourself inside your head?"

This is a question I often ask children in order to find out what they are thinking. A common answer might have been, "I say to myself, 'I hope she doesn't call on me!'" or "I wish I could go home." But Jeremy replied, "I say 'Hi!'"

I continued, "You say 'hi' — to yourself?" Jeremy nodded.

"And then what do you say?" I asked.

Jeremy replied, "I say 'hi' back." Jeremy was talking about the voices inside. Later he drew pictures of faces that went with the voices, and wrote what else they said. One voice was telling him to go find his brother and take care of him.

The teacher's behavior had probably reminded Jeremy of someone else whose movements had actually been threatening to him, and perhaps to his brother. The teacher had unknowingly triggered some anxious feelings, which caused switching inside for Jeremy.

* * *

Adam had just gotten into trouble at school, which was unusual for him. During recess, he punched his friend Peter. He explained tearfully to his teacher that he and Peter had been arguing, and then "Peter called me a dummy!" When Adam got home after school, he and his mother discussed the note his teacher had sent home with him. In trying to recall the incident, Adam discovered that the voice he had heard saying "Dummy!" had come from inside his head, rather than from Peter. Adam had been unaware of this angry part of himself that called him names and seemed angry with him.

Sometimes the "voices" of different personalities are so distinct as to be discernible even to outsiders when the child switches personalities.

Matthew's foster father reported that he heard Matthew talking to himself when he was playing in his bedroom. He also heard Matthew answering himself in a different voice.

* * *

Merrie came to therapy one day with a very quiet demeanor, and gave me a hug. Speaking more softly than usual, she picked out the puppet she had earlier labeled "scattered" to show how she was feeling. We picked an activity and Merrie started painting at the easel. As she dipped the brushes, Merrie's voice changed, along with her manner. She was suddenly loud and boisterous, gleefully piping, "I'm going to drive you NUTS!"

In addition to hearing voices, visual hallucinations may occur; these too may be related to old trauma. The child may think he sees something now that happened at a time trauma was occurring. In other cases, a personality who is seldom out may expect to see something that was present the last time he or she was out and imagine that that "something" is there.

Jeremy was telling me about something that scared him. "One night I woke up and went downstairs in the dark, and I thought I saw some vomit in the hallway that the dog threw up. But I checked the rug and it was dry! Then I remembered that our dog threw up a long time ago."

The personality who got up that night had last been up when the dog *was* sick—perhaps this part was originally triggered to come out by the smell or sight of the vomit, reminding him of an earlier traumatic time. Though it was months later, this personality was at first unaware of the passage of time since he had last been up at night; he expected to see—and convinced himself he saw—the same soiled spot in the hallway.

10. *Discipline problems at home; poor learning from experience.* Because of the presence of several personalities that take turns being in the body, or that influence the part who is "out" from the inside, a DID child may have poor memory both of behavior that gets him into trouble and of the consequences that follow. While one or two parts may experience the consequences of misbehavior, others do not — so they repeat the misbehavior over and over.

Monica's mother reported that she'd tried behavior contracts "loads of times," but they never worked. Monica would agree to them, and then within a few days do exactly what she'd agreed not to. When that happened, Monica usually denied she had made an agreement, covered by saying it wasn't fair anyway, or denied she had broken any agreement or done the alleged misdeed. Her behavior was radically changeable in other ways as well. One week Monica was cheerful and helpful around the house and followed the rules; she reported that she felt very good about that. The following week she was caught shoplifting. Distraught, she cried, "I don't know why I did that!"

Similar problems may occur in therapy. The therapist may think the child is gaining, and then find that she seems to be starting over because the small patient appears to have "lost" what was once learned. Children who are dissociative enough to have fairly strong amnestic barriers between inner parts will not be able to pass around among the inner system what they have learned from one personality's experience — whether that experience is discipline at home, therapy at the office, or just plain everyday skills.

Jeremy's mother commented, "Sometimes I think I'm not talking to the real Jeremy." Jeremy often forgot his mother's careful instructions, looking blank — as if he'd never heard them. He also seemed not to understand how his behavior was connected to his parents' reactions. "My dad gets mad at me for no reason," Jeremy told me. His parents would try to set rules for what was allowed, or what chores Jeremy was expected to do, but found that Jeremy simply couldn't seem to follow through, no matter what punishments or rewards they used.

Of course, this inability to generalize from one experience to the other, which happens in an inconsistent manner, is very difficult and frustrating for the child's caregivers. I find that parents come in with similar stories: "He did something he knew he wasn't supposed to do, and I told him off again. He had consequences—I sent him to his room. He was very upset and said he'd never do that again. The next day he does the same thing! And he stands right there and tells me he never heard me say not to do it, and he never did it before!" Some children use more blaming than denial to cope with the situation, with statements such as, "Well, it was your fault!" or "You always blame me for everything! Why doesn't (sister) ever get punished?" These defensive remarks cover for the fact that the child may not really remember the misbehavior in question at all.

11. Regressive behavior (acting younger than the child's age). DID children usually have personalities who were split off at a younger age than the child is now. Those personalities may not be apparent often, but show up occasionally when the child is stressed—particularly if the stress is caused by something resembling old trauma in any way or evokes in the child a feeling similar to what was experienced during trauma.

As mentioned earlier in this chapter, DID children usually have symptoms of PTSD; when they are triggered by something in their environment resembling old trauma, they may feel and behave just the way they did when the original trauma occurred. For instance, if a child was physically abused as a toddler, and used to cope by cowering under a table, hiding under a bed, sucking his thumb, or crumpling up in tears, then later in life that child may regress to the same behavior when he experiences conditions that cause the same feelings of helplessness and anxiety. The later-in-life trigger may not be nearly as big or as threatening as the earlier abuse, but can cause the same coping reaction.

The behavior of younger personalities will appear younger than the child's chronological age and may show lower developmental skills. Sometimes the therapist can witness switching to a younger personality by observing a decline in the child's behavioral or language skills or in the child's drawing ability. Figure 2.3 is an exam-

Figure 2.3 Pencil drawings by Merrie, age 8, showing differences in developmental levels as she switched from part to part.

ple of how different developmental levels can show up in drawings as the child switches from part to part.

Regressive behavior can be more difficult to detect in children than in adults, especially when the child is very young to begin with. Reverting to behavior of a lower developmental level is often perceived by parents as "just being childish," "mood changes," "whining," or "having a bad day." However, once they become aware of what to look for, parents and teachers make excellent observers.

Jeremy's teacher reported that one day at school Jeremy seemed "strangely wound up." At one point he "just fell off his desk chair and landed on his back. He lay on his back for several minutes with his feet sticking up in the air, saying nothing." She left him alone, and he eventually got up and sat down again.

* * *

Monica's mother noted that Monica occasionally became very frightened or overwhelmed. She said, "Sometimes I find her curled up on the floor of her room, sucking her thumb, or rocking herself. Sometimes she also gets food on the walls, or draws with crayons on her walls. Of course, that makes me really upset."

* * *

Matthew had recently begun wetting and soiling his pants during the day. His foster father complained that Matthew also used "baby talk" with him and refused to act his age.

12. *Family history of dissociative disorder.* Many DID children I have worked with have at least one parent, and sometimes two, with observable symptoms of a dissociative disorder or an exceptional ability to dissociate under stress. While a parent or another family member may not have been diagnosed as MPD/DID, one of the child's caregivers may provide information that suggests the possibility of one. The ability to dissociate may be generational in some families (Braun, 1985); in such cases, dissociation may be passed down in families as a coping mechanism, right along with the cycle of abuse or trauma. One family member having good dissociative abilities increases the likelihood that he or she will pass those abilities on to a child, either biologically or by modeling—or

by the necessity brought on by the continuation of the cycle of abuse down through the family generations. If you have an adult client with DID, and that client has children, it would be wise to evaluate the children for a dissociative disorder.

I suspect that a dissociative disorder is not as difficult for a child to develop as one might think. In one childhood case of DID that I have treated, the child had experienced several isolated incidents of sexual molestation by peers before the age of six and lived in a family atmosphere of high anxiety and tension, where dissociative skills could have been modeled or inherited or both. In another case, a child with "dissociative disorder not otherwise specified" had experienced some sexual exploration at age four or five by slightly older peers, and a summer of molestation by an adolescent relative at age seven. Neither of these children had a history of chronic sexual abuse extending over years, nor any physical abuse or sadistic (cult) abuse.

RITUALISTIC ABUSE OF CHILDREN

What is ritualistic abuse? We define it as follows.

> Ritualistic abuse (also called ritual abuse) is any kind of abuse done in a ceremonial or systematic form by a specific group. The group can be described as a cult or any organized (usually religious) group that performs purposeful rituals that have specific meaning to that organization. (Bryant et al., 1992, p. 245)

Ritualistic abuse does occur. If you work with children who show signs of trauma (see Chapter One), chances are some of them will have been exposed to ritual abuse. I believe that with any child you diagnose or suspect of having DID, it is important to check out the possibility of ritual abuse. This does not mean you will *find* ritual abuse whenever you look for it, any more than you will discover DID whenever you observe dissociation in a child.

What are some indicators of ritual abuse in a child's history? The clinical data available show some commonalities across reported cases (Young, Sachs, Braun, & Watkins, 1991). The child may show heightened fear or dread around the time of Christian holidays such as Christmas, Easter, or Halloween, which are also occasions for satanic ceremonies. The child may show an antipathy toward birthday celebrations, or fear of her own approaching birthday. Drawings may contain symbols that suggest cult involvement, such as pentagrams and crosses. I have observed that children who have experienced cult acitivities also seem to like to draw cartoonlike faces or characters that look particularly menacing, bizarre, or evil. Ritually abused children may have unusual fears, as of mirrors or small enclosures; they may show unusual problems with certain everyday activities such as eating, bathing, and sleeping.

Ritual abuse can be very difficult to diagnose; child vicitms seldom disclose such trauma spontaneously. Why? Perpetrating groups usually begin to involve and indoctrinate children who are under age five; besides instilling fear of punishment or death if victims remember or tell what happened, the methods used guarantee dissociation, particularly in young children.

> [D]rugging, hypnosis, dissociation-producing trauma, and terrorization of the child combine to produce a dissociative barrier truly daunting to the clinician. . . . [T]he immature personality structure in the child less than six years old cannot prevent amnestic barriers from being erected in response to the abuse. . . . [A] history of ritual abuse beginning before age six is extremely unlikely to be remembered by the child or spontaneously disclosed to anyone. (Gould, 1992, p. 208)

Catherine Gould (1992) has published an excellent checklist for indicators of ritual abuse in children (see Table 2.2), which can be converted into questions for gathering information about the child's history. It will be necessary to ask the child's caregivers about the possibility of ritual abuse. Talking with the child's teacher may also be helpful—*unless* the school is suspected as the source of the abuse. Gould (1992) addresses the dilemma that the clinician encounters just in obtaining information.

> The clinician often has no way to know for sure whether the parents of a child who turns out to have

Table 2.2
Signs and Symptoms of Ritualistic Abuse in Children.
From Gould, 1992.

1. Problems associated with sexual behavior and beliefs:

    A. Child talks excessively about sex; shows age-inappropriate sexual knowledge; uses words for sex and body parts which are not used in the family.

    B. Child is fearful of being touched or of having genital area washed; resists removing clothes for baths, bed, etc.

    C. Child masturbates compulsively or publicly, tries to insert finger or object into vagina or rectum.

    D. Child pulls down pants, pulls up dress inappropriately.

    E. Child touches others sexually, asks for sex, interacts in an inappropriately sexualized fashion. Child is sexually provocative or seductive.

    F. Child complains of vaginal or anal pain or burning when washed, pain when urinating or defecating.

    G. Semen or blood stains are evident on child's underwear.

    H. Child "hints" about sexual activity, complains someone is "bothering" him/her.

    I. Child refers to sexual activity between other children, or between him/herself and another child, in the abusive setting.

    J. Child states someone removed his/her clothes.

    K. Child states someone else exposed self to him/her.

    L. Child states someone touched or penetrated his/her bottom, vagina, penis, rectum, mouth, etc.

    M. Child states (s)he was made to touch or penetrate someone's bottom, vagina, penis, rectum, mouth, etc.

    N. Child states that sharp objects were inserted in his/her private areas.

    O. Child states (s)he witnessed sex acts between adults, adults and children, adults or children and animals, etc.

    P. On examination by a pediatrician specially trained to diagnose sexual abuse in children, child relaxes rather than tenses rectum when touched; relaxed anal sphincter, anal or rectal laceration or scarring.

Table 2.2 (*Continued*)

Q. On exam, blood or trauma around genital area; enlargement of vaginal opening, vaginal laceration or scarring in girls; sore penis in boys.

R. On exam, veneral disease.

S. Female child refers to being married, states that she is married, is going to have a baby; or, child states she will never be able to have a baby.

2. Problems associated with toileting and the bathroom:

A. Child avoids bathroom; seems fearful of bathrooms, becomes agitated when has to enter a bathroom.

B. Child avoids or is fearful of using toilet; has toileting accidents because (s)he puts off going; develops chronic constipation.

C. Child of toilet-training age is fearful and resistant to being toilet trained.

D. Child avoids wiping self because it is "too dirty"; child's underwear is soiled because (s)he will not wipe, or due to relaxed anal sphincter.

E. Child avoids bathtub; fears bathing; resists being washed in genital area.

F. Child is preoccupied with cleanliness, baths; changes underwear excessively.

G. Child is preoccupied with urine and feces; discusses it compulsively or at meal times; becomes agitated while discussing it. Child uses words for bodily wastes that are not used at home, especially "baby" words. Child compulsively discusses or imitates passing gas.

H. Child acts out in toileting behavior, eliminating in inappropriate places, handling urine or feces, dirtying an area or sibling with bodily wastes, tasting or ingesting wastes.

I. Child draws nude pictures of self or family members urinating or defecating.

J. Child talks about ingesting urine or feces, having it put on his/her body or in his/her mouth, being urinated or defecating upon, or having any of these things happen to someone else.

(*Continued*)

Table 2.2 (*Continued*)

3. Problems associated with the supernatural, rituals, occult symbols, religion:

   A. Child fears ghosts, monsters, witches, devils, dracula, vampires, evil spirits, etc.

   B. Child believes such evil spirits inhabit his/her closet, enter the house, peer at the child through windows, accompany the child, torment or abuse him/her or watch to make sure (s)he keeps secrets, inhabit the child's body, and/or direct the child's thoughts and behavior.

   C. Child is preoccupied with wands, sticks, swords, spirits, magic potions, curses, supernatural powers, crucifixions, and asks many or unusual questions about them. Child makes potions, attempts magic, throws curses, calls on spirits, prays to the devil.

   D. Child sings odd, ritualistic songs or chants, sometimes in a language incomprehensible to the parent; sings songs with a sexual, bizarre, or "you better not tell" theme.

   E. Child does odd, ritualistic dances which may involve a circle or other symbols. Child may costume him/herself in red or black, take off his/her clothes, or wear a mask for such dances.

   F. Child is preoccupied with occult symbols such as the circle, pentagram, number 6, horn sign, inverted cross, etc. Child may write backwards, inverting all the letters and/or writing right to left.

   G. Child fears such occult symbols, becomes agitated or upset in their presence.

   H. Child fears attending church, becomes agitated or upset in church, fears religious objects or people, refuses to worship God.

   I. Child states that (s)he or someone else prayed to the devil, threw curses, made potions, performed ritualized songs or dances, called upon spirits, did magic. Child states that (s)he or someone else wore ghost, devil, dracula, witch, etc., costumes, used ceremonial wands or swords, had their body painted (usually black).

4. Problems associated with small spaces or being tied up:

   A. Child fears closets or being locked in a closet.

   B. Child fears other small places, e.g., elevators, becomes agitated if forced to enter one.

Table 2.2 (*Continued*)

- C. Child closes pets or other children in closets, or otherwise attempts to entrap or confine them.
- D. Child states that (s)he or someone else was confined in a closet.
- E. Child expresses fears of being tied up, states that (s)he or someone else was tied up.
- F. Child expresses fears of being tied (usually by one leg) and hung upside down, states that (s)he or someone else was hung upside down.
- G. Rope burns are evident on the child.
- H. Child attempts to tie up other childen, pets, parents, etc.

5. Problems associated with death:

- A. Child is afraid of dying; states (s)he is dying, or fears (s)he will die on his/her sixth birthday.
- B. Child states that (s)he is "practicing" to be dead, or is dead.
- C. Child is afraid parents, sibling, other family members, or friends will die.
- D. Child talks frequently of death, asks many questions about illness, accidents, and other means by which people die. Questions may have an overly anxious, compulsive or even bizarre quality.

6. Problems associated with the doctor's office:

- A. Child fears, avoids visits to the doctor; becomes highly agitated in or on the way to the doctor's office; refers to "bad doctors," or otherwise expresses mistrust of the doctor's motives.
- B. Child is excessively fearful of shots; may ask if (s)he will die from the shot.
- C. Child is excessively fearful of blood tests; asks if (s)he will die from blood tests or whether someone will drink the blood.
- D. Child fears taking clothes off in the doctor's office; asks whether (s)he will have to walk around naked in front of others.
- E. Child behaves in a sexually seductive way on the examining table, appears to expect or "invite" sexual contact.
- F. Child states (s)he or someone else received "bad shots," had to take clothes off or have sexual contact with others, drank blood, or was hurt by a "bad doctor."

(Continued)

Table 2.2 (*Continued*)

7. Problems associated with certain colors:

   A. Child fears or stongly dislikes red or black (sometimes orange, brown, purple); refuses to wear clothes or eat foods of these colors, becomes agitated in the presence of them.
   B. Child states that black is a favorite color, for peculiar reasons.
   C. Child refers to ritualistic uses of red or black that are inconsistent with what (s)he has experienced in church.

8. Problems associated with eating:

   A. Child refuses to ingest foods or drinks because they are red or brown (e.g., red drinks, meat); becomes agitated at meal times.
   B. Child expresses fears that his or her food is poisoned; refuses to eat home cooked food because (s)he fears the parents are trying to poison him/her; refers to poisons of various types.
   C. Child binges, gorges, vomits, or refuses to eat.
   D. Child states that (s)he or someone else was forced to ingest blood, urine, feces, human or animal body parts.

9. Emotional problems (including speech, sleep, learning problems):

   A. Child has rapid mood swings, is easily angered or upset, tantrums, acts out.
   B. Child resists authority.
   C. Child is agitated, hyperactive, wild.
   D. Child displays marked anxiety, e.g., rocking, nail biting, teeth grinding.
   E. Child feels (s)he is bad, ugly, stupid, deserving of punishment.
   F. Child hurts self frequently, is accident prone.
   G. Child is fearful, withdrawn, clingy, regressed, babyish.
   H. Child's speech is delayed or regressed, speech production drops, speech disorder develops.
   I. Child has "flat" affect, fails to respond in emotionally appropriate ways.
   J. Child has frequent or intense nightmares; fears going to bed, cannot sleep, has disturbed sleep.
   K. Child has poor attention span, learning problems.

Table 2.2 (*Continued*)

10. Problems associated with family relationships:

   A. Child fears the parent(s) will die, be killed, or abandon him/her.
   B. Child fears (s)he will be kidnapped and forced to live with someone else.
   C. Child is afraid to separate from parents, cannot be alone at all, clings.
   D. Child fears the parent(s) no longer love him/her, are angry and wish to punish him/her, or want to kill him/her.
   E. Child seems distant from parent(s), avoiding close physical contact.
   F. Child "screens out" what the parents say, failing to retain information they give.
   G. Child becomes excessively angry or upset when told what to do or "no" by the parent(s), tells them "I hate you" or "I want to kill you"; threatens them with bodily harm, physically attacks them.
   H. Child talks about "my other mommy," "my other daddy," or "my other family" (in the cult).
   I. Child expresses fears that a sibling or pet will be killed, kidnapped, molested.
   J. Child physically attacks, initiates sexual contact with, confines, puts excrement on or threatens a parent, sibling, or pet.
   K. Child states that someone said his/her parents would die, be killed, abandon or try to hurt the child. Child states someone said (s)he would be kidnapped.

11. Problems associated with play and peer relations:

   A. Child destroys toys.
   B. Child acts out death, mutilation, cannibalism, and burial themes by pretending to kill play figures, taking out eyes, pulling off heads or limbs, pretending to eat the figures or drink their blood, and burying them.
   C. Child's play involves theme of drugging, threats, humiliation, torture, bondage, magic, weddings and other ceremonies.
   D. Child is unable to engage in age-appropriate fantasy play, or can do so for only brief periods.

(*Continued*)

Table 2.2 (*Continued*)

E. Child hurts other children, sexually and/or physically.

F. Child's drawings or other creative productions show bizarre, occult, sexual, excretory, death or mutilation themes.

G. Child is extremely controlling with other children, constantly plays "chase" games.

H. Child talks to an "imaginary friend" who (s)he will not discuss, or who (s)he states is a "spirit friend."

12. Other fears, references, disclosures and strange beliefs:

   A. Child fears the police will come and put him/her in jail, or states a "bad policeman" hurt or threatened him/her.

   B. Child is excessively afraid of aggressive animals, e.g., crocodiles, sharks, large dogs, or poisonous insects; states (s)he was hurt or threatened with such animals or insects.

   C. Child fears the house will be broken into, robbed, or burned down, or states someone threatened that this would happen; may wish to move somewhere else.

   D. Child fears "bad people," "robbers," "strangers," or states (s)he had contact with such people; watches out the window for "bad people."

   E. Child discusses unusual places such as cemeteries, mortuaries, church basements, etc., or states (s)he or others were taken to such places; displays seemingly irrational fears of certain places.

   F. Child alludes to pictures or films of nude people, sometimes with references to sexual acts, unusual costuming, animal involvement, etc.; fears having pictures taken, or strikes provocative poses; states (s)he was a victim of pornography.

   G. Child discusses drugs, pills, bad candy, alcohol, mushrooms, "bad medicine," or injections in an age-inappropriate manner; may refer to drug or laxative effects, or state he was given a substance. Upon returning from an abusive setting, child's eyes may be glazed, pupils dilated or constricted; (s)he may be difficult to rouse and may sleep excessively.

   H. Child fears his/her own blood, becomes hysterical, thinks (s)he is dying.

   I. Child excessively fears violent movies.

   J. Child believes or fears there is something foreign inside her chest or stomach, e.g., satan's heart, a demon or monster, a bomb, etc.

Table 2.2 (*Continued*)

K. Child talks about animals, babies, human beings confined, hurt, killed, mutilated, eaten, etc.
L. Child experiences constant illness, fatigue, allergies, and somatic complaints, e.g., stomach or leg pains.
M. Marks or burns are noted on the child, as well as unusual bruises, sometimes in patterns.

---

been ritually abused are involved in the abuse. However, it is reasonable to assume that parents who have voluntarily sought help for the child are or were not involved in the child's victimization. The vast majority of child ritual abuse cases encountered in clinical settings have been perpetrated outside the home, usually in day care. Occasionally, a parent who has an undiagnosed multiple personality disorder resulting from his or her own early history of ritual abuse will seek clinical services for a child who has been abused by a cult in which the parent is unwittingly still active. In cases of this type, there is a healthy and caring part of the parent who is seeking to rescue the child from a situation that may be almost impossible to escape without extensive professional help for the whole family. (p. 210)

There are some excellent sources of information already available on diagnosis and treatment of ritual abuse in children: *Ritual Child Abuse: Discovery, Diagnosis and Treatment* (Hudson, 1991), "Diagnosis and Treatment of Ritually Abused Children" (Gould, 1992), and "Play Therapy with Ritually Abused Children, Part I and Part II" (Gould & Graham-Costain, 1994a, b).

Other resources for the interested therapist are *Ritual Abuse: What It Is, Why It Happens, How to Help* (Smith, 1993), *Cults That Kill* (Kahaner, 1988), *Ritual Abuse: Definitions, Glossary, the Use of Mind Control* (Los Angeles County Commission for Women, 1991), *Michelle Remembers* (Smith & Pazder, 1980), *Suffer the Child* (Spenser, 1989), and *Recovery from Cults* (Langone, 1993). A book about ritual abuse in preschools that can be used judiciously with some children is *Don't Make Me Go Back,*

Mommy (Sanford, 1990). This last book and the one by L.A. County Commission for Women may be helpful to the child's current caregivers.

CONFIRMING DID WITH PARENTS OR CAREGIVERS

How do dissociative children end up in my office? With the kind of abuse that is frequently found or reported in the literature as a precursor of DID, it is unlikely that many perpetrating parents would bring their children to see a therapist. But it does happen. Or, sometimes a parent who has sought treatment for dissociative identity disorder will recognize that the child also needs help as she herself starts to get better.

More often, DID children arrive in the office a different way. Some have already been removed from an abusive home and are staying with other relatives or foster parents. These children and families may be required by Social Services to provide some counseling for the child. More often, the foster parents or relatives initiate counseling for the child who, following an adjustment period in the new home, has begun to act out severely. Some DID children are brought for therapy by a divorced parent, who knows the child suffered abuse either by a relative or by the other parent. Sometimes that child has already had treatment for physical or sexual abuse, but dissociative symptoms are still present. And other children are brought in by a divorced parent who is aware that the child may have been overpunished by the divorced parent, but is unaware of the extent of the abuse that occurred.

I have seen just as many DID children who were physically and sexually abused by a female as by a male. I have met more than one nonabusive father who was alcoholic or who worked out of town during the child's early years, and was therefore unaware of the mother's abusive behavior and unavailable to the child as a safe haven during the marriage. However, following a divorce, these fathers began a new relationship, perhaps even a new career, gave up drinking, and got "new eyes." After several months of being new observers, they began to notice a problem: "What is wrong with my child?"

What do the parents notice? Caregivers report rather similar stories about what it is like to have a DID child at home. A severely dissociative child is not easy to parent:

"She seems depressed. Lately she's even been hurting herself. "Sometimes when she's done something wrong she says, 'I don't deserve this or that, or I don't deserve to live.' I don't know why her self-esteem is so low."

"When she's angry, she scares me. It's like she's a different person. She's even gotten a knife out of the kitchen drawer and threatened her brother with it. She's just totally out of control."

"At times she's just whiny and clingy, like a four-year-old, and she uses babytalk. I get so frustrated with that."

"Everything has to be done his way or he's not happy. And he has to do it a certain way. If I try to explain another way to do it, or try to help, he just gets furious."

"She gets a lot of headaches and stomachaches, but the doctor can't find anything wrong with her. I think she's just manipulating me."

"She has several friends, but they're mostly younger. And she tends to end up acting like them sometimes, which is strange. But I think she likes younger children so she can be in charge."

"He really doesn't have friends—just plays with his brother."

"She's nervous a lot. Has trouble sleeping, and doesn't like to go to bed. Getting her to bed is a nightly problem. And nightmares. And she refuses to sleep on sheets, I don't know why. She's done that for years."

"She still has problems with the bathroom, and hates taking a bath. Anything to do with the bathroom takes her forever. And sometimes I'll find soiled underwear under the dresser, like she hides it from me."

"He wets the bed a lot, even still has problems pooping his pants."

"He doesn't feel pain a lot of the time. If you spank him he'll say, 'It doesn't hurt,' and he won't cry. And he also gets bruises and cuts from time to time, but doesn't know how he got them."

"He forgets things a lot. Can't remember to bring home his homework; he'll do some at home, and then forget to turn it in."

"She gets in fights at school, but says the teacher always blames her."

"He never gets into trouble at school — but at home it's a different story."

"She breaks the rules constantly, and then says it's my fault because I never tell her what to do. She never listens to what I say. Or she totally denies she did anything wrong, even though I just saw her do it. She tries to manipulate everybody in this house so that nothing is her fault. I know I shouldn't spank her, but I simply don't know what to do!"

"We have tried everything we can think of, and nothing seems to work. We've tried behavioral contracts, stickers for rewards, time-outs, taking away privileges. We're exhausted and angry all the time. If something doesn't get better, I'm going to go crazy."

As you can see, no one symptom alone would be significant enough to indicate a dissociative disorder; in fact, most of these complaints would describe children who had other types of problems. When they are taken together, however, a picture of DID emerges.

How do you present dissociation and DID to parents? The Child/Adolescent Dissociative Checklist is an excellent start. When checklist items fit the child and describe what the parents have been seeing, two things are accomplished: the parents feel validated in their observations and their concerns; and they begin thinking in new ways about behaviors they've seen as negative for a long time. This allows the parents to open up to new ideas about how to help the child.

I present dissociation to parents as something that we all do to some extent. I talk about a dissociative continuum and describe forms of dissociation that are common to most people (see Chapter One). I give concrete examples of how DID might affect the child's development and capabilities—how it will look at home. This gives parents much relief and hope for change, as they realize there is a reason their child exhibits certain behaviors.

Reframe the negativity caregivers experience from the child as that child's attempt to protect herself, based on old strategies for surviving trauma. Parenting an extremely dissociative child is very difficult at times, if not most of the time. Parents need lots of support, education about dissociation and how to handle it, and outlets for their own frustrations.

Some parents fear that dissociative identity disorder means their child is "weird"; some even imagine that the child is a small "monster" to be feared, as if the child were more powerful than the adult. This is not so. It is important for parents to learn that dissociation, as a defense in the form of DID, is a particularly elegant coping mechanism used by extremely bright children to get through times of trauma and to handle overwhelming feelings of anxiety. Nothing more, nothing less.

A child with DID can heal from the trauma and learn new coping skills. To do so, however, the child requires a caregiver with some knowledge of how to view her realistically and positively— someone with patience, someone who can accept the child where she is, and *whoever* she is, right now. A dissociative child especially needs a caregiver who is willing to provide a safe, secure home with clear boundaries, structure, consistency, and lots of love. Most parents will need ideas and support about how to provide such structure and boundaries, while paying attention to the child's special limitations due to dissociation (see Chapter Six).

CONFIRMING DID WITH THE CHILD CLIENT

I think it is important for the therapist to validate the existence of dissociative identity disorder herself, by observation of corroborating symptoms in the therapy room (i.e., witnessing switching, unusual forgetting in session, or trance states) and by confirming it with the child himself—no matter how conclusive the history she may have received from the parents. The child client's thoughts and feelings are not only relevant but important, from the beginning to the end of treatment.

Gaining and maintaining the child's trust are the foundation of the healing process. The child's own acceptance of her inner system, along with the denial or verification of having personalities, is simply part of the therapy. The therapist must start where the child is in her thinking and feeling, which is usually in denial and defensiveness. Rarely do children begin therapy by acknowledging, "Yes, I have parts! How did you know?" They usually start with, "No, I don't forget things."

If the child is very young—say, under eight or so—she may not know that her inner world is different from that of any other child. It may not even occur to her. The family she knows, and the world she knows—inside and outside—is ALL she knows. Below is an example of confirming the presence of separate personalities with a child. April's story continues from an earlier anecdote.

April's aunt had heard her swearing at her cousins, and April had denied the behavior. "I didn't do it! But why would Aunt Bea lie about me?" April wondered. I gently confronted her with the possibility that there might be another part of her she doesn't know, a part of her that gets angry and does things she wouldn't do. I suggested that her angry part might be trying to protect her when she feels scared at her aunt's house, which is a home she's not used to.

April acknowledged that she does feel scared sometimes when she stays with her aunt. We talked about the reasons. April continued thoughtfully, "And I don't remember going to a restaurant with them this weekend, but my aunt says we went." I got out some doll figures and explained how people have different parts inside. April picked out parts for herself that she was aware of today: an angry one, a scared part, and a confused one. This was her first attempt at accepting the possibility of having other parts.

The following session, a different part of April was evident. She wanted to play dress-up, donning a wig, hat, and veil. She urged me to dress up, too, cracking jokes as she plowed through the clothes trunk. I noticed that this part of April was more outgoing and humorous.

During the third session, April was unable to remember and tell me anything we had done together last time. She had no memory of playing dress-up. April looked down at the floor. "I'm afraid you won't like me anymore if I did those other things, the things I don't remember. I don't want to have parts—I wish I'd never been born." Tears spilled down her cheeks. I told her I liked her, and I liked the other April, too.

Then April gathered her courage and said she'd like to show me the stories she'd written down about the sexual abuse that had happened to her. "But I thought if you knew about my past, you wouldn't like me anymore." This was another good step. I reassured her again that she is likable, and that what happened to her was not her fault.

Here you can see the process that April went through to begin to validate that she had separate personalities—not only to me, but also to herself. A child like April who is old enough to know she is different from others may try to cover up and appear "normal" so she can fit in and be loved and accepted.

DID children may unwittingly give other kinds of evidence of the separateness of personalities, besides observable switching. They often have parts of differing ages and developmental levels. When a particular personality is "out," the child perceives herself to be older or younger, taller or shorter, heavier or skinnier.

Merrie, age eight, demonstrated her changing self-perception by her comments to her foster mom at home. One day, after watching a rerun of Bonanza *on TV, she declared proudly: "I followed along with the story all by myself! Pretty good for somebody in kindergarten!" (She was then in third grade.)*

On another occasion, Merrie was watching TV during the evening with both her parents. She had been allowed to wear one of her mom's long nightshirts to lounge in, with the admonition to just stay on the sofa and not try to walk in it. During a commercial, Merrie quickly swung her feet to the floor and stood up. Forgetting the long gown, she started to walk, and immediately tripped on the hem, falling flat on her face. "Oops!" said an "older" Merrie, "I keep forgetting I'm so short!"

* * *

Adam, age nine, commented to me early in therapy , "Sometimes I think I'm in kindergarten." (He was then in fourth grade.) Bending his knees and holding his hand out palm down, he added, "I see from lower down." He noted that sometimes he can't see over the kitchen counter at home, as if he were smaller and shorter. His mother later verified that sometimes Adam asks her to get an item on the kitchen counter for him, even though it is well within his reach.

Sometimes dissociative children, like adult clients, show changes in handwriting or in handedness when switches in personality occur. Some DID children also use different names for themselves, depending on which part is out, or have a history of wishing to be called by a different name.

Kristie, age 14, automatically shifted the pen to her left hand when certain parts drew pictures. I asked her if she ever remembered using her left hand before. She said she used to write with her left hand until she was five or six years old.

* * *

Merrie's school papers sometimes showed different handwriting. In the example shown in Figure 2.4, Merrie's writing style changes, as does the direction of the storyline.

* * *

Jeremy's school journal shows changes in handwriting style and pressure; internal dialoguing among his personalities is also evident (see Figure 2.5).

* * *

Adam's parents remembered that when he was in kindergarten his teacher told them that he had asked her to call him "Jerrod." There happened to be a popular little boy in his class with that name. When Adam was five years old his parents began using a new babysitter whose child was also named Adam. Adam's parents and his new babysitter called him "Adam James" (adding his middle name) in order to tell them apart. By age six Adam was showing

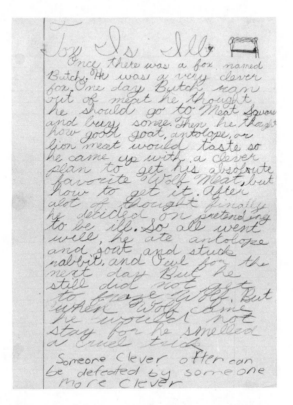

Once there was a fox named Butch. He was a very clever fox. One day Butch ran out of meat he thought he should go to Meat Square and bury some. Then he thought how good goat, antolope, or lion meat would taste so he came up with a clever plan to get his absolute favorite Wolf Meat, but how to get it. After a lot of thought finally he decided on pretending to be ill. So all went well, he ate antolope and goat and stuck rabbit, and Owl for the next day But he still did not get to buese Wolf. But when Wolf came he would not stay for he smelled a cruel trick

Someone clever often can be defeated by someone more clever

Figure 2.4 School composition by Merrie, showing changes in handwriting.

temper outbursts of kicking and biting, which he blamed on "the other Adam."

* * *

During the second month of therapy, Merrie wanted to play dress-up. In her best director's manner she stated, "I'm going to be Diane, and you be Lou." With a sigh of inevitability, she added, "I've been Diane all day." Then she glanced at me from the corner of her eye to see what my reaction would be. "OK," I replied, "I'll call you Diane." As Diane, Merrie enacted the story of a harried mother who had twin girls named Linda and Melinda, and a boy child, an "alien" who was always getting into trouble.

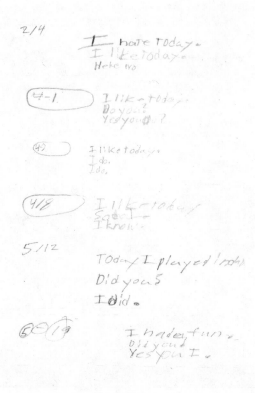

Figure 2.5 Entries from a daily journal for school, kept by Jeremy, age 9. Note the internal dialogue going on within each entry and the changes in handwriting. Many entry dates were inaccurate.

In her play, Merrie was showing me many of her parts; one was "out," but the others were portrayed as characters in the story. Following the play, we talked about parts. I used the animal puppets to give her examples of the kinds of feeling and ability parts we all have. Then Merrie selected several of the puppets to represent parts of herself, which she gave adjectives to, such as happy, or silly, or scared.

For ideas and techniques on explaining dissociation and parts to children, see Chapter Six on treatment of DID. A useful resource for explaining DID and dissociation to older children is Eliana Gil's little book, *United We Stand: A Book for People with Multiple Personalities*. While this is a book geared toward adults, the first ten pages or so can be helpful with children.

Take your time when you're diagnosing a child and watch for signs. Start with the information that the child herself gives you. The only way to get confirmation from a child on some things is to ask. For example, you can't find out if a child hears a voice in his head if you don't ask. Very, very seldom will a child, even in the most permissive environment, say to you, "By the way, did you know I hear voices in my head? It's very confusing because they're arguing all the time." Children don't often volunteer information of such vulnerability.

In working with young children, very often the therapist must be able to see the child and her behavior, and at least suspect *what it means*, before the child will be able to confirm the meaning. The therapist must *go ahead of the child* and give her permission to be who she is before the child will be able to acknowledge and accept who she is. Children are dependent on others for feedback about what is acceptable and permissible and what is not. We learn who we are initially by the mirroring of ourselves we receive from the adults in our lives (Miller, 1981). This makes it important for the therapist to tread carefully.

A therapist who works with children must know about many possibilities for diagnosis, match those possibilities with her own observations of the child, as well as with the child's history — and then corroborate it with the child. Yet the therapist must always be open to other possibilities, reevaluating the child, reassessing the clues with every session, so as not to impose a misdiagnosis on a child. By the time they see a therapist, most dissociative disorder children have already been given distorted or negative mirroring of who they are and why they feel and behave the way they do. It is important that when they enter therapy they be treated with respect, their thoughts and expressions validated and observed with care.

Chapter Three

BEFORE YOU START:
TREATMENT ISSUES IN WORKING
WITH DISSOCIATIVE CHILDREN

Almost by definition, dissociative children are anxious; they use dissociation to cope with that anxiety. Severe dissociation usually indicates chronic or long-term anxiety or greater impact from trauma. For the anxious child, any new situation or any contact with an adult, even a "helping professional," may feel stressful. The therapy structure, the child's contacts with networking professionals, and the therapist herself all need to be nonthreatening and protective in order to provide as much safety as possible for the child at that moment.

THE THERAPY SETTING

For anxious, dissociative children the therapy setting should be neat and not overstimulating. It helps to have a regular storage shelf or container for each item; each toy should have a fairly stable "place of its own." To feel safe, anxious and/or abused children need a structure that stays constant from one time to the next. I have worked with children who are aware, within one minute of entering the playroom, of any new toy sitting on the shelf, or of the absence of one that is normally there, even something as small as a Playmobile doll figure. This is not really surprising, since hypervigilance is a symptom of anxiety and post-traumatic stress. Consistency—of the setting and of the rules in the therapy setting—is in and of itself therapeutic. The best discussion I have read about the literal and metaphoric use of the "therapeutic space" is found in Donovan and McIntyre (1990, Chapter 6).

Materials that are useful to have on hand in the play therapy room include the following:

- A sturdy table and comfortable chairs for children
- Art materials, such as paper, crayons, markers, tempera paint and brushes
- Clay (the kind used for pottery) and tools for pounding, shaping, and rolling
- Sand tray and a variety of small objects to make scenes
- Puppets and a sturdy screen to hide behind
- Dollhouse with furniture and figures
- Wooden building blocks, string

Stick to toys that are not easily broken. It is also important to have only toys that are generic rather than figures associated with specific story characters from cartoons or movies. Generic toys allow the child to project her own experience onto them. For ritually abused children, certain materials in addition to those commonly used are helpful for the sandtray or dollhouse:

- Playmobile human figures of all ages and sizes
- Playmobile pirate and medieval castle figures and small accessories
- Long capes for doll figures, or pieces of cloth that can be used for wrapping and draping
- Miniature candlesticks, bowls, and weapons
- Wooden blocks and sticks of various lengths and sizes to reconstruct settings as needed

THE THERAPY STRUCTURE

I ask the current caregivers to come in with the child for the first session and express their concerns; I also ask the child how he or she thinks and feels about being here and about the issues caregivers bring up. I watch how child and caregivers interact. Starting with a good history from the current caregivers and any other professionals (doctors, teachers, social workers) involved in the child's life, I continue by observing the child's process both at the beginning of my contact with him/her and throughout treatment. This helps me know when and where to be directive, to intervene, or to confront—and when I need to pull back and get more information.

Ongoing Assessment

The therapist needs a good working knowledge of normal child development, of how trauma and abuse affect children, and of how children think. With this background information one can usually come up with a pretty reasonable hypothesis about the child's feelings, cognitive errors, etc., from which to base interventions. However, it is just as easy to be wrong, since each child and every home situation are unique. That is why it is crucially important to keep an open mind, to constantly observe the child you work with and what he tells you verbally and nonverbally in play, and to be willing to adapt your interventions to new information.

Confidentiality

I believe a child should have as much confidentiality as possible. Having the current caregivers and child together for the first session gives me an opportunity to go over my therapy rules and my policy about confidentiality. I let children know I will not repeat their words to parents without their permission, but that I will keep the parents informed as to what issues the child is working on, and on his or her progress. Things often come up during therapy with the child that cannot be kept confidential (abuse, suicide thoughts, plans to run away) or that in my estimation need to be shared with caregivers. I have not encountered a single child who was unwilling to have material shared with *safe* caregivers when disclosure was presented as necessary or helpful in order to solicit the caregivers' input or assistance in providing safety or making something better.

ADDRESS SAFETY FIRST

No anxious, dissociative child is going to be able to give up familiar defenses unless he feels safe enough to do so. No child who uses dissociation to cope with trauma or abuse will be able to heal from that trauma and learn to use different coping methods without first feeling secure. Donovan and McIntyre point out that verbal reassurances of safety are rarely enough for a child; children must experience safety and environmental protection in order to feel safe (1990, p. 73). It is often counterproductive and may be downright harmful to do therapy without addressing the issue of safety for the child. Some children will be unable to change their dissociative behaviors because the world outside the therapy setting remains too uncertain or too traumatizing; other children may learn new behaviors in therapy that are not safe to use outside that setting.

> In working with abused children it is an error to rein-
> force behaviors that may precipitate attacks at home.
> For example, one child client was encouraged to ask
> questions and say how he felt in therapy. The clinician
> failed to alert the child that the new behavior could be
> received differently in different settings. When the child
> was reunited with his natural family, his mother, threat-
> ened by her perceived inability to provide information,
> would slap him each time he asked a question. . . . The
> therapist needs to help the child understand that some
> behaviors may provoke different responses in different
> settings. (Gil, 1991, p. 80)

Sometimes caregivers who are not physically or sexually abusive use words, tone of voice, or behaviors that cause the child to *feel* threatened. Some families seem to make strides in cognitive under-standing but show little change in internal family functioning, maintaining a chaotic household. These families may be too dys-functional to provide a setting in which the child can get well (Dell & Eisenhower, 1990).

> If the family is unresponsive and continues to organize
> around multiple crises, the most helpful interventions

> will be those designed to help the child cope with the
> realities of the environment. (Gil, 1991, p. 41)

Children who have perfected a dissociative response to the point
of having or beginning to form separate personalities with amnestic
barriers between them (DID) have usually had to cope with overwhelming trauma or loss. To attempt in therapy to remove that
defensive style of living without assuring the child's continuing
safety is potentially damaging, to say the least (Dell & Eisenhower,
1990; Fagan & McMahon, 1984). Therapy, however, can be helpful even in a situation where the child is temporarily unsafe or
cannot be made completely safe. Techniques that allow the child to
stay in the dissociative mode work well (see Chapter Five).

Assuring a safe environment for a child in treatment is not always easy, and may require intervention by several parties. Therapist observations, reporting, and follow-up may be crucial to the
process.

DISCLOSURE OF CHILD ABUSE

Like other children who are brought in to see a counselor, dissociative children may present initially with anything from no symptoms
of child abuse to many symptoms that would indicate the possibility of abuse. Although both PTSD and DID children may present
with some symptoms of abuse, they may not disclose abuse until
well into treatment. There are several reasons for this.

One reason for the delay in disclosure is the time needed to
build trust between the therapist and an extremely anxious child.
"Clinical" or "pathological" dissociation is an indicator of high
anxiety or of a personality organized around coping with anxiety.

A second reason may be the child's living situation. The child
may be living full-time with a safe parent but still be required by
the courts to visit a once abusive or currently abusive parent. Or,
though the current home may be safer than the abusive home, the
child may still experience emotionally hurtful behaviors that remind her of the former abusive situation, triggering fear and dissociative coping. If the child is currently living with a perpetrator, she
may fear loss of her parent, her home, her parent's approval, and

therefore loss of her own well-being, if she discloses the abuse to an outsider. Most children who disclose abuse have some regrets after doing so. Delayed disclosure and retractions are common symptoms of the child abuse accommodation syndrome (Summit, 1983).

A third reason for the lag time in disclosure of abuse with DID children has to do with dissociation itself. When a DID child has separate parts or personalities, some parts carry the memories of trauma, and others don't. The dissociative process protects the child from awareness, from registering the feelings or the pain. Other personalities who do know about the abuse may be in denial, coping by believing that "nothing bad ever happens." The personalities who actually suffered the abuse may be hidden away inside behind safe amnestic barriers; the information they carry may be quite unavailable to those personalities who are talking with potentially protective adults. It will take time for the effects of trust and therapy to make the hurting personalities and the information they carry available for disclosure.

REPORTING CHILD ABUSE

This part of the process may also be difficult for children with dissociative symptoms—and again, most abused children do use dissociation to some degree (Gil, 1991). The child is often asked to repeat the disclosure of abuse to a police officer or protective services social worker, or to a physician who examines the child for abuse. Fear and anxiety may cloud the child's memory of a previous disclosure or block verbalization of information disclosed by one part in a child's personality system. Due to state-dependent learning, information stored or retrieved in certain settings may not be available to the child in other settings (Putnam, 1991b).

For DID children some planning strategies may help, if time allows. If therapy has progressed far enough when disclosure occurs, the child may be able to decide ahead of time which of her parts feels brave enough and strong enough to talk to the police officer or social worker, and which parts can comfort and reassure those who might feel frightened. If the abuse was originally stored or disclosed by a very frightened or a very young part, the child can make an inside "tape recording" or "video" (of the information, pictures, feelings, etc.) so a stronger personality can retell it later.

Although more professional people are becoming aware of dissociative disorders in children, the therapist's input on the child's symptomatology may still be necessary to clarify the child's disclosure. Some experts believe that the diagnosis of DID alone may be enough to warrant suspicion of child abuse (Coons, 1985; Elliott, 1982). However, the sometimes clear, sometimes hazy memory of the dissociative child can cause authorities to feel frustrated in their attempts to get evidence for an investigation. An example may illustrate some of the problems encountered with reporting abuse of dissociative children.

Matthew, age six, was a DID child who had a history of serial short-term parenting by several mother and father figures. When he began to disclose about physical abuse, Matthew could describe an object and how it was used, but could not initially be consistent about the abuser or the setting. The assertive "Matt" part had certain information that shy "Matthew" did not, and vice versa. Matthew was unable to confirm his own statements from one discussion to the next.

Dissociation may also distort the child's narrative version of what actually happened; his recall of the abusive experience may be mixed in with his dissociative defensive tactics. Dissociation is a protective mental process that allows the helpless child imaginary control of or distance from the abuse; it lets the child make the abuse seem to happen to someone who is "not me" or to make himself into someone or something magical enough to take control of the abusive situation. Here is an example from Gil (1991) about a five-year-old child:

> At the preliminary hearing Johnny was articulate enough to state that Larry had "hurt his bottom." Upon cross-examination he was asked, "What did you do when Larry hurt you?"; Johnny replied, "I stabbed Larry's eyes, broke his knees, and pushed him off a mountain." Johnny's case was dismissed because he was not seen as a credible witness even though there were medical find-

ings conclusive of sexual abuse. There was little doubt that something sexual had happened to the child, but it was difficult to ascertain exactly what it was and who the perpetrator was. (p. 107)

NETWORKING WITH OTHER PROFESSIONALS

DID children seldom arrive at the therapist's office in the arms of family or friends who are the originators of the child's trauma. In some cases a nonabusive parent may bring a child in for help following a divorce from an abusive parent and a change in lifestyle. However, DID children do often end up in the county welfare system following removal from their homes by protective services. Many young clients may be in foster care or adoptive homes when they begin treatment. Teenagers may have severe symptoms of conduct disorders, personality disorders, PTSD, and substance abuse (Dell & Eisenhower, 1990). Untreated, they may end up in long-term residential care for emotional problems or in juvenile detention facilities for criminal behaviors. Any such child in the county system who has a history of abuse, neglect, or severe loss should be evaluated for a dissociative disorder by a qualified professional. Dissociative children *can* be treated. Children whose history includes abuse may be eligible for state victim assistance funds, which will pay for psychotherapy services (see Appendix A).

The therapist of a DID child will need to keep in contact with the child's physician, with his teacher, and (if he is in the county welfare system) with the child's social worker, foster care provider, probation officer, etc. These professionals will most likely need to know something about DID, how it looks in this particular child, and how it works. They will need some guidance about how best to deal with the child, given his symptoms.

ABUSIVE CAREGIVERS

When the child is living with an abusive person, she needs her dissociative defenses. The same applies when the child has legally sanctioned visitation with an abusive relative or has to spend time with any person who triggers severe anxiety. When the outside world is too threatening, the child needs her inside safe place, with its protective "walls," its locked-up memories, and its buried feelings.

The DID child in this kind of situation will be slower to work toward communication and cooperation among the personalities. Memories of trauma may be too threatening to the inside defense system, and integration shouldn't be attempted. It is more helpful for the child to have the personality system, with its protective amnestic barriers, intact (Kluft, 1986).

When traumatization is ongoing or when triggering is severe enough to recapitulate old trauma for the child, then safety becomes the main issue. Therapy can only be helpful if the therapist works toward gaining a safe environment for the child. Networking with county child protective services is important. Sometimes safety can be achieved when the child discloses abuse. Nonabusive parents who have custody or visitation may be of great help in separating the child from an abuser or in providing safe supervision for the child. In some cases, involving family court mediators or scheduling a hearing in court over custody or visitation arrangements may be necessary to bring about safety for the child.

Nonabusive parents often need lots of support in order to bring about such structural family changes. Sometimes they, too, feel threatened. And sometimes, even after the best attempts to provide distance for a child from a current or formerly abusive relative, separation cannot be legally obtained. Counseling or support groups for the nonabusive caregivers may be helpful. Also, a national organization called Mothers Against Sexual Assault (MASA) provides consultation and support either in local groups or by telephone to therapists and clients who may be in the process of finding legal assistance to provide a safe environment for children. (For a list of national resources for support and information, see Appendix A.)

Should the child's therapist work with caregivers who have been identified as perpetrators of abuse toward the child? Certainly those caregivers should be in treatment and have their own therapist. Certainly the child's therapist and the family's therapist should consult. In many cases, reunification of the family is a goal of social workers overseeing the case. However, the child's safety should take priority.

In my opinion the child's therapist should not try to be the parents' personal therapist as well. Trust issues arise on both sides that can easily block the child's progress in therapy. For the same reason, a family therapy format with the perpetrator and child together in the same room does not work either (Terr, 1989). The power differential has already been abused and will contaminate the safe feeling of the therapy setting for the child. Parents who perpetrate are needy people who exhibit dysfunctional defenses; they need and deserve a therapist of their own. But more importantly, the safety and trust of an abused child are at risk. Even when a caregiver has inflicted only "mild" abuse (and I use the term cautiously) or when there has been, for example, a single episode of abuse in the "distant" past, a child may never truly trust that caregiver again. So when a relative is in denial of his or her own abusiveness, or when abuse has been stopped only by law enforcement, the child's safety and need for trust become major issues in the treatment. Sachs (1986) notes that any family intervention can only be useful if "there is some means for verifying that the abuse cycle has been stopped" (p. 164). Such verification is difficult; even with monitoring, the therapist may discover much later that a perpetrator continued to be abusive (Gil, 1991; Sachs, 1986).

When the caregiver has been or is a perpetrator of abuse, I believe child and caregiver benefit most from separate therapists who keep in touch or, if necessary, from occasional conjoint family sessions in the adult's therapy room with the child and the child's therapist present to hear what is being said. That way the child always has an advocate of her own and the child's therapist doesn't have to cross boundaries and become the parents' therapist when parents must confront their own personal issues, their own histories, and their own needs. And the child's therapy room remains a safe place for the child.

WORKING WITH A CHILD WHO
HAS CONTACT WITH ABUSERS

Under circumstances where authorities lack sufficient evidence to remove a child from an abusive environment, where a child is court-ordered to visit an abusive or formerly abusive relative, or where the nonabusive caregiver is at least temporarily unable to prevent some contact or threat of contact by a perpetrator, the child will feel the lack of safety. For example, a child who has been sexually abused by a relative who was incarcerated following the child's disclosure may legitimately fear reprisal or renewed abuse upon this person's release from prison. In some cases, former perpetrators have been known to harass their families and to file for visitation rights or reunification following completion of their sentences, putting the child and family through emotional turmoil and financial distress as they fight such a petition in court. The child's fear or anxiety under such conditions is realistic.

When a child *must* visit a relative who is a current or former abuser, the therapist can work with the child and nonabusive caregivers to provide the maximum safety possible. Hopefully, the visiting relative will be required to be supervised during the visit by another safe adult. Nonabusive caregivers can certainly do their best to bring this about. The child may also gain some security by making up a "safety plan" in advance of the visits that provides options should she feel threatened in any way during the visit. Nonabusive parents, foster parents, social workers, etc., can be in on this plan, in which all parties understand that the child is to call a "safe" person on the telephone to terminate the visit at once and collect the child, or that the child is to go to a certain location that has been designated as safe (e.g., a neighbor's house, a grocery store) and telephone to be picked up.

For the DID child who must visit unsafe relatives or wait in suspense for a court ruling on visitation, the tension will cause some chaos in the inner personality system and provoke protective maneuvers from certain parts (see following section on the abusive cycle). During these times the therapist can work with the child to put nurturing personalities in charge of comforting scared personalities. The child can also learn to use "safety measures" inside that help strengthen the child's inner defenses during an anxious time (see section in Chapter Six on "Building Cooperation Between the Personalities"). This involves a purposeful control of dissociative barriers, which can in itself be therapeutic.

ABUSIVE CYCLES RECREATED
IN NONABUSIVE FAMILIES

Dissociative children may hide their anxieties, their sadness, and their anger; they may steal, throw tantrums, act out destructively, and then dissociate those behaviors and any negative feelings that accompany them (see Chapter Four). This is typical even of children whose symptoms fall short of dissociative disorders. Over time, these behaviors may evolve into a pattern or cycle of coping with difficulties at home or school.

A child who has been abused carries around a set of habitual expectations and responses specifically designed for survival; she must provide herself with a sense of safety and control in situations where she has none. This pattern of learned responses makes up what is called a "trauma bond" (Herman, 1992; James, 1994), which characterizes the abused child's relationship with the abuser and her approach to future relationships. Attachment problems may complicate relationship difficulties (James, 1994; Rila, 1992).

With the DID child the possibilities for recreating an old abusive pattern among nonabusive people may show an added dimension, due to the possibility of cycling within the child's inner system. Just as adults with DID have an inner coping cycle (Bryant et al., 1992), children with DID may show a sequence of switches from one personality to the next in a pattern designed to cope with chronic anxiety and trauma. For example, when anxiety is triggered, the child's pattern may be to go from acting frightened, to belligerent, to violently destructive, to tearful, to curled up sucking a thumb, to ingratiatingly helpful—mood changes often accompanied by switches in personality states within the child. While this pattern may seem dysfunctional, it has its origins in survival. In some cases, the child's behavioral changes may have followed the abusive adult's behavior changes; in other cases, the child's behavioral changes may have helped to alter the environmental tension by signaling or triggering the chaotic adult to change behavior. This may be particularly true if the dissociative child's caregiver was also dissociative and given to rapid shifts in mood or behavior.

New caregivers, as well as nonabusive biological parents, may find that they, too, can be triggered, sometimes by the child's dissociative behaviors, into behaving defensively. We are all human beings; our weaknesses, unmet needs, and unresolved emotional conflicts can rise up to greet us when we least expect them—especially under stress. If nonabusive caregivers were *themselves* traumatized or abused as children, their own learnings about relationships and coping will contribute to a complicated mix of fears, hopes, expectations, and reactions between themselves and the child.

Environmental conditions may trigger the dissociative child's anxiety, which is followed by dissociative behavioral reactions; other family members may in turn respond with anxiety and anger of their own. This can create a destructive pattern or cycle in the family. No longer just a sequence of feelings and behaviors involving individuals, the interaction between family members can catalyze into a *family* dynamic that feels quite abusive to everyone. A crisis usually erupts. The whole family must often be involved in therapy to interrupt the pattern. The following is an example of a DID child's inner coping cycle occurring within the family's coping cycle.

When Monica was triggered in her family, she reacted with explosive, controlling coping behaviors that her mother and older sister responded to first with pleading, and then with angry counter-controlling maneuvers. Everyone played "Gotcha" in an effort to feel better, but underneath it all each person was scared. The family's fearful pleading implied that Monica did have control over her mother and sister; their retaliatory angry behavior increased Monica's anxiety, while reinforcing Monica's belief that she was "bad." Reframing Monica's angry behaviors as attempts to feel in control when she became overwhelmed with anxiety helped her family to see Monica differently. I explained that Monica could deescalate only if her mother remained calm, in control of herself, and refused to "point a gun" figuratively back at Monica when Monica "fired" at her mother. Mother noticed that when she was able to do this, Monica often reverted to crying, which was easier to handle and felt less threatening to all involved.

When the DID child feels overwhelmed with anxiety, her inside system of personalities naturally falls back on coping patterns that have been used before under anxious, traumatic circumstances.

Screaming, hitting, or withdrawing can all be defensive behaviors a child uses to feel more control in a scary situation. "Provocative" behavior may also be seen as an attempt to stimulate enough internal arousal to activate the body's protective chemical numbing or analgesia, which would lower her overwhelming anxiety (James, 1994; van der Kolk, 1994).

Nonabusive caregivers can fall right into a dysfunctional pattern with the child, particularly if they are not aware of their own "stuff." However, if the parents do not take the dissociative child's difficult behavior personally, and instead begin to question where the behavior fits into an old pattern, they may come to a better understanding of why the child copes this way.

Merrie had a boy part named "Arnie" who walked with a strut, lied to Merrie's foster mother, and was generally very manipulative. When her mother commented on Arnie's behavior, this part replied, "That's how I have to be. I don't have any thoughts—I'm just here to torment you!" When anxiety hit in a particular way, Merrie's "Arnie" part came out to cope in this way, as he had when Merrie lived with her natural mother. We speculated that if Merrie's foster mother were to continue to react with boundaries that were nonpunitive, Merrie's "Arnie" part would not need to resort to the usual behaviors, and, with therapy, Merrie might broaden to more positive ways of coping.

When you work with the DID child and her current family, think of yourselves as a *team* of pioneering detectives in an uncharted land. Identifying the dysfunctional patterns the family and child get into is a major accomplishment, similar to discovering the atom: you have unearthed the secret of the nuclear family "fission"! Now you can get on with creating something better for everyone. It will take time and patience, and in many cases a lot of hard work, but it can be done.

Caregivers must maintain their own sense of calm and control when the DID child is behaving chaotically. Caregivers may need to practice or role play with each other or the therapist privately in order to be able to do this. It helps to be able to view the child's angry outburst or destructive behavior not as a personal attack but as the child's way of communicating: "I am overwhelmed, I am frightened, I have to protect myself." If the parent reacts with frightened or angry behavior *of his own*, the DID child will often respond in one of three ways: (1) increased explosive behavior; (2) frightened, regressive behavior (cowering, thumb-sucking, etc.); or (3) shutting down, going blank. While a parent may feel better seeing behaviors in the second or third categories, any of these three reactions means the child feels overwhelmed and powerless.

Parents of a DID child must learn to react calmly and nonpunitively in the face of the child's anger and anxiety. Boundaries or rules must be appropriate and consistently maintained without the use of force, threats, put-downs, or guilt. It's a tall order! But only then can the DID child come to trust the adult and learn to believe that her feelings are acceptable and her existence on the planet earth is safe. The child will also need to learn to tolerate and express her own feelings safely, and to reinterpret what her own and others' feelings mean, now that abuse has stopped (see Chapters Four, Five, and Seven).

Quite literally, people in power who have traumatized the DID child in the past have demanded that the child be what they want rather than who the child really is. The message is, "Don't be." The child has metaphorically died to herself many, many times through trauma until she can honestly say, "The bad stuff didn't happen to me; that wasn't me, it was someone else." The dissociative child has taught herself to believe that she is sometimes "me" and sometimes "not me," when the need arises. By adulthood, a client may report, "It's hard to know if I really do exist" (Bryant et al., 1992). To a child, if it's not safe to be emotionally or physically who I am, then it's not safe to "be."

Nonabusive parents of an abused child are asked to do an awful lot of reparenting. Parents must find it in their hearts to accept the child's "huge" feelings, while offering them behavioral ways to express those feelings nondestructively. For the DID child this acceptance is even more imperative. If caregivers cannot bring themselves to believe that the child has a right to feel angry, enraged, terrified, hateful, mean, sad, whiny, etc., then their reactions will show their rejection and disapproval—which in the abused child's eyes will amount to the same situation he experienced when he was being traumatized. The *words* parents use with a DID child must match the kind of consistent, accepting, but firm behavior described above. Words also must be nonpunishing and nonthreatening in order to decrease the child's anxiety. Otherwise the child will continue to need dissociative defenses.

Anger was a difficult feeling to deal with in Matthew's family. The foster father held his anger in, and occasionally went long periods without talking. The foster mother yelled when she was angry. Matthew stomped his feet. The father stated his belief, "Sometimes Matthew has no right to be angry!" The mother yelled when Matthew angrily balked at going to his room. During a therapy session, Matthew showed his unconscious awareness of the rules for "being" in his family during his play with me.

Matthew made a sandtray scene containing trees and houses, several moms and dads, and three children. He placed several animals in his picture, and put three small ones in a cage, commenting, "They have to stay in the cage because they haven't been trained yet." In the storyline that ensued, one of the little animals tried to escape because it was hungry. Matthew made a bigger "trained" animal prevent the little one from escaping. Later he stated, "Now he's learned his lesson," and he allowed the little animal to stay outside the cage with the other animals.

Excellent teaching resources exist for caregivers who want to learn new skills. *The New Peoplemaking* (Satir, 1988) teaches parents how to make positive changes in family patterns of perceiving, feeling, and behaving with each other. *Parent Effectiveness Training* (Gordon, 1970) sets the tone for the kind of parent communication that works best with an anxious child and teaches parents how to actively mirror the child's feelings without being blaming or hurtful toward the child. *Between Parent and Child* (Ginot, 1965) and *The Parent's Handbook* (Dinkmeyer & McKay, 1989) are both helpful guides to communication and discipline and offer many examples.

DISSOCIATIVE PARENTS

As noted in Chapter Two, one of the predictors of a dissociative disorder in children is a parent who has a dissociative identity disorder. If a DID parent is not in treatment, he or she may have an extremely difficult time parenting, since many of the adult's personalities who have roles in the outside world may be teenagers or younger. The child of a DID adult may end up at times playing the parent role to the mother or father.

Kluft (1985a) recommends that any child of an adult DID client in treatment be evaluated. The ability to dissociate to this level tends to run in families, and can be generational (Braun, 1985). While a majority of adults with DID experienced physical, sexual, and emotional abuse as children, not all of these same adults will abuse their own children. One study found only nine percent of the children of DID parents were abused by their DID parent or the parent's spouse (Coons, 1985). A DID parent who is in treatment will have the opportunity to become more aware of his or her parenting behaviors from the perspective of the other personalities, and to learn how he or she projects feelings and beliefs from past experience, much of it stored in the unconscious, onto the child.

Projection involves ascribing our own feelings, thoughts, behaviors or experiences—especially those that are negative or problematic—to other people and situations, and then reacting to those people or situations according to what we "see." Projection is, of course, a common defense mechanism. To the extent that we all have "parts," integrated or not, identification with and projection onto our children occur with all parents. Many parents find that their children restimulate their own unresolved childhood conflicts at particular ages and stages of their development. For example, a five-year-old girl may remind a parent of her own childhood feelings of shame and self-denigration if she herself was abused at that age. A teenage son may remind a parent of a similar-looking relative who was abusive or negative.

A parent with DID may not be able, until some time into her own treatment process, to become aware of dissociated personalities that think, feel, and behave in ways that the parent did as a child. The biological child may behave, or look, or sound like one of the parent's own younger personalities with whom she has not yet made peace. Prevented from developing a continuous sense of self during her lifetime, the DID adult may feel repeatedly off balance as she tries to meet the challenges of parenting. The switching among her many and varied personalities may prevent her from being consistent and dependable in her parenting or even in her role as a parent in the family. Instead, the DID parent may find herself "reliving" her own childhood over and over in her home, with or through her own children. Conflicts and mutual frustration between parent and child may ensue.

Like other parents of DID children, dissociative parents will need lots of support and parenting information about how best to help their child. In turn, the child will need to know that the parent is also dissociative, and what that means. In some cases, both parent and child can be said to be getting well together. However, it is important that the child not be inadvertently coached into being available to support and/or comfort the parent who is also in treatment (although some "helping out" is natural).

I drew a picture for Adam to illustrate how his mother had parts inside. Adam said that his mother had three mothering parts that he knew of. He called them "Mama," "Mom," and "Mommy," and responded to each of them differently. With the personality called "Mama" he could be silly and have fun. "Mom," on the other hand, was often strict or angry; Adam often coped with that part by saying "I love you," upon which his mother would often switch into her "Mama" part. The part Adam called "Mommy" he described as younger, shy, and quiet; he often acted as helper for this mother part.

Learning new roles as parent and child is a difficult process that occurs over an extended period of time. When they live in the same family, dissociative parents and children get to know their own parts and how those parts interact within themselves, as well as in the outside world. While everyone might wish for the parent to begin functioning most of the time as an adult so that the child can truly feel free to be a child, this is not always possible, especially in the initial stages of treatment for either party. I find it is best to give both parent and child validation for doing their best and to cheer on each new awareness and each new positive behavior change as it occurs, without demanding total or immediate changes in life-style. As long as neither parent nor child is abusive, violent, or threatening toward each other or other family members, they can take the time they need to learn the fine art of being parent and child. (If abuse is occurring, reporting has to occur, and the legal system enters the family system. Supervised parenting or co-parenting with a nonabusive spouse may be necessary if the child is to remain in such a home, as would be the case for any abusive parent.)

When one child in a family has DID, siblings may be also dissociative. Indeed, in my own experience, it is not uncommon to find the whole family dissociative to some degree. This certainly adds to the family's difficulties around communicating clearly and maintaining consistent rules and boundaries. Everyone tends to forget who said what when, and to whom. Being uncertain of what was said, dissociative parents may guiltily give in on boundaries instead of being firm — or be overly strict, forgetful of earlier negative consequences of their actions or changes made earlier in the rules. Holding family meetings to discuss house rules and to resolve family problems may help. Any resulting house rules should be put in writing, dated, and posted for all to see. Before meting out consequences for misbehaviors, the parent can find out how the child felt about the situation and also confer with a spouse; this promotes teamwork and can head off prolonged conflicts and anxieties on all sides. Again, the family members can be encouraged to see themselves as detectives, experimenting and learning what will work and what won't.

Chapter Four

DISSOCIATIVE SYMPTOMS:
A TREATMENT OVERVIEW

Some children seem to dissociate feelings such as sadness, fear, or anger without showing behavior problems that concern adults. Other children use behaviors to dissociate uncomfortable feelings— behaviors that may also have to be dissociated because they create additional problems. Dissociated feelings and dissociative behaviors invariably appear in childhood post-traumatic stress disorder, dissociative identity disorder, and dissociative disorder not otherwise specified. As noted in Chapter One, they may also occur in other childhood disorders, such as conduct disorder, oppositional-defiant disorder, and childhood anxiety disorders. My approach to treatment of children's dissociative symptoms is fairly similar across most of these diagnoses; specific techniques are just as applicable to DID as to milder dissociative symptoms (see Chapter Five).

The conceptual framework I draw from is a mixture of client-centered beliefs about people, family systems and social learning theory, and Gestalt techniques. In my experience, therapy is a process that evolves within a trusting relationship between child and therapist and caregivers. I believe it is important to know the child's history; we are born with all the equipment we need for life, but the inner blueprint for our personality is impacted by our external world as well. Our early experiences reinvent themselves as parts of us, continuing to affect the way we relate to ourselves and the world around us.

Virginia Satir's concept of parts in all of us, our "many faces," is extremely useful in working with children. Every human is a jigsaw puzzle of interlocking parts inside; some of our parts we know consciously, and some we don't know or are only vaguely aware of. Each part is important to the whole, and affects the others. We all learn very early in life which parts of ourselves are accepted and liked and which are not. Those that are not approved of we tend to wish away, or disavow. This is similar to what Gestalt therapists call "disowning." When we feel scared or stressed, we learn what internal or external maneuvers will take care of us and bring some sense of safety and control. Dissociation of the "bad stuff" is one of those defenses. I refer to "dissociation" in this broad sense, to mean disowning or putting out of awareness certain feelings, behaviors, body sensations, or thoughts that cause anxiety.

Oaklander's Gestalt therapy is effective with dissociative children because it emphasizes making contact with ourselves, being "present" with ourselves, and getting to know the parts of ourselves we are "out of contact" with. It also facilitates contact with the environment, being aware of the information coming in through our senses, which in turn makes us "alive" to our bodies. Dissociative children have gradually taught themselves to disconnect from contact functions. Within the safe therapeutic space, the child can begin to reconnect with feelings, behaviors, and experiences and come to terms with them, regaining the lost parts of herself.

DISSOCIATED FEELINGS

Disowning feelings is a defense that all of us use from time to time, even as adults. Many of you have probably experienced the sudden death of a relative or a dear friend, or have watched someone close to you go through it. You may have noticed that you or your friend went into shock right after the news and wished the death hadn't happened. Most of us move from that protective state of numbness and initial denial onward to grieving. However, some people never seem to allow themselves truly to grieve a loss—they stuff their feelings inside or sidestep them by taking care of others involved in the loss. Of course, that doesn't mean the feelings of loss cease to exist inside; that person simply doesn't allow himself to feel them. When a person disowns grief feelings, he may say to himself or others, "It's for the best," "I have to be strong," or "What's the point of crying?"

Children often see that adults are uncomfortable with feelings of sadness, fear, and anger. Many parents would also rather not see their children feeling sad, angry, or scared, and routinely send children messages to that effect. The result is that children come to believe that these feelings are not allowed, shouldn't be expressed, and are "bad." Children often hear things like, "What are you afraid of that for?" or "Don't cry! Be a big boy now." Regarding anger, the messages are even more confusing; the child's anger is often met with reciprocated anger: "Don't you talk back to me, young lady!" or "There's no need to get mad about it, just do it." Anger is often the hardest feeling for parents to accept, both in themselves and in their children.

Some children seem to disown their anger by swallowing it, becoming very compliant and pleasing. Other children's disowned anger shows up in acting-out behaviors or in displacement onto another person such as a schoolmate or a sibling. Disowned anger may also be turned inward in self-blaming or self-injury. In any of these methods, the anger is not expressed directly and clearly; instead, the child finds ways to cope with feeling badly about a feeling that others disapprove of, stopping the anger from being directed at the person with whom the child truly has an issue. Children who have been traumatized may have an even greater need to dissociate or disown feelings than children who have not. Expression of feelings may have been prohibited by a bigger person, who was in control while the trauma occurred. For example, during a violent molest, the child may have been told not to cry, not to fight back, not to show the normal feelings of fear or anger that anyone would commonly experience during such a trauma. Or, the child may have discovered for *herself* that the only way to keep any sense of control was not to cry or show fear, even if an abuser wanted her to. She may have taught herself to dissociate such feelings.

A child who has been traumatized may also dissociate feelings that become too "big" in and of themselves because of the traumatic experience. The child may not be able to cope with the intensity of the fear, rage, sexual feelings, or shame; dissociation may become a useful way of defending against those feelings and making them manageable. Children may become quite adept at dissociating feelings if the trauma is chronic or recurrent (Terr, 1994).

Ten-year-old Brian had a little sister who had died several months earlier after a long illness. Brian's parents were concerned that he was always pleasant, helpful, and adultlike since then—too much so. When Brian came in to see me he made a king out of clay and placed him on his throne. "The king feels very happy," he said. Asked if the king ever had other feelings, Brian replied, "Nope, he never has any other feelings—only ever happy ones." I asked if he ever felt mad or sad. "No," said Brian, "always happy." Then I asked Brian, "What do you think would happen in real life if we never could feel mad or sad?" Brian thought a moment. "I guess we'd be happy all the time?"

And this is indeed how children try to make themselves happy all the time: by "not having" any of the bad feeings. I told him how mad and sad feelings are helpful, and why babies are born with the ability to feel all their feelings. This information was new and surprising to Brian.

Children often don't want to feel mad, or sad, or scared—these are considered feeling "bad." But owning and expressing "bad" feelings can be both healthy and beneficial. To explain this to children I might say, "If we couldn't feel pain and remember the hurt, we might burn our fingers over and over on a hot stove; if we couldn't feel scared even of really dangerous things, we might run out into the street after a ball when a car is coming. Feeling scared is our inside warning bell that says, "Watch out! Danger ahead! Be careful!"

To explain about anger I might say, "If we could never get mad we might let the school bully torment us again and again; being mad helps us try to protect ourselves by getting away, by telling the teacher, or even by hitting the bully back. Sometimes we may be angry when we see someone else getting hurt or someone being mean to an animal. Anger is the part of us that says, 'Hey, that's not fair—I don't like that!' Anger can help us feel strong enough to try and make things that aren't fair *more* fair.

"And feeling sad means we care about something. We feel sad about a stray dog that is cold and hungry or a friend who is hurt and in trouble. What would life be like if a best friend didn't miss *us* when we were not at school? Or if no one cared about animals at all?"

Happiness feels good and love feels good; these two are "easy" feelings and we all like having them. But scared, angry, and sad feelings are just as much about being human as happiness and love are. Children are often quite surprised to find out the "good" side of these "bad" feelings. Violet Oaklander also teaches children how expressing feelings—and withholding feelings—affects the body. When feelings want to come out and aren't allowed expression, they can make the body "sick" by causing a headache, a stomach-ache, or tight, sore muscles (Oaklander, 1988).

Children can be encouraged to access their disowned or dissoci-ated feelings through play therapy. The following is an example of how a child can discover and get acquainted with feelings that he finds either unacceptable or too hard to handle.

Brian made a sandtray scene that had lots of trees, and a child playing in a playground. He stated that the boy in the scene was very happy; the trees were happy too. After commenting that it's important to know what it's like to be happy, I asked what this picture would look like if there were something about it that was un*happy. How would the picture be different? Brian looked at his scene and decided to remove all of the trees. "Why?" I asked.*

"Because," said Brian, "if you don't take the trees out, the boy will play on them and break the limbs." He added broken trees.

"After the trees are broken, then how does the little boy feel?"

"Sad. His parents don't care that the trees are gone, and the policemen don't care either." This seemed to give Brian another idea. After rummaging quickly through the toys, he placed lots of policemen and other emergency hospital workers in the picture standing by, "just in case something should happen that we need them."

"What does the little boy have to play with now?" I asked.

"Well, he can play with the statues in the park."

Brian then made the boy doll climb up onto the statues; but by climbing on them, he knocked the statues over and broke them, too. It seemed that everything Brian's sandtray "boy" touched or might touch would be harmed. Although Brian's real-life words and behaviors were full of smiles and cheerfulness, play therapy allowed the disowned sadness and fears to surface.

I made up a different story to follow Brian's, using some of the elements Brian had given me to work with from his own sandtray story. His story showed me that many of his feelings of fear and sadness were related to feeling responsible in some way for bad things that happened. A feeling of hopelessness also permeated his story; trying to play only brought more pain. Without asking Brian to own up to feeling responsible, sad, and hopeless, I tried to reframe some of the beliefs I saw underlying those feelings, staying within the metaphor he had given me. Here is my story:

"Once upon a time there was a boy who had several toys and a pet pig to play with. The pig ran away and got lost in an old, abandoned playground. This old playground used to have play equipment and trees to climb, but now the equipment was all broken and the tree was dead and lying on the ground half buried. The boy went to find his pig and discovered it nosing around the playground. An old man was busy sawing up the dead tree limbs. The boy asked the old man how come the playground equipment was broken. 'Well, it was pretty old, and the city decided to take it apart so the little kids wouldn't get hurt playing on it. Good thing, too—it was all rusted up,' said the man. The boy looked at the tree he was sawing up. 'And how come the tree died?' he asked. 'Well, that's another thing,' the old man began. 'There were a couple of kids who used to like to play on that tree, and one of them climbed up on it and came crashing down, because the tree branch broke. Luckily, the boy wasn't hurt. Poor little guy thought he broke the tree branch, and felt real bad. Come to find out, that tree was diseased—sick—had been for years, and it was almost hollow. One day a strong wind came and just blew that tree over. It had died,

you see. Wasn't the boy's fault at all. And now it'll make good kindling wood for my fireplace.' The boy crouched down near the log, where his pig was sniffing. There beside the old tree trunk was a tiny new plant with just three leaves. The boy had an idea. He dug up the little plant and took it home; there he made a little hole in the backyard and carefully patted the soil around the new roots. He wasn't sure what kind of plant it would turn out to be — it was a mystery plant. But it grew and grew. And what do you think it grew up to be? Yup. A shady tree for climbing.

"Eventually the city cleaned out the old playground and built a new one with brand-new equipment and lots of trees. They hauled out the dead tree roots. But the boy wanted to remember the old tree where he had found the new plant growing. So he put a little rock by a bush in the new playground to mark the spot. And it stayed there forever."

Brian was just beginning his work to reown his sad feelings. With time, parental support, and continued therapy, Brian might learn to tolerate and express his intense feelings more openly. For dissociative children, addressing difficult feelings metaphorically in play allows them to access those feelings with a sense of safety (see Chapter Five).

BEHAVIORAL PROBLEMS

Lying

Lying can be a dissociative mechanism that children use to defend themselves when they experience too much anxiety about a "bad" feeling or a "bad" behavior. Many very young children can dissociate from what they are doing, saying, and feeling almost instantaneously. A two-year-old who takes the forbidden cookie when Mommy isn't looking and then gets caught may solemnly protest, "I didn't take a cookie!" even when the half-eaten cookie is in her hand. What parent hasn't experienced a similar episode with a youngster? This behavior may be considered "lying," but it is more often quite unconscious dissociation.

For an older child, lying is a form of denial, which is a dissociative defense. A child's denial is often a defense against a behavior or a feeling that the child feels anxious about. His behavior may cause him anxiety because he fears an adult's anger or disapproval (punishment) or because he doesn't want to feel his own guilt feelings about what he did (or felt).

Parents often perceive the lie—this wish to avoid the outside and inside consequences of a misbehavior—as "manipulation": "He's just lying because he doesn't want to get caught." Or parents may see the lie as a direct assault on the parent-child relationship. Parents often feel hurt by the child's lying: "I trusted you to tell me the truth—how can I ever trust you again?" Parents may feel so angry and hurt that they fail to realize what the lying really means: that the child is defending against something that feels frightening, that he is struggling to cope, and that he is using a defense tactic that isn't working well. And he may be using it unconsciously, rather than purposefully.

Six-year-old Marc was out playing in the park with another child while his mother and her friend sat on the grass and chatted. In a moment of anger, he picked up a sizable rock and threw it at his playmate. His mother severely reprimanded him, and told me about the incident at the next session. She recalled, "When I asked him, 'Why did you throw the rock?' he replied, 'I didn't—that was the other Marc, the one who spells his name different from me.'" By the time I talked to Marc about it in session, he didn't remember anything about the incident at all.

Marc may have wanted to immediately disown his behavior after doing it or to disown the angry feeling that preceded the behavior. He may have been trying to avoid his mother's anger, or he may have tried to avoid the feelings of guilt and disapproval that would follow his own awareness of his anger and his behavior. In any case, Marc dissociated his anger and his behavior immediately after experiencing them.

In therapy we played out the angry feelings and angry behavior in a story similar to Marc's real-life incident. During the play, Marc was able to recognize the story character's anger and the reality of his behavior, even though the story character denied the behavior as Marc had done. In a subsequent session, Marc had a question.

Looking at the "Feeling Chart" of children's faces depicting differ-ent feelings, he asked me: "If I take a cookie when I'm not supposed to, and say I didn't take it—but I really did—what feeling is that?" We decided it might be a scared feeling or a sneaky feeling. Marc was getting the idea.

For children who have been traumatized by abuse, lying may be even more than a defense; it may be a survival tactic. A child may learn to lie about certain feelings or behaviors to avoid abuse. Or he may learn to deny to himself and others that there has even been abuse, in order to keep the family intact ("Mom says if anyone finds out, Dad will go to jail and we won't have any money"). When the abuser is a parent, the child both loves and fears him or her, so denial of abuse (lying) protects both child and parent. Disavowal of the abuse, or learning to deny and lie, is part of the child abuse accommodation syndrome (Summit, 1983).

Ruthie, age 15, lied about all kinds of things—things that mattered and things that didn't matter. It had gotten to be a habit. Ruthie came in to see me with her grandmother because she wanted to stop lying. "I don't know why I keep doing it," she said with frus-tration. Ruthie had lived with her grandparents for the last several years. Her natural mother had physically abused her when Ruthie was small, and had been stopped by county intervention; now Ruthie saw her mother only on vacations.

When I asked Ruthie to tell me about living with her mother, Ruthie noted that her mother used to hit her a lot. "I never told anybody, not even my grandma. If anybody asked me how I got hurt, I just made something up." One day her teacher noticed a bad bruise and wanted to call her mother. Ruthie said, "I burst out crying because I didn't want her to call my mom—I'd get in worse trouble." So the school called protective services.

I reframed lying as something that had been useful and helpful to Ruthie to keep her from getting hurt much worse by her mother. This was something Ruthie could understand. She stopped putting herself down for lying. Realizing finally that her grandparents now would not allow her mother to hurt her physically again, and that she even had the option of not visiting her mother, Ruthie was finally able to stop lying.

While the child is learning which feelings or situations in her life (past or present) stir up enough anxiety inside to trigger dissociative denial, parents can help with a few behavioral interventions at home. Focusing on the betrayal of trust that they feel and hoping to "hear the truth," many parents fall into a pattern of *asking* the child whether he has misbehaved (e.g., lied about something), even when they already have good reason to suspect that he has. ("Did you put away the lawn mower like I asked you?") This has the effect of "setting up" the child to lie to the parents again, since the child still hopes to avoid the bad feelings and bad consequences of the original misbehavior. Parents can better help the child by simply confronting him firmly about any misbehavior, including lying. ("I discovered that you did not put away the lawn mower as I asked you to.") Parents may need reassurance that it is more helpful *not* to believe the child who has a history of lying to them, and to set clear and consistent consequences for misbehavior.

Stealing

Stealing is another behavior that often involves dissociation. Like lying, stealing has a powerful moral "shouldn't" attached to it, and therefore stealing also carries a lot of shame. Most often the two behaviors are combined; stealing is usually followed by lying about the stealing.

As with lying, a parent whose child steals may often feel personally affronted or betrayed, saying the child has "broken my trust." In addition to the disapproval of stealing, the parent's personal hurt adds guilt and shame to the family dynamic and to the child's inner experience. Genuine guilt about stealing is, of course, a positive thing, but if stealing is a dissociative defense then it is the child's attempt to block his own awareness of something inside that is very powerful and that causes him tremendous anxiety. The feelings of guilt that follow will usually not suffice to encourage the child to change his behavior. Guilt about this coping behavior (stealing) may be something he's willing to put up with. Or, as often happens, he may learn to dissociate the guilt feelings too, thereby compounding the problem.

Fourteen-year-old Paul stole money regularly from his siblings and his parents. They were angry and hurt, and no one in the family felt they could ever trust him again. In fact, they wanted him to "suffer" in paying them back, feeling he had made them suffer when he stole from them.

Paul stated that he knew he stole, and he knew when he did it; he spent the money on things he wanted. He recalled no feelings about his stealing until after he spent the money, at which time he occasionally felt guilty, but thought to himself, "Oh well, it's already spent, so there's nothing I can do about it." While describing his thoughts and feelings in the presence of his family, Paul was visibly ashamed and embarrassed about his behavior.

However, while the family and I were discussing the problem, a new wrinkle appeared. Father mentioned that Paul had stolen more recently than the last time Paul recalled doing it. "I didn't tell you about missing money from my tool cabinet this week," commented Father.

"I didn't take that!" Paul exclaimed. "I haven't stolen since a month ago."

"Well, I don't know who else could have taken it," Mother frowned.

I asked, "Paul, you don't remember taking money from your dad's workroom this week?"

"No," Paul repeated irritably. "The last time I did it I took twenty dollars from my brother."

Father turned to me. "I keep money in this little box in the basement tool cabinet, kind of like an emergency fund," he explained. "It's mostly quarters. The kids know where it is."

"Yeah," Paul admitted.

Father continued, "Most of the quarters were gone, and only pennies left."

Paul tilted his head thoughtfully, and his expression changed. "I did take it. I remember now. Yes, I did."

"You didn't remember taking it, but now you do?" I asked.

"Yes," said Paul, nodding.

"How did you retrieve the information?" I pursued.

"I pictured that little box, and the workroom in the basement, and I saw myself taking it."

"How much money was it, then?" Father wanted to know.

After a moment Paul replied, "About eight dollars."

"That's exactly right!" exclaimed his father, surprised.

Paul had dissociated his stealing behavior without even knowing it. By his own account, he probably also dissociated his feelings about stealing much of the time, since he could remember only feeling guilty sometimes right after spending the money. Then he used denial again to re-dissociate the guilt: "It's too late to do anything about it."

What might a child who steals be defending against? Stealing, particularly if it is chronic, indicates a child with an important need that is not being met. It may be a need for parental attention and affection, for example, or for peer approval and belonging. The discomfort of having such a basic need unsatisfied may be too anxiety-producing to keep in awareness (especially if the child believes it may be his fault that he doesn't get what he needs). Stealing can be a metaphorical solution. The child can dissociate from the need and the uncomfortable feelings about it *and* "get something" for himself at the same time.

Sometimes stealing can provide the child with a "high," a temporary thrill that feels exciting and good ("I did it! I got away with it!"). The internal chemical rush that accompanies stealing for some children can become quite addictive. Stealing can become habit-forming, just as using alcohol or drugs can. As such, addictive behavior is often dissociative behavior that allows the child to numb extremely uncomfortable feelings. Some children experience such a deep "low" welling up or such a vast emptiness inside that it requires a considerable "high"—even one that carries severe social consequences—to mask it.

The child's attempt to find attention, approval, belonging, or escape hides deeper, more devastating feelings: feeling invisible, unloved, without a place; feeling hurt, unhappy, and angry; feeling severely depressed, empty, or just plain "all wrong." These are powerful feelings that may be so anxiety-provoking or so over-whelming that the child tries to mask them or satisfy them with stealing. She cannot let herself know that she feels so invisible or unloved or "wrong," lest she feel more depressed and anxious. Nor can she let herself know she steals, or she will feel too guilty and ashamed. These are "bad" feelings that children (as well as adults) don't like to have—so they try to put them away from their aware-ness or disown them. Maybe then they won't exist, just like Brian hoped in the example given earlier.

I have found many young stealers to use this double technique: they steal in order to cover up or dissociate from a "bad" feeling inside, and then dissociate the stealing behavior, resulting in a "lie" to cover what they have done. With help, they are able to discover what that bad feeling is and then to face it and find better ways to handle it. Fortunately, stealing is often visible enough to call the parent's attention to the child's difficulty and allow help to inter-vene.

In therapy, reframing the behavior helps the child realize that stealing is an attempt to get something good for himself—some-thing he really needs: attention, affection, belonging, etc. The ther-apist can give the child permission to need things; all people have needs. Stealing then changes from something horrible to something meant to help; the child himself changes from "a bad person" to one who is trying to find ways to feel better. The resulting self-acceptance, combined with outside support, enables the child to begin to tolerate the anxious, "needy" feeling, to look for other ways to meet that need, and ultimately to replace stealing with something more satisfying.

The parents of a child who steals may be suffering inside as well. A parent may feel so personally responsible for and implicated by the child's bad behavior ("I must be a bad parent if my child steals") that he is overwhelmed by his own anger, hurt, guilt, and shame. Family members all benefit from sharing these feelings with one another and realizing that each of them is hurting. Reframing allows parents to see what the child's behavior is really trying to tell them: that he or she feels very needy and anxious.

Parents usually feel relieved when they find something they can do that helps. When a child is lying and stealing, the parents must maintain a firm stance about stealing, which includes providing appropriate consequences. They may need support to do this. Some parents are so eager to trust again that they help the child back into denial before the core problem can be addressed. It is important that the parents *not* trust the stealer again until he has made amends in an appropriate way and until he has refrained from stealing for an extended period of time.

I had been working with Tonia, a 12-year-old girl, for several sessions. Her mother let me know one day that she had become sure that Tonia was stealing from others at home; the things she took ranged from money to perfume to her sister's new birthday gift. When I asked the mother to confront Tonia about it, Tonia initially denied the behavior emphatically and accused her mother of being unfair and "blaming everything on me." However, once her mother gently told her she wanted to help, Tonia hung her head and admitted to stealing. Her body slumped, and her face suffused with red — one could almost see the shame filling up.

Alone with Tonia, I asked her to draw a picture of the part of her that steals. She drew a picture of "Freddy" (see Figure 4.1), a little boy who looked quite babyish and stood with his fingers in his mouth. A toy umbrella dropped from his other hand. Tonia told me, "This part thinks he can't get things that he wants just by asking."

"What does he want the most?"

"He wants attention," Tonia replied. Then we thought of possible ways to get mother's attention. Tonia wrote:

> *"Steal things,*
> *Scream and yell and act real mad,*
> *Say I need a hug,*
> *Ask her if we can go to the mall,*
> *Tell her I'd like to look for books*
> *at the library."*

Tonia was amazed to find that she had so many choices available to her for getting attention, most of them positive. Her mother affirmed that she was willing to listen to Tonia's requests for attention and that most of the time she could either supply Tonia's want

Figure 4.1 Drawing by Tonia, age 11, of "Freddy," a part of her that steals. Freddy appears to be much younger than 11, and is shown dropping a toy umbrella.

or make plans to provide it at a later date. After finding out that her Freddy part needed attention, and that she could actually have it in good ways, Tonia decided to accept that part of herself and stopped stealing.

✻ ✻ ✻

Heather, age 13, had spent the last seven years of her life in foster care. The current foster parents brought Heather in to see me when she was caught shoplifting several times, as well as stealing from others in the family. Heather had admitted to shoplifting, and felt remorseful, but she had vehemently denied stealing at home until some missing items were discovered in her pockets.

In therapy, Heather confessed that she felt ashamed of her behavior and promised herself she would stop — only to do it again. Over a period of time, a pattern emerged. Heather often felt jealous of her foster mother's natural children and their relationship. At the times she felt most left out, unwanted, and unloved, she stole. As Heather became more comfortable talking about these feelings to me, she was gradually able to share them with the foster parents, who were sympathetic. Although the family structure changed very little, Heather found that confronting her feelings and talking about them helped her accept them. Her stealing behavior stopped.

Sexualized Behavior

Sexualized behavior may occur as a symptom of post-traumatic stress, when the child has been sexually molested. Occasionally it may also appear when there has been no sexual abuse. For example, a child may use masturbation to release anxiety and tension inside that result from extreme tension in the home.

When a child has been molested, sexual feelings in the child may have been stimulated during the abuse. Sexual stimulation may have been paired with feeling helpless and trapped. The resulting mixture of excitement and pleasure with shame and humiliation can be very confusing for any child. And for some children, the combination of anxiety, physiological arousal, trauma, sexual stimulation and/or release, and dissociative numbing can become a post-traumatic behavior pattern aimed at decreasing anxiety.

Angela, age five, was discovered fondling a younger cousin during a family get-together. She had also sexually touched a little boy at kindergarten in the previous month. Angela was reenacting her own previous trauma, a common type of behavioral memory (Terr, 1990). Repetition of one's own abuse by doing it to someone else may be a child's unconscious attempt to gain control of an experience that felt disturbing and in which she felt powerless. Angela did not remember her sexual behavior afterward, and, in fact, she may have acted it out in a dissociated state.

Angela had many opportunities in therapy to play metaphorically about the sexual abuse that happened to her. As Angela recreated her experiences using doll figures, I verbalized feelings she acted out, and also provided ways for her to express and comment on the feelings being shown in the play, so that she could learn to accommodate those feelings. We also changed the story and the ending at times so that Angela had a chance to express thoughts and feelings that had to be stifled during the abuse. After a while, she no longer needed to act out sexualized behavior.

Post-traumatic play and reenactment are often quite literal, compulsive representations of the original trauma. This type of play contains no true playfulness, and is often without feeling. Replaying the trauma in therapy allows the therapist to see and understand the child's experience, and allows the child a chance to gain a sense of control over the experience in a safe setting. However, continued repetitions of post-traumatic play without therapeutic intervention can have more negative than positive effects, reinforcing the feelings of anxiety and helplessness (Gil, 1991). Continued post-traumatic reenactment can "set" the trauma cycle into harmful dissociative behavior patterns that become part of the child's personality style (Burgess, Hartman, & McCormack, 1987; Terr, 1990).

In therapy, interrupting post-traumatic play with opportunities to feel, comment, or change behaviors allows the child to complete the traumatic experience. The curiosity, excitement, guilt, and other feelings that were stimulated can be named and put into the context of the trauma. Stories and play allow the inner dissociated conflicts that underlie post-traumatic reenactment to surface, be evaluated, and resolved.

Lynette, age nine, had been sexually abused. Her foster mother worried about her habit of masturbation. Lynette told me, "Sometimes I can't sleep at night, and I lie awake and think about the past, and then I masturbate to feel better. Sometimes I do it in the daytime too. But afterwards I feel sad and lonely."

Lynette had taught herself to dissociate from the fear and trauma and to "go with" the good feeling during the sexual abuse she experienced; years later, she was still using the good part of the bad experience to mask other disturbing feelings when they surfaced. However, the dissociative behavior (masturbating) didn't take care of the problem now that the abuse had stopped; it only added more sadness, loneliness, and anxiety. Lynette needed to talk (or play) about the old trauma until much of the anxiety, sadness, anger, and shame about it was resolved. Until that could happen, the

*feelings were too big to be carried consciously and had to be disso-
ciated. She would also need to learn other ways to relieve anxiety
and loneliness.*

* * *

*Connie had been sexually abused by an older relative at age six. At
15, she now often found herself fighting off sexual advances from
boys in high school, and feeling helpless to defend herself. She also
tended to pick boyfriends who depended on her to help solve their
problems at home and school. Although she was flattered by their
attentions, these boys often wanted more from her than she really
wanted to give.*

*Therapy helped Connie become aware of conflict inside that
kept her in unsafe relationships. In a dialogue with her "sad" part
about the abuse that had occurred earlier, Connie discovered that
she felt drawn to pity the older boy who had molested her, and
wished she could help him. These feelings contributed to her dilemma about setting good boundaries for herself at 15. The dialogue went as follows:*

*Speaking as her sad part, Connie told me, "Connie shouldn't be
so mad at Bob [the abuser]. I feel very sorry for him, and pray for
him. God understands his pain, and so do I. I have to be the big
person here. I forgive him; I don't want him to hurt anymore. I
hope he turns his life around."*

*I commented, "You really care about Bob. And you have a very
loving heart. It sounds like you feel close to God; you can see when
people are hurting, and you feel for them."*

"Yes," Connie replied.

*After a pause, I continued. "I want to tell you something. Connie
was just a little girl when Bob hurt her. She was so scared and
little, and she didn't think anybody could help her. She had angry
feelings, an angry part of her, that tried to protect her, and
couldn't. Bob threatened little Connie and hurt her, and he was
bigger. A lot bigger. Connie needs your love and sympathy too.
She needed somebody to care for her when that happened, and to
care about her now. Did you know that?"*

*Connie looked at me consideringly. "I didn't think of that be-
fore."*

We talked about caring for oneself, and feeling love for one-

self—even for the parts of us that are angry and disappointed that we couldn't be big enough and strong enough to protect ourselves when we were little. Connie was able to see how caring for herself was different from being selfish or inconsiderate of others. This insight enabled her to see her friends—particularly boys—in a new light; she began to realize she could care about other people without crossing the line into ignoring her own wants and needs.

Aggressive Behavior

Aggressive behavior toward others is often an outgrowth of children's disowned anger. As mentioned earlier, anger is a feeling that many families have difficulty allowing and expressing. In addition, children often tell me that anger feels "violent" or that expressing it seems to them like "violence." Such is the intensity and power of a child's experience of anger.

Children have fears of doing harm to someone they love and whose approval and care they need if they express this violent feeling directly to a parent. They may even have fantasies about the violence they would like to inflict, which may increase the fear— and guilt—they associate with feeling angry toward a parent. So the "violence" children feel inside may be disowned partially or completely if parents fail to provide acceptance and model positive channeling of aggression.

What happens to the aggressive feelings when they are disowned? The child may displace them onto a sibling or peer, acting the feelings out with a safer object than the parent; he may use a passive-aggressive means of expressing the inner "violence," such as verbal teasing or sarcasm; he may try to swallow the anger entirely, leading to feelings of depression; or the child may turn the violence inward and direct those feelings on himself (see below, "Self-destructive Behavior").

Emotions have been observed in very young infants. The capacity for anger or rage is inborn, a part of being human (Izard & Malatesta, 1987). When an uncomfortable stimulus reaches a sufficient intensity, it triggers an internal "affect system," and the body reacts by tensing muscles in ways that are commonly experienced as anger; this stimulus-response pattern occurs whether we are consciously aware of those emotions and body sensations or not (Nathanson, 1992). Though we try, anger cannot be excised; it cannot even be ignored or shoved out of awareness without cost. Acting-out behaviors can be seen as an attempt by the body to bring the inner system some sense of balance when the child cannot own or express anger (Oaklander, 1988). The child may dissociate not only her angry and aggressive feelings but also the aggressive acting out she uses to cope with them.

Danny, age eight, was very fond of his fun-loving mother. He was also very angry with her; after his parents divorced, she rarely came to visit him and failed to keep many promises. Danny was afraid of losing her love, and defended his mother fiercely with excuses for her behavior—excuses that often duplicated her own exactly. The school sent home note after note about the fighting Danny initiated at school, and finally threatened to suspend him if something didn't change. So Danny's father brought him in to see me.

Danny was unable to consciously own his anger toward his mother for some time. But in play therapy a make-believe child did get angry at his make-believe mother; Danny made a "mother" doll out of clay and pounded that mother again and again for her negligence toward the child doll. His acting-out behavior at school and daycare dropped to zero.

Sometimes a child needs permission to accept her aggressive feelings. Confusion or fear about feeling angry and acting angry can occur particularly in children who have experienced physical and/or sexual abuse. An abusive adult may express his or her own anger intrusively and hurtfully toward other adults or children in the family. This is the experience of a child who has either witnessed or been the recipient of physical violence. The perpetrator may have been angry, "mean," or aggressive, but the victim may not have been allowed to be angry or fight back. If she did, she may have been hurt more in the attempt.

Children who have experienced these confusing messages about anger and aggression need to know about safe ways to express angry and mean feelings—they need to know that not everyone who is angry hurts another person or gets hurt. They may need to hear that aggressive feelings can be good and helpful, just as anger can. Feeling angry and "violent" signals a wish to defend and protect ourselves when others truly threaten us. Angry aggression, when directed at someone we are really angry at for a good reason—*and when it is expressed in a safe way*—may be empowering. Pottery clay is a wonderful medium for expressing these angry, rageful, and "fighting" feelings.

Cindy, age five, had been molested by an uncle. In therapy, we made the uncle out of clay, and Cindy smashed her abuser with a rubber mallet over and over until she felt finished. "Now I'm bigger than him!" she cried gleefully.

❖ ❖ ❖

Maria, age 10, was often aggressive toward others at home and at school. However, Maria was afraid to express her rage at a relative who had physically and sexually abused her. One day in therapy she made a very metaphorical story in the sandtray. Maria used blocks to create a house, and various mineral rocks to represent the characters, "Scared," "Love," and one bad man. Here is her story:

"Scared locked the door of the house so the bad man can't get in. And Scared is sitting on top of Love so Love can't get out either. But the bad man [a black rock] keeps them both in the house— they're trapped. The man leaves to go visit his other lands, and while he's gone, Scared gets out and plays with the other (scared) parts. Love also comes out to play. But then the man comes back and is angry with them for getting out. See, the man had put the Love in the house in the first place—but he wanted it all for himself."

Love and Scared obviously didn't like being trapped, but they seemed at the mercy of the bad man. I commented on the absence of angry or mean parts living in the house with Scared and Love, parts with angry feelings about what the bad man was doing. Reframing "mad" and "mean" as powerful and able to give Scared and Love some help, I added two sharp rocks to be on the "house" team, with Maria's permission. We then played out a different ending for the story.

In a subsequent session, Maria told another story showing her progress in directing her anger at the perpetrator. The characters

*were called "Bad, Ugly, Love, Scared, Mad, and Mean." Maria
was working in clay, and used clay figures for the characters in the
story. (Note: Maria's abuser went by the name of "Sandy.")*

*"Once upon a time there were two villages, one with a big foun-
tain of water and one with only dry sand. Bad and Ugly are asleep
in the sandy, dry village, because they're lazy. Love, Scared, Mad
and Mean are dancing and singing in their village around the fountain of youth. All Bad and Ugly have to play with is a pet sandbag.*

*"Mean is the sheriff of their village. Love and Scared stay around
the fountain to stay young. Then Bad and Ugly wake up. Love and
Scared are guarding the water, but they take a lunch break. Bad
and Ugly come to steal the water; Mad and Mean see them and put
them both in jail. The pet sandbag comes and takes a little bit of
the water, and then gets young and HEAVIER and BIGGER.*

*"But the sandbag doesn't know that Love and Scared are coming
back on duty, and they squeeze all the water out of the sandbag.
Then Mad and Mean lock him up. So Mean watches over the jail
and Mad helps Love and Scared demolish the sandbag. They rip it
open and throw all the sand out and stomp it into the ground. Bad
and Ugly get fined $100 each for letting their pet steal the water.
Love, Scared, Mad, and Mean each pound and smash Bad and
Ugly." (Maria carried this out with a hammer on the clay figures.)*

*"The fountain of youth is precious, because if you're young you
can play, and when you're old you can drink the water and do all
the things you didn't do when you were young." (This might be
Maria's attempt to comfort herself for her childhood losses.)*

Self-destructive Behavior

Aggressive expression of anger is fairly common in children, especially when they are unsure of how to express their anger in more
acceptable ways. Social and parental disapproval or punishment of
the child's aggressive feelings may increase the child's need to "get
rid of" them. One way to keep anger and aggression from going
onto others is to point them at oneself.

A certain amount of guilt accompanies most children's violent
feelings toward a loved one, especially if the child is young enough
to be fairly egocentric or to imagine that violent thoughts themselves may cause harm to others. Depression and self-blame often

occur when rage is "huge" and the child's inner mandates against feeling and expressing the rage are very strong. When the child has "punished" herself enough with self-blame or injury (releasing the angry and aggressive feelings on herself), a feeling of relief may follow, which helps numb the anxiety about having the "bad" feelings. Hurting oneself can elevate the child's anxiety level enough to activate the internal chemical changes that *alleviate* overwhelming anxiety—becoming part of a self-perpetuating dissociative cycle (van der Kolk et al., 1991).

Natalie, 11, had lots of anxiety about anger. Her parents brought her in for therapy because she was having tantrums followed by suicidal thoughts and wishes. A neurological checkup found nothing amiss. Natalie hit herself, pulled at her hair, and pinched and scratched herself, saying "I hate myself." She explained to me, "When I'm mad, I say things I don't mean, and then I want to die."

One day Natalie was at home with her mother and brother when she "went into a rage that went out of control," according to her panicked mother. Natalie had started out by fighting with her brother. Then, grabbing a knife from the kitchen, she held it to her own chest. After mom wrestled the knife from her, Natalie sobbed hysterically, saying she was afraid she might hurt herself or her little brother.

Natalie and her mother came in to see me the next day. Her mother reported that Natalie seemed like "a different person" during certain angry episodes, and that her eyes looked glazed. Mom also commented that Natalie refused to use the other more acceptable ways to vent her anger that we had already talked about and tried out, such as drawing or telling someone what she was angry about. Natalie looked away and covered her face. "Being angry is evil," she said.

Natalie's rage frightened her mother, who seldom raised her own voice. Perceiving the importance of being "good," Natalie had decided that the anger she felt must be bad—even monstrous. Full of shame and fear, she dissociated herself from her "evil," angry part.

In a subsequent session, Natalie drew her angry part as a monster with evil eyes, sneering and laughing at her. "When I am bad or mad I say really bad things, and I hear at church that the devil is looking for who he can take hold of." I explained that her angry part was just a normal part of her, something every little baby is born with, and it's not really bad or evil. But an angry part might get to thinking it is evil, especially when people want to get rid of it. Then the angry part starts to feel hurt and feels mad at its owner, too. Natalie began to get acquainted with her anger; we talked and played out scenarios about things that made her sad and angry, both past and present. She wrote out a conversation with her angry part on paper. It turned out that the angry part of Natalie wanted to be liked, and was willing to be helpful.

Natalie wrote to her angry part, "I have been scared of you. Why did you scare me?"

"I was mad at you. I'm sorry, I shouldn't have done that."

Natalie concluded, "I thought you were evil, but not now."

Natalie's self-destructive thoughts and behaviors diminished with more acceptance from herself and her family. She still raged and cried from time to time, but felt more control just in owning the anger as hers.

WORKING WITH PARENTS

When children feel it necessary to dissociate feelings or behaviors in order to cope with their anxieties about them, the parents can usually help by examining their own anxieties, expectations, and rules. Do they feel anxious and uncomfortable or upset and angry when the child is angry, sad, or scared? How do the parents *show* these feelings about the child's feelings? Do the parents' feelings and behaviors about the *child's* feelings show approval and modeling for healthy expression of feelings? Or are the parents' feelings and behaviors more apt to show disapproval and/or punishment of the child's expression of angry, sad, or scared feelings? Are power and control important priorities for the parents? If so, then power and control will be important needs for their children, and emotional safety will be an issue.

Because children *are* young and dependent, they need safety and support to make changes. Dissociation is a coping skill born out of feeling *unsafe*. When parents can support the child in new ways, allowing and encouraging the child to express herself and get her needs met in healthy ways, the outcome can be particularly positive. But if a child has little outside support besides the therapist, the process may be difficult and slow. A child's progress in treatment depends on her age, how much trauma she has been through, and how safe her environment is now. With good support, many children thought to be "hopeless" can confront their unmet needs, mourn their losses, and move past dissociation as a defense.

Most parents were not given permission, acceptance, or good modeling for expressing "negative" feelings when they were children. Intervention at the family level, looking at the family's generational rules and beliefs about anger and other emotions, can be extremely helpful in mending old hurts and misconceptions that may be playing out in the current nuclear family. I find that older children and teens really enjoy and appreciate a generational perspective on the family dynamics. When parents begin to understand their own feelings and beliefs better, and when children can share in that understanding, the level of blaming in the family decreases and mutual support and empathy increase.

Some parents may need to learn to express their own feelings in new ways. If the parents' behavior is abusive, this is absolutely essential. Again, the child cannot feel safe enough to look at what is troubling him, or trust the parent to do so, while that child must spend energy coping with abuse. If the child is to remain in the home and get better, the parents also must get better.

However, even without abuse in the home, a child may feel so anxious or emotionally unsafe that she turns to dissociation to cope. Nonabusive parents, too, may need new ways to express feelings. While some parents embrace this kind of new learning, others find that it feels very risky or difficult, given their own past learnings and current ways of coping. These parents may benefit from therapy just for themselves. However, I have found that even if (nonabusive) parents are unwilling or unable to make major changes in their own ways of feeling and expressing emotions, if they are able to genuinely encourage the *child* to do so — and if they can maintain appropriate boundaries — it may be enough.

Parents may also need support and information on setting ap-

propriate limits. Following a new understanding of the reasons for
dissociative behaviors and a message of permission to feel feelings—even "bad" ones—parents will need to provide some limits
for behavioral expression of feelings and encourage the child in
new ways of handling difficult feelings like anger. The therapist
can model active listening, good communication, and appropriate
consequences. One excellent resource for parents in learning these
skills is a book called *The Parent's Handbook: (STEP) Systematic
Training for Effective Parenting* (Dinkmeyer & McKay, 1989).
The authors present children's misbehaviors as arising from feelings
of discouragement rather than "badness" and give many, many
anecdotal examples of how to listen, how to talk to kids, and how
to apply suitable consequences.

As mentioned earlier, disowned feelings often have to do with a
person the child cares about and depends upon the most—a parent
or caregiver. Even if the child has not been abused, he may feel
quite wounded by his parents emotionally. Sometimes parents do
make every effort to acknowledge their failures and mistakes and
successfully make significant changes in their current thinking and
behavior—only to find that their child needs more time to nurse his
wounds. Such a child may successfully confront his own behaviors
and disowned feelings and yet remain unable to trust the parent
right away. It is important for both parent and child to know that
this is OK. Trust takes time.

Once old wounds are validated, a child may appear "stuck" for
a while in being angry with the parent, or unhappy, or unloving.
These feelings are hard for parents to face every day, and they
can inspire the return of parental guilt, hurt, or angry frustration,
especially if the parent had hoped for an improved "attitude" in the
child. But this is *not* the time to give up. Parents must hang onto
their new skills of permission-giving, accepting, and encouraging
appropriate expression of the child's true feelings. These "hard"
feelings may have been the same ones the child had been too anxious to let himself feel or express to his parents before—these very
feelings! The child may be testing to see whether his parents can
really handle this, or whether the child must go back to protecting
himself and his parents by dissociating and disowning his feelings
(and therefore, his "self"). The fact that he is now showing these

feelings (in spades) is testimony to the changes the parents have made in allowing that to happen.

What can a parent do when a child stays in an unhappy or unloving mode or an "I'm mad at you" stance for a period of time? Keep doing active listening (mirroring), and keep setting clear boundaries and consequences. Sometimes there may be nothing the parent can do in the moment to make the child feel happy, loving, cooperative, or different—if the child really needs to show the parent his angry, *un*happy, *un*loving, or hurt feelings. Trying to get the child to feel differently only creates a control issue and makes the child feel helpless and unsafe again. Parents need to know that they can stay in charge as parents and still be accepting and encouraging of their children's feelings and self-growth.

REPLACING DISSOCIATION WITH EMPOWERMENT

Children who dissociate their feelings of sadness, anger, or fear carry around a lot of anxiety that they don't know any other way to handle. The "bad" feelings themselves cause the child anxiety; the behaviors they use to mask those feelings (lying, stealing, destructiveness) may cause guilt and shame, which lead to further anxiety that has to be dissociated. While these children may look manipulative and powerful to their caregivers, inside they are feeling powerless and discouraged. If parents are willing and able to support their child in new ways of coping, establishing an atmosphere of safety in the home, the child can take the first step toward giving up dissociative defenses.

Next, reframing negative coping behaviors as attempts to protect or take care of oneself allows the child to accept herself in a positive way. Being angry must be reframed as a positive emotion; lying, stealing, and aggressive behaviors can be presented as efforts to meet important needs. Once the child opens to the possibility that she is not "bad," and that her intentions are not bad either, she can begin to admit other choices for expressing feelings and meeting her needs.

Discovering and making new choices can feel very empowering to children. Sometimes a child only has to see the choices to begin trying them out, as in the case of Tonia. Others will need modeling and practice to incorporate new choices into their personal repertoire.

Connie wanted boys to stop taking advantage of her. As her therapy progressed, she became more and more aware that her own behavior contributed to being used by others, but this realization did not immediately open other choices to her. Meeting others' needs was very familiar to her, but when asked how to meet her own she drew a blank.

Connie and I role played frequently so she could learn new choices by watching and practicing. Initially, I asked Connie to play the part of the aggressive or intrusive boys she ran across in her life, and I played the part of "Connie" to show her some new possibilities. Then we reversed roles. Sometimes we reversed roles again, so Connie could see how she looked and sounded in her new assertive role. (I played "Connie" attempting to be firm and self-protective.) She noticed that her first efforts at assertiveness looked and sounded "wimpy" or gave ambiguous signals that might appear to a boy to mean "go ahead." Anger and what felt to her like "meanness" were parts of herself that Connie began to reown and use to help her make truly assertive responses to unwanted sexual advances and unwanted attention from boys. Then she began to feel her own power.

Because she had been molested as a young child, Connie particularly needed the support and protection of her parents as she began to change. The process of reowning her scared, sad, and angry feelings and incorporating them into new self-protective behaviors was quite a risk for Connie and required lots of courage. Her parents backed up Connie's complaints about schoolmates by confronting school personnel when needed. When Connie wanted to "ditch" persistent young males on the phone or when she was out with friends, her parents offered themselves as alibis ("My dad says I can't stay/can't talk," etc.). Her parents helped create a safe home base. With such loving support, and her own new insights and skills, Connie blossomed from a frightened victim into a powerful young woman.

Chapter Five

ASSESSMENT AND
TREATMENT TECHNIQUES

The advantage of play therapy is that it enables us to use make-believe and metaphor—which are in themselves dissociative processes—toward therapeutic ends. Because dissociative processes are so much a normal part of what children do and how they think, using that same mode in therapy feels comfortable to them.

> With children the process of retrieval and reintegration may itself remain largely dissociated from immediate conscious awareness. This is not to say that children never follow the adult model . . . [b]ut we must repeatedly remind ourselves not to impose an adult discursive style upon the child. For many children such an interactive style will be foreign and very anxiety-provoking. (Donovan & McIntyre, 1990, p. 68)

I believe that in most cases awareness assists change, and that children derive a greater sense of self and a more solid foundation for self-esteem if they are able to "own" their own feelings, thoughts, and behaviors. However, children do not *have* to understand their behavior consciously in order to change it. Feelings and thoughts are often powerful without being conscious, and change can occur by being routed solely through the unconscious. This is what I call going through the child's "back door." In fact, when the therapist is staying present with the child using the metaphor of play, the most effective interventions may originate from the therapist's own "back door" as well. Therapy may facilitate significant changes inside the child without the therapist being consciously aware of what the child specifically finds therapeutic.

> With one child I made a baby out of a piece of clay, told her it was she, and made believe I was giving it a bath. The child felt happy and satisfied, and that evening she suggested to her mother that she begin to take showers. (She had previously refused to take baths *or* showers.)
>
> If this child had said, "I'm aware that I miss being treated like a little baby again now that my baby brother is on the scene, and I won't take a bath until someone recognizes this," I would probably "understand what happened." All I really know is that I was able to give the child an experience that was satisfying to her and that allowed her to feel secure enough to easily take another small step toward growing up. (Oaklander, 1988, p. 60)

Many children are able to face up to a difficult feeling, a powerful negative belief (e.g., "It's my fault my mom left me"), or a dysfunctional behavior only after doing some projective work in art or play. Staying in the dissociative mode permits children to show, rather than tell, the therapist "where it hurts," and to feel safe while they make changes through unconscious processes. Some children seem never to get to the point of conscious awareness, but still make significant changes by working only in the metaphor.

ASSESSMENT: CREATING A PICTURE OF THE CHILD'S INTERNAL PROCESS

Assessment of the child's process is ongoing throughout treatment. By allowing the child to set up a scenario "in play," the therapist can watch the child's process. For younger children, the dollhouse is often useful; for children age 12 to 16, the sandtray may be more acceptable. Either medium aids the therapist in assessment by showing where the child's inner conflicts lie and allowing the child to recreate a relational problem or traumatic experience that may cause him too much anxiety to address directly ("Daddy loves

Bobby more than me" or "Mommy hits"), to show which feelings, thoughts, or behaviors the child accepts in himself and which he disowns, and to illustrate an unspoken belief underlying a dysfunctional coping behavior ("It's my fault bad things happen").

Using the dollhouse, I may start by asking the child to set up the rooms however he wishes and to people the house with whatever kind of family he wants. I observe his energy level, his movements, the way he does things. Many children begin naturally to talk about the scene they have created, or to act out a scenario with the dolls. If not, I may ask some questions:

- "Does this family have a mom? A dad? Kids?" (I note how the constructed family is the same or different from the child's real family.)
- "Is it daytime or nighttime in this house right now?"
- "Where will you put the mother doll? What is the dad doing? And the kids?"

Following the initial set-up, the therapist can switch to play, talking to the doll figures rather than directly to the child. Sometimes I even say, "I'm going to talk to this little boy right here in the bedroom upstairs. Little boy, . . . " I may then coach the child, "You be the boy's voice," or I may hesitate after my initial question or comment and whisper to the child, "What does he say now?" using the child's answers to keep the dialogue going. Sometimes the child will say, "You be [the daddy] and I'll be [the boy]." This works just as well. If I know something about the child's real-life daddy, I'll play him that way; otherwise I will ask the child for cues about how the father figure would behave.

Another way to start is for the *therapist* to set up a family scene or other potentially significant context using information about the child's background. Staying in the "pretend" mode, the therapist then asks questions like those above, always directed to the doll figures, and always in an appropriate "pretend" voice. Moving right into playing rather than talking to the child directly allows the child to dissociate from real life one step further, "becoming" immediately the play figure of the child, or the mom, or the sister, etc.

Once the scene is set, the therapist can find out how everyone in the pretend family is feeling or how the house is feeling (or the dog or cat, etc.). To keep the child within the safe space of the metaphor, it usually helps, especially early in treatment, for the therapist to refrain from crossing over into commenting or questioning about "real life." Other types of questions I find useful within the play interaction:

- "What happens next?"
- "So it's nighttime and everyone is in bed. Then what happens?"
- "And what does [other doll character] do then?"
- "And then how does [doll figure] feel when [other figure] does that?"
- "Let's pretend. You be the [doll character's] voice. What is he saying right now?"

Questions can be interspersed with play dialogue, so the child doesn't feel interrogated. In early sessions, if the child doesn't answer a question or says "I don't know," it is wise not to push but to accept the child's limit as to how much she is willing to respond. It is more important to provide safety. Reflective listening, with comments back to the child regarding the overt and covert feelings he is showing, may be helpful during this process if the therapist stays matter-of-fact and does not demand agreement from the child or the child's play character.

Another possible direction is to simply allow the child to play with the figures in the scene he has created. This approach may be the safest and least intrusive way to start with traumatized children. It also allows the therapist a chance to observe how the child moves, thinks, and feels, and to get a sense of how the child perceives and experiences his world. The storyline that evolves from what he makes the doll people do and say reveals what is going on inside or real-life experiences, past or present.

In setting up a sandtray scenario, I may ask the child to create a picture of anything he'd like *and* to put one or two animals or people in his scene. I sometimes ask the child to create a family scenario using animal figures or human figures. Possible questions to ask would be similar to those listed above:

- "Tell me about your picture. What is this you've made over here?"
- "And what's happening in your picture?"
- "How do the animals/people/trees/cars, etc. feel? This one? And this one?" ("Of course we know cars don't really have feelings; but if we could pretend they did, what would this car here be feeling right now?")
- "Do these animals/people know each other?"
- "How do they feel about each other?"
- "How does this one feel right now?"
- "You be [this animal's] voice. What would he say right now if he could talk?"
- "Could I ask the [animal/tree/car] something? I'll ask, and you be the [car's] voice and say something back to me."
- "I bet you've watched a video that you play on a VCR. And you can make the movie stop by putting it on 'pause,' and then push 'play' to make it keep going. If your picture was part of a movie you made, and we put the movie on pause, maybe we could see this scene you made right here. Now if we push play again so the story keeps going, what will happen next in your movie?"

The pictures and story the child creates, what he shows or fails to show, as well as his responses to the therapist, can be quite revealing. For example, sometimes a child will leave out a family figure that I know exists in the child's actual family, stating, "In this house, there isn't going to be any daddy." Putting this statement together with the child's history can give the therapist clues. It may indicate inner conflict about a "daddy" figure in real life, e.g., the wish that he could really make the dad "go away," or simply acceptance of the reality of an absent father.

When children create a family scene, I sometimes run across the statement "pretend that didn't happen," which is a clue to anxiety and dissociation. Sometimes the child senses that his play has revealed too much or looks too much like real life.

Merrie is one of the DID children whose story is mentioned in Chapter Two. Early in her therapy, Merrie sets up a story in the sandtray. There are two mothers who are neighbors, and both mothers have five children. Mother #1 is nice and pretty; mother #2 is strict and has rules. All the kids like to play at Mother #1's house; that family has a nice yard, toys, boats and other indicators of wealth. However, when one of the little girls comes over to play and whines a lot, Mother #1 "banishes her to Cleveland — the mother owns the whole world." At school, Mother #1's favorite child, "the aerobics kid" who likes to exercise, gets sick. The sick child goes to see the school nurse; a doctor comes in and gives her a shot, and then laughs. Merrie then makes Mother come to the school and laugh at the child also, and give her more shots. "She's going to need surgery," says the mother doll. (At this point, I ask how the little girl doll is feeling; Merrie wants me to be the girl doll.) In a little girl voice I say, "I'm scared! I don't like shots!" Merrie suddenly stops short, looking at the sandtray scene. "Pretend that didn't happen," she said, looking anxious. "They didn't give her shots." Later, when I asked Merrie if she ever had surgery, she looked completely blank.

Merrie showed her experience of the world and how she coped with it in several ways in this sandtray scenario. Merrie was living with her foster father and mother (Mother #2) and experiencing conflicting feelings about her natural mother. She described Mother #1 as "nice and pretty" but showed her behaving like a sadistic despot who exiled a whiny child and laughed at a hurting one. The child's helplessness was vividly portrayed by the comment that Mother "owns the whole world." My question about how the child felt and my portrayal of it were too soon or too much. My question about real life at the end also made Merrie too vulnerable at that point. Merrie was afraid to acknowledge that the child felt frightened and that "mother" frightened her. It was apparent from this short example that in Merrie's experience of mother-child relationships it was not OK for the child to have needs. It was also apparent that Merrie had experienced mother as sometimes nice, sometimes cruel—thus very confusing. It would be useful to explore with her foster parents whether this child had ever had surgery or serious illness, or even whether there were any indicators of ritual abuse in her history.

"Pretend that didn't happen" is seen in children with milder dissociative patterns as well. An example follows.

Danny was a child with a neglectful mother who didn't keep her promises. One day Danny painted a picture and created a story about a blue "Y" (two blue intersecting lines in the painting). In his story, a bully with a little brother showed up, and the blue Y called the bully names. Then the bully's father and the blue Y's father asked, "Who started this fight?" Danny made the blue Y lie about what happened. But when blue Y's father found out he lied, Danny said, "Pretend he didn't say it—he didn't lie."

Here Danny showed his denial and discomfort about recognizing lying behavior, wanting to dissociate from the whole issue. Any story the child creates can tell the therapist where the child is stuck.

ART

Art provides a medium and a method for children to express what is contained in the unconscious. For dissociative children art can be especially helpful, because when the child becomes involved with the paint or clay and the process of creating, she enters naturally into an altered state of consciousness, allowing unconscious material to be projected onto her work. Art can also be useful as an assessment tool.

Artwork provides the therapist with a chance to observe the child's process, whether she is drawing, painting, or using clay. Is she timid, worried about making mistakes? Or is she bold or haphazard in her movements? Is she anxious or relaxed? Is her style cramped, small, and neat? Or is it messy and careless, needing lots of space or material? These are all clues to the child's inner state and her way of interacting with and in her environment.

Specific types of drawings, such as the House-Tree-Person

(H-T-P) and Kinetic-Family-Drawing (K-F-D) are very helpful in assessment (Burns & Kaufman, 1972; Jolles, 1971). The child's manner of drawing, the focal points of the drawing, and the emotional content are all clues to the child's inner world. Drawings can provide information about how the child perceives and interacts with important people in her life, as well as how she views herself (Burns, 1982). Preoccupation with sexual themes or body parts, or extreme concerns about self-protection may be clues to physical or sexual abuse (Burgess & Hartman, 1993; Wohl & Kaufman, 1985). Figures 2.1 and 2.2 in Chapter Two are examples of drawings by children who had histories of such trauma.

Like play therapy, art allows the child to express herself metaphorically, which feels safe; the therapist can then encourage the child to enlarge on or interact with the drawing or the clay sculpture, increasing the opportunities for self-expression and awareness. Oaklander (1988) offers a variety of interventions to use with artwork of all kinds. Of these, the ones I use most often are similar to the comments and questions I use in play therapy.

- "Tell me about your picture/sculpture."
- "Tell me more about [this part, object, color, shape] over here."
- "If this [object, color, shape] could talk, what would it say?"
- "Pretend you are the [object, color, shape] and tell me about yourself (e.g., 'I'm a circle with lots of blue ink in me'). What are you used for, or what do you do? How does it feel to be [object, color, shape]?"

These interventions can be tailored to fit the child. Open-ended, nonspecific comments are better for the early stages of treatment and for children who are very anxious; questions that encourage conscious awareness and emotional connections are helpful for children who have had time to become more comfortable with themselves and the therapist.

Ann, age 10, had a history of physical and sexual abuse. One day, while working with clay, she decided to make an ashtray, hoping to take it to school to use in a skit. When she had finished, we talked.

"Pretend you are the ashtray, and tell me about yourself," I suggested.

"Well, let's see. I am an ashtray, and I'm gray and I have cracks in me. Some of the cracks were made from birth, due to my mom. (But those are OK, Mom!)" she added with a giggle, although her mother wasn't present. She continued, "Some of my cracks are from cigarettes that are too hot, grinding into me." Ann stopped and looked at me. "That's abuse," she said with a wry face. After looking at the ashtray in silence a moment, she began blowing off some bits of dry clay on the surface.

"Ashtray, what is it like to have air blowing on you?" I asked.

"I like it. I have a blower to blow the ash off, because it's hot and it hurts," Ann replied. Then she smoothed out the cracks in her sculpture, especially where the cigarettes would lay. "There," she said, "that's so the ashtray won't hurt while it's doing its job. Now it doesn't need a blower anymore to cool it off."

In her sculpture and her verbal "translation" of it, Ann metaphorically described her pain, distinguishing between unintentional and deliberately inflicted injury. She also validated her self-worth and activated her own nurturing to help in the healing process.

REFRAMING

Reframing is both a technique and a process. The therapist reinterprets the negative or blaming meaning of a particular feeling, thought, behavior, or experience as something positive. Most feelings and behaviors children have learned to perceive as "bad" can be reframed as helpful, protective, or attempting to satisfy needs. Negative meanings of hurtful experiences, such as "It was my fault," can also be reframed into meanings less burdensome and binding for the child.

Once the child has begun to show what processes are characteristic of him, and under what circumstances or triggers he needs to use his internal distancing, the therapist can begin reframing and offering new options. This can be done either by staying in the medium the child is currently working with or by using another. Reframing often needs to be repeated in various ways and offered over a period of several sessions, allowing the child time to assimilate the new information. Following is an example of how reframing can become an ongoing process throughout the course of therapy.

Sandra, age eight, was a quiet, compliant child who seemed much older than her age. Her mother had been seriously ill for several years, and Sandra was already a great help around the house. However, she had few friends and worried about leaving her mother's side. Her interactions with me in therapy revealed that she was quite uncomfortable with playing. She seemed to have disowned even being a child and having childish wants and needs. In addition to challenging Sandra's egocentric beliefs about her mother's illness, I began reframing playfulness, "selfishness," and childishness as normal and OK.

When we played board games, Sandra initially apologized for winning, bringing her role of caretaker into the therapy sessions. But I crowed gleefully over my wins and encouraged her to do the same. We had contests to see who could brag the best and snort the loudest. In artwork, Sandra started painting with brushes and progressed to fingerpainting. She began to have favorite games and activities and ask to play them. We practiced leaving the playroom "just a little" untidy when she left. After a few months, Sandra was even able to have a pillow fight in which she tried to "get me" in earnest. Her mother reported that she began to ask about having friends over and had developed an interest in riding her bike—even to the school playground several blocks away.

INTERACTIVE STORYTELLING TECHNIQUES

Many children, especially in the ages from four to twelve, are eager to help create a story along with the therapist. If the child starts a storyline, the therapist can finish it; if the therapist starts the story, the child can add to it; or therapist and child can agree to take turns creating the story. Being part of the child's story gives the therapist a chance to insert cues and see where the child will go with them, which helps in assessment. It also gives the therapist an opportunity "midstream" in the child's process to reframe and create new choices. The therapist can also make a "sequel" to the child's completed story, using Gardner's (1977) technique of keeping the same cast of characters and creating a different ending.

Stories can be acted out using clay figures, sandtray scenes, the dollhouse, or puppets. Very young children (ages three to eight) love puppet shows where the therapist conceals herself behind a screen; they become very involved with the puppet characters and in their interactive "helping." In this way children can safely recreate a situation that in real life causes them much anxiety. Through the safe medium of play they are free to try out hidden feelings or new ways of responding and, with the therapist's interventions, find new solutions to their problems.

An example of this occurred with Danny, the child with a mother who broke her promises. I created a puppet story to simulate his real-life external and internal conflict. Through interactive storytelling, Danny initially recreated his own dissociative pattern and his wish to believe that his mother was not really neglectful or untruthful ("Pretend she didn't lie"). However, the puppet character (due to my input) continued to have a problem that was not resolved with Danny's usual style of coping. This forced Danny to tolerate a little of the anxiety that he usually sidestepped by pretending things were different. As our puppet story continued, Danny had an opportunity to try on another way to cope with the anxiety. (If the child were unable to come up with other possibilities, the therapist would have a story character suggest one or two.) In Danny's case, he was able to nurture the puppet character (developing the self-care part of himself) through his distress and help him find a different solution. Following this session, Danny's play involved stories of people or animals that "lied," and comments about those lies. Instead of denying that people sometimes lied to him, or pretending people and events were different, Danny was assimilating the reality of his situation and perhaps also attempting to desensitize himself to it.

How to Create a Story Metaphor

Therapeutic storytelling is a calculated "back door" technique. To be effective, the therapist's story must incorporate the major aspects of the child's inner conflict and the parts of himself involved in that conflict; also, the story must forge a path for the child where he has not been able to go himself. Sometimes children will work along quite well for a while, showing increasing awareness and ability to verbalize needs and feelings, and then hit a block—a vulnerable spot. Other children need to do all or most of their work through the unconscious because of anxiety, lack of safety in the environment, or simply because of the child's individual style. When thoughts and feelings are so scary that children cannot verbalize or process them consciously, a therapeutic story can "talk for them."

Usually, as I mentioned earlier, I build a story from a piece of material the child has just given me in his or her play. Sometimes, however, I like to give more thought to a story's creation. In those cases, I choose a metaphor carefully and structure the story to reframe a larger issue. For the interested clinician, Mills and Crowley (1986) discuss at length how to create story metaphors for children. I use a less complicated method, which seems to work well.

Here are the steps I use to creating a story. After some practice building little stories from the child's dollhouse or sandtray scenes, formulating more complicated stories is not difficult.

1. Start with the inner conflict the child shows in her play themes. If there are several, pick one only per story. This will become the foundation for the therapist's metaphorical story.

2. Pick characters to represent symbolically the various *important* aspects of the conflict. You may have to simplify the theme somewhat, or make two separate stories if there are many conflictual elements, so the child can absorb one or two main points at a time. When choosing a symbol to represent the child herself, pick one you know the child identifies with, preferably something for which the child has already indicated a preference (Mills & Crowley,

1986). For example, if a child particularly likes German Shepherd dogs, build a story around a German Shepherd dog; if she adores chocolate, make a story about "The Little Chocolate Cupcake."

3. Use as many sensory modalities in the story as possible: taste, sound, sight, smell, emotion, touch, inner feelings such as pounding heart, heavy legs, etc. This allows the child to "get into" the story with you, and makes the story seem real. When you are telling or reading the story aloud, use your voice to create sensory expressions: fast or slow, loud or quiet, big or little, hard and soft, happy or angry, sad or tired, etc.

4. Have the child relax on the floor or chair, with eyes closed if she wishes. Or let the child draw while you tell the story. Either way helps the child go into trance as she listens to the story. And the story itself will put the child into an altered state, so that information and learning can be assimilated through the child's unconscious.

5. Create the same conflict the child experiences, using the metaphor.

6. After presenting the conflict of the story, and approximating the child's experience metaphorically with the opening scenario, the storyline can:

   (a) reframe the problem situation in a new light;

   (b) allow a disowned part of the child (as a story character) to emerge and demonstrate a feeling the child is afraid to express or own;

   (c) have a story character take an action the child denies, rejects in himself, or thinks he can't do;

   (d) say something the child might like to say but can't;

   (e) challenge the child's erroneous belief about self or others.

7. The story should offer a resolution or partial resolution of the original conflict, which will allow the listening child to experience either an increased ability to tolerate feelings, a reduction in anxiety, or a change in the way she perceives/experiences/acts on/gives meaning to the central problem. Possible story resolutions might include:

(a) a different outcome than the child has expected occurs, since the story characters offer the child new options.

(b) the child (in the story character) makes a different decision, expresses a new belief, or takes a different action than the child usually does;

(c) external help or resources become available and help the child (story character);

(d) a helper part of the child or inner resource aids the child in the story.

Breanna, age eight, was brought in by her mother. Mother, who had worked outside the home most of Breanna's life, felt guilty for leaving her in daycare. Breanna showed lots of anger at home, but was clingy when her mom left her at school, the sitter's, etc. In therapy sessions, Breanna's play themes showed "bad" little children who were rejected and abandoned. Following is a story I created for her using mythical creatures and a magical theme. Such a theme works well for many children but is not advised for children who have been exposed to ritualistic cult abuse.

"Once upon a time there was a kingdom at the foot of a high mountain, which sloped gently down to the ocean. The royal castle was nestled down in the valley next to the sea. Now, the King was a nice man, and everyone liked him. But the Queen was sad—no one knew why. She moped around the castle all day and never went out. The Queen was said to have a beautiful baby, but she never took the baby out either. She was just very, very sad.

"In the village of this kingdom, there were two girls who were friends: Jill and Pam. The girls liked to play up in the mountains by a pond. They especially liked to catch frogs and go fishing with their fishing poles. Not many other children knew about their special place to play, so they had the pond all to themselves.

"One day a big, black crow flew over them and circled awhile. Then suddenly it swooped down and said, 'CAW, CAW, CAW!' The crow was so loud that it scared the frogs, and the fish, and even the squirrels and deer ran away. Pam was mad. 'Go away, crow!' she said. But Jill stood thinking about it for a while. The *next day, the same thing happened. This time, the girls got a good look at the crow: it was HUGE. That frightened Pam. She thought the crow was mad at them for some reason. But Jill thought maybe the crow was crying. When the crow showed up at the pond the third day, the girls stopped going there to play, and played at home instead.*

"Then the big crow flew down into the village, and went from house to house, almost as if it was looking for someone. Soon the whole town knew about the big bird. The crow even flew up to the Queen's window in the castle—which made the Queen cry even more. And that made the King mad! He offered a reward to whoever would kill the huge crow.

"When Jill found out about the reward, she felt sad. People tried to shoot the crow, but missed it. Everyone in the village seemed angry about the crow and even scared of it. People started staying indoors whenever the crow was around. And because of that, their crops went untended, and the cows didn't get milked, and pretty soon there wasn't food to sell at the market. Jill kept thinking and thinking. Finally she decided, 'I'm going to find out what's the matter with that crow.' She trudged back up the hill to the pond by herself, and waited.

Sure enough, here came the big crow. It sat on the ground near Jill and began to CAW loudly. 'I'm not afraid of your voice,' said Jill. Then the crow flew up, circled over Jill's head, and lunged at her. She could feel its feathers brush her leg, and saw the crow's piercing black eyes. Now she did feel scared.

"'Why are you doing that?' cried Jill. 'I only want to help. I don't think you're really a bad crow at all. But if you don't stop, the King will hurt you.'

"Then the crow came to her, opened its beak, and began to speak. 'I've looked for you everywhere. Only you can help me.'

"'Why?' asked Jill.

"'I have had a spell put on me, and only someone with a kind heart can help me,' said the crow.

"'How can I help you?' said Jill.

"'You must let me ride on your shoulder and carry me to the Queen. Then the spell will be broken.'

"'But somebody will kill you if you try to go in the castle!'

"'*You must not let them! Please help me!*' *pleaded the crow frantically.*

"*So Jill sat the big crow on her shoulder, and petted it. The crow started to cry. 'No one has ever petted me before. Most people think I am bad and ugly. And most people are mad at me or scared of me. But I have never hurt anyone.*'

"'*I know,*' *said Jill. 'You are not a bad bird at all, and I don't think you're even ugly, either. Your feathers are real shiny. You are very sad, though. I like you, and I'll take you to the Queen.*'

"*Jill walked and walked. It took her all day to walk to the castle, and she had to pass right through the village. People in the village shouted nasty words at them, or ran inside their houses. Some men wanted to shoot the crow, but Jill said, 'You'll have to shoot me, too.' So they didn't. Even Pam tried to talk her friend out of going to the castle, but Jill just kept walking.*

"*By evening, they got to the castle and knocked at the gate. The crow sat at Jill's feet by the door. Guards answered, and immediately surrounded Jill and the crow. They pointed all their swords at the crow, and put their arrows in their bows, ready to strike. The King came downstairs. When he saw the crow there, he was very angry, and commanded the guards, 'Shoot!'*

"'*Stop!!*' *cried Jill. Nobody moved as Jill bent to pick up the bird.*

"*Then, something unbelievable happened! When Jill bent to get the crow, the crow was gone! And in its place was a tiny little baby. The baby was a girl, and she was wrapped in a pink and lavender blanket. The baby was asleep, but all the shouting woke her up, and she started to cry. Jill picked up the baby and held it tenderly. 'Poor baby—you weren't really a crow at all! I wonder who put such a mean spell on you?' She gave the baby her finger to suck on, and smiled.*

"*The Queen appeared in the room. 'What is going on?' she demanded.*

"*Jill curtseyed with the baby, who was not crying anymore. 'Do you know anything about this baby, Madam?' she asked.*

"'*That's my baby!*' *gasped the Queen. 'A wicked witch took her away from me and said I would never see her again.' The Queen took the baby in her arms. 'My poor baby! Did that witch hurt you? I missed you so much! All the time you've been gone, I've thought about you and missed you.'*

"*Jill told the Queen, 'She only put a spell on her. The baby was the big, black crow that came to your window.'*

"*Every voice in the room stopped. There was total silence. Everyone stared, and their mouths dropped open.*

"'*It only took someone to be nice to the crow and keep it safe, and pet it, and bring it back to the castle. It never was a bad crow, mister King. It was your baby,' explained Jill.*

"'*Well!' exclaimed the King. 'Guards — outside!'*

"*The Queen hugged Jill. 'Thank you so much. You are a very brave and wise young girl.'*

"*The King and Queen and their baby lived happily ever after, and the baby grew up to be a beautiful princess. And when she was old enough, Jill and Pam taught the princess to catch frogs and grasshoppers, and how to fish in the pond. And they made friends with any crows that came by to watch!*"

In this story, the two girls, Jill and Pam, represent two parts of the real child, Breanna — a part that is afraid, and a part that is nurturing. The crow represents Breanna's rejected (baby) self. The nurturing self accepts the baby self, reframing it as not ugly or mean or unworthy, but misunderstood. The baby self is drawn back into the child's positive self-concept. This story was followed by immediate observable changes in Breanna's play themes and in her behavior at home, and she began to develop her ability to nurture herself.

USING GESTALT DIALOGUES

Once the child's disowned parts are identified, a Gestalt dialogue with the disowned part is useful (Oaklander, 1988). Ask the child to pick a puppet to represent parts of herself or to draw a picture of a (negative) part of herself. If the child is not ready or able to confront herself in this way, the therapist can start a dialogue between two figures in a story scene, two parts of a clay sculpture, two figures in a painting, etc. Since the child projects herself into any work, any part of it can represent a part of the self symbolically. As such, it is all useful therapeutic "fodder." Then the therapist can help the child get to know that part.

Some therapist prompts might be:

- "What do you want to say to your _____ part (or doll/clay/painting figure)?"
- "What would your _____ part say back to you?"
- "How do you feel when your _____ part says that?"

As therapist, *you* can also ask to talk directly to this externalized part. For example:

- "_____ part, how do you feel when [child] says 'I hate you'?"
- "What would you like from [child]?"
- "Is there another part of [child] who could help you?"

Andy, age eight, felt bad about getting any grade below a B in school. I asked him to draw a picture of a part of himself that gets bad grades. He did and titled it, "A dumb part who doesn't understand anything." (See Figure 5.1.)

"Tell your dumb part what you don't like about him," I suggested.

"I don't like that you're so dumb," Andy declared. "I want to throw you out."

I continued, "Dumb part, would you tell Andy what you'd like to say?"

As his dumb part Andy replied loudly, "I'll always be here—you're never going to get rid of me!"

Then Andy didn't know what to do; the two parts had reached an impasse. We talked more about trying to get rid of a dumb part and wishing we never made mistakes. We also talked about people being good at some things and not as good at others. Everybody has a "dumb" part. I made a "fairy godmother" come to talk to the dumb part, something Oaklander (1988) suggests using to represent an accepting, nurturing part. The fairy godmother said, "It's OK if you don't always know everything all the time. I guess that's the way most people are. Nobody can know everything."

Figure 5.1 Drawing by Andy, age 10, of his "dumb part, the part that doesn't understand."

Andy decided to change his picture a bit. He apologized to his dumb part, and then wrote on the picture, "I'm sorry, fairy godmother, that I was mean to him."

Other examples of Gestalt dialogues appear in Chapter Four. Once the child has come to know and accept a part of herself that she formerly saw as negative, there is less need to dissociate that part. Acceptance of the disowned part allows greater self-esteem to develop, anxiety to decrease, and new ways of coping to emerge.

USING DREAMS

Dreams can be a powerful source of information and learning that the child gives to herself. Oaklander (1988) cites Perls on the significance of dreams:

> The dream . . . is a message of yourself to yourself, to whatever part of you is listening. The dream is possibly the most spontaneous expression of the human being, a piece of art that we chisel out of our lives. And every part, every situation in the dream is a creation of the dreamer himself. . . . Every aspect of the dream is a part of the dreamer, but a part that to some extent is disowned and projected onto other objects. (Perls, 1971, p. 27)

Abused and traumatized children may have more frequent nightmares than others, some of them symbolic repetitions of trauma (Terr, 1990). Dreams, arising from the unconscious, are the mind's attempt to process material that stimulates anxiety in the child. Therefore, dreams often deal symbolically with issues and feelings that the child dissociates from consciousness in waking life. Using dreams as part of therapy allows the child to access her unconscious, her own "back door" for learning. I have found that both good dreams and bad ones can hold very positive content when framed as ways to help the child learn something about herself.

Many children have dreams of being chased by monsters or

scary things that they can or cannot get away from (another dissociative process). I may ask the child to draw the scary dream character and talk with it as if it were a negative or disowned part. This
is a way to discover what that part of the child wants, needs, or
feels. Before those needs or feelings can be accepted, the negative
part's positive motives must be recognized.

A frightening dream character may also represent a perpetrator
or another scary aspect of trauma the child experienced. Sometimes
post-traumatic dreams show the child what aspects of a trauma
remain unresolved, what questions are unanswered, or what still
causes internal anxiety and conflict. In such cases, drawing or recreating the dream in play scenarios may help illustrate and clarify
the conflicts. The child may also benefit from exercises that help
her gain a feeling of relief or control over the traumatic situation.
The child can draw the scary monster and destroy it by scribbling
it out with a dark crayon and tearing it up. Or she may draw a
different ending to the dream, in which a helper part of the child or
someone or something more powerful comes to her aid. Young
children need to know that the adults in their lives will protect
them once trauma has been disclosed.

Frightening aspects of a dream that do not obviously represent a
perpetrator can often be reframed into positives. This helps drain
the fear out of the nightmare and enable the child to see how the
dream is trying to help her own or learn something important in
her life. Some examples follow.

*Connie, 15, related a scary dream she had. "I was a french fry,
being eaten by a big, fat man. He was ugly and awful. But I slipped
out of his grasp and got away, and landed on the floor. When the
french fry landed on the floor, it turned into me—the way I really
look. Then the man threw apples at me, and I was dodging them.
And I saw that the apples had bombs inside of them. So I stomped
on the apples and crushed the bombs before they could explode."*

*Connie had been sexually molested as a young child, and when
she started therapy, had difficulty fending off unwanted advances
from boys (see earlier anecdote in Chapter Four). Although this
dream was experienced as frightening, it showed how "grounded"
Connie was becoming (she turned into herself when she landed on*

the floor). The dream commented on her increasing ability to see threatening people and things for what they really were and to protect herself. After working on this dream, Connie realized she was taking back her power.

* * *

Jeremy interpreted his own dream one day, following a question, "Why do I only have bad dreams when I'm at home in my room, not when I'm staying over at anybody else's house?" As we talked, Jeremy became aware that he felt the most secure at his own home. "Oh!" said Jeremy. "Dad is the brown bull in my dream, and the [abuser] is the white one!" I asked what he meant. Jeremy explained, "In a dream I had, I was playing outside a house and two big bulls were fighting. One bull was huge and white and mean, with horns that curved in. There was a brown bull that was just regular size—but the brown bull was stronger. He laid out the white one! Then me and the other kids ran into the house, and the brown bull went in the house, too. The white bull started to knock down the wall, but the brown bull came out of the house and shot the white bull with a gun. The brown bull is my dad, and the white bull is the bad guy."

Jeremy's interpretation showed that he felt protected and not overpowered by his father, who was "regular size, but stronger." Jeremy had found a safe place in his world.

* * *

Kari, age nine, told me a nightmare she'd just had that week. She wasn't eager to tell it to me, afraid that it would mean something bad might happen, but she gradually settled in and told me the dream story step by step, as I drew it on paper.

"In the dream," Kari began, "I was with my dad visiting a big cave where a lot of tourists go. It was dark in the cave and dusty on the floor. My dad didn't say anything. I looked and saw a pretty cross laying on the ground, and I picked it up. Then in the dream, I went downtown, and there were three people there. I showed them the cross I found and they said, 'The devil will haunt you.' Then I woke up."

I asked, "How did you feel when you woke up?"

"Scared."

"How did you feel in the dream when you found the cross?"

"Happy!" Kari smiled. "It was really pretty and sparkled."

"And how did you feel in the dream when you heard what the three people said about the cross you found?" I continued.

"I felt sort of sad, and mad too," Kari replied. I wrote these feelings on the picture as Kari told me.

"What were you sad and mad about?"

Kari paused. "Well, I thought it was nice that I found the cross, and I liked it, and those people thought it was something bad. But I didn't think so. It made me feel bad. It wasn't very nice of them to say something mean."

"So you thought something different from the three other people, and felt different. In real life, do you sometimes think differently from other people?" I asked.

"Yes!" Kari exclaimed. She gave some examples, and her feelings about that.

I continued, "Was the devil in your dream?"

"No, the people just said he'd haunt me."

"Was God in the dream?"

"God is everywhere," Kari stated.

"Where would you put God in this picture we drew of your dream?"

"In the cross!!" Kari drew a face on the cross to represent God.

"How do you think God—the cross—would feel in the dream?" I asked.

"God doesn't have feelings—He's all-powerful," Kari said. I explained how it might be possible that God has feelings, if God cares about people. "Then God would feel happy I found the cross and hurt about what those people said," Kari replied.

"Well, let's look at this picture of your dream again," I said, taking an objective tone. "The girl in the dream finds a cross, and God is in it. So the girl in the picture is finding God then?"

Kari's eyes lit up. "Yes!"

Asked what parts of the dream she'd like to keep, and what parts she didn't want to keep, Kari decided to keep everything but the three people, and she crossed them out with X's. Then she added a light in the cave, noting "It's hard to find God in a dark cave."

Kari really enjoyed reframing her nightmare. "When I tell you

*things, I feel better," she said. She took the drawing of this dream
home to save. Many scary nightmares can be turned into positive
discoveries by tapping into the child's own inner wise self; as with
Kari, the child may be able to connect more solidly with her own
strength.*

ROLE-PLAYING

Role-playing can help the child become aware of a dissociated feeling when the work of therapy is just beginning. For example, a
teenage boy may say, regarding a fight at school, "I wasn't scared."
When we role play what happened, however, I may reverse roles to
show him himself, accenting the downcast eyes, half-turned shoulder, and hunched body. I ask what feeling I look like I am feeling.
The teenager reports with surprise, "Scared!" When the boy reen-
acts the scared posture, he may be able to report where he feels
scared in his body this time. And then we have a start on reclaiming
the dissociated feeling. As with other forms of play therapy, it helps
for the therapist to act out the more vulnerable feeling parts before
asking the child to do it; this gives the child a chance to become
accustomed to hearing, seeing, and feeling those parts.

Role-playing is also a useful technique to help children learn
healthy, assertive ways of coping after they begin to reown those
dissociated feelings, thoughts, and behaviors. We may start by
brainstorming all the possible ways to feel, or think, or behave in a
certain situation that comes up for the child. We write all the
possibilities down. If the child is unaware of other choices, ask her
to describe how TV or movie characters might react. As therapist, I
add possibilities I think up as well, making sure we have some
relevant choices available.

Then we try out those choices. I often initiate role-plays by
asking the child to play the role of the antagonist—the pest, or the
bully, or the friend being mean. I play the more vulnerable role of
the child, to model the various options. After each exchange, I ask
the child how it felt being on the other end of my behavior. Then I
may ask how that new behavior looked to her, or how she would
feel about trying that option. We then pick the one she feels most

comfortable with and replay the scene, with the child playing her-self and me playing the challenger. Again, I ask how it felt to do the new behavior, and how she felt *about* doing it. We do it again, until the child has her own words and the behaviors feel a bit more comfortable.

It may help to reverse roles one more time to show the child how she looks again, so she can see whether her behavior really looks effective, or assertive, and how she might be perceived by someone else. End the role-play by having the child play herself in her new (assertive) behavior as strongly as she can, noting voice, posture, facial and body expression, and words. Then set up how and when she will practice the new behavior outside the session. If necessary, adult family members may help give permission and support for the new ways of coping.

In play therapy, the child is encouraged to project her inner processes onto the play objects. This enables the therapist to ob-serve the child's hidden beliefs, feelings, or unverbalized experi-ences—that is, elements of the child's inner conflict. The therapist reframes a child's disowned feeling or behavior as something posi-tive and more easily acceptable to the child. Therapy then provides the child with opportunities to see how that part of herself can be owned and expressed in safe, appropriate ways. The child's errone-ous beliefs can also be challenged through play metaphors, allow-ing the meaning of negative or traumatizing experiences to be re-framed. The creative therapist can invent many ways to modify the above techniques to fit his or her own personality and style.

Chapter Six

BEGINNING TREATMENT WITH DISSOCIATIVE IDENTITY DISORDER CHILDREN

The course of treatment with children who have a severe dissociative disorder, i.e., dissociative identity disorder (formerly multiple personality disorder), is both more complex and often lengthier than therapy work with children who have lesser degrees of dissociative symptoms. However, many of the techniques and procedures are the same. Treatment for DID children generally proceeds through the following steps:

1. Assuring a safe home environment
2. Getting to know the inner personalities
3. Building cooperation between the personalities
4. Abreaction and cognitive processing
5. Sharing memories and feelings throughout the inner system
6. Integration of personalities
7. Post-integration work

The first step, assuring a safe home environment, takes priority in treatment with DID children (Kluft, 1986). Children who are currently living in traumatic conditions need their dissociative defenses. The various issues involved in addressing safety in the home and in the therapy setting have already been discussed in Chapter Three. Steps two through six may overlap quite a bit; the treatment process with DID children is orderly, but not completely sequential. This chapter will cover steps two and three, which are tasks that usually occur in the beginning stages of treatment. Chapters Seven and Eight will cover the remaining four steps outlined above.

Many children, especially very young ones (under age five), may not have fully developed DID or fully formed personalities. Some may have what Fagan and McMahon (1984) call "incipient" multiple personality disorder or DID "in progress." In those cases, there may be no need to delineate the parts and work on building communication to the extent described in this chapter. However, these techniques have worked well with the DID children I have seen in my office, who have ranged in age from six to fifteen. I find that children with DID usually have less rigid amnestic barriers between parts than adult clients and often find it easier to build awareness and communication within the system.

DEFINING INNER PERSONALITIES AS PARTS

When I talk to children about personalities, I refer to them as "parts." I do not call personalities different "people" inside; children are very concrete thinkers and can get confused when adults use incorrect words. Using puppets or doll figures, I explain parts as something we all have:

"I have a Happy part, and a part of me that feels Scared sometimes, and a Mad part. I feel sad sometimes, so of course I have a Sad part. And I have parts of me for doing different things, too. For instance, I have a Counselor part—that's what I'm being right now! And I have a Teacher part, because I teach school sometimes. I have a Shy part sometimes around people I don't know very well, and I have a Friendly part, the side of me that likes to have fun with other people. Let's see, I have an Embarrassed part because that's how I feel when I goof something up. Do you get the idea? All the different ways we feel and think and behave can be parts of us.

"We can use these puppets to represent our parts. I might pick this little dog (puppet) for my Happy part, and this mouse for my Scared part. Mice run away and hide when they feel scared, don't

they? And maybe I could use this wolf for my angry part: 'Gr-r-r!'
See how that works? Now you try it. What parts do you know
about that you have inside?"

Children catch on quickly to the concept of having parts. For
DID children it is a way to normalize the separateness they experience among the inner aspects of themselves. I find that children
show integrity in their choices of descriptive self-parts, never copy-
ing mine. Below are examples of the types of self-descriptors DID
children give in the very early stages of identifying their own parts.

Merrie

The twin sisters: Always happy / always sad
Turtle puppet: scared part
Grandpa puppet: my nasty part

Monica

Turtle puppet: my shy part
Shark: mad part
The Queen: keeper of the jewel
The King: tells everybody what to do
Puppy: embarrassed and ashamed
Kitty: satisfied part

Once the child has picked out symbols for his inside parts, in
play therapy the therapist, as well as the child, gets to know those
parts. The child's inside parts may come out to "be" that part as
the child is playing.

One day several months into treatment I took out the puppets and
explained "parts" to Jeremy. He readily admitted at this point that
he lost his place during his school day sometimes or failed to re-
member what his parents told him to do. Jeremy named a couple
of his own parts of which he was aware, including a "worry part"
that thought something bad might happen to family members.
Later we took out old pictures he had drawn for me; he did not

remember most of them, including a kinetic-family-drawing he'd done.

We used the turtle puppet to talk about scared feelings. Jeremy stated, "I don't ever feel scared!" But when I asked him what the turtle does when the turtle feels scared, Jeremy said, "He pretends he's Superturtle!" As he threw the turtle puppet into the air several times, Jeremy noted, "The turtle feels scared of being thrown into the air, but he pretends he's flying." (This is an accurate description of many dissociative children's method of coping with fear.)

Before the session ended, I suggested that Jeremy create a place where worried and scared parts didn't have to feel nervous. Jeremy built a big, solid house out of Lincoln logs and called it "A Safe Place." He put one small doll inside and said, "That's me." He decided at this point that there was no one else safe enough to allow inside the safe house with him. We left the log house standing in a corner of the room when Jeremy left to go home.

Switching

DID children may or may not switch from personality to personality within a session. When they do, the therapist soon learns how to differentiate parts.

Some children use overt or covert mannerisms to signal a switch, such as blinking, looking down then up, closing then opening eyes, looking away then back, smoothing hair back with fingers, etc. Others don't use observable switching signals but show a change in rhythm, tone, or loudness of voice; still others show a subtle-to-distinct change in behavior or activity. Because some personalities were split off or failed to integrate at an early age, they may have the voice and mannerisms of a younger child.

Caregivers are usually able to discern switching sooner than the therapist, since they live with the child. They can pass on clues to the therapist about the characteristics of various parts. Often the children themselves are very savvy, even at a young age. As Merrie, age eight, told me early on, "All the parts aren't here all the time every day, you know. And there are different ages." Within the safety of the therapy setting, children will soon feel comfortable telling the therapist which part is out in the world at that moment. For example, Matthew, age six, came in one day and stated matter-of-factly, "I have a different name than Matthew. Call me Matt. I'm not the same person as Matthew."

When personalities are not as confident and/or confrontational as Matt, the therapist can help by asking the child to pick out a puppet to represent herself today, or to "show me which part is here today." This is helpful for children who do not have names for their various parts or who are just learning to acknowledge to another person who they are when they are "out." By the time they can do this, however, most children are able to acknowledge how much or how little they know about other parts and what they do when they are in control.

TYPES OF PERSONALITIES

Children will show in their play the interaction inside (or lack of it) between the parts, and also the interaction between certain parts and family members at home. The therapist can begin to see the roles the child's various parts play within the inner system and the roles some play (or used to play) in the outside world. Children often choose names or descriptive attributes for various parts of themselves through identification with television characters or comic book heroes, etc. This makes sense if we realize that imagining he is someone or somewhere else or has incredible powers may be the helpless child's only sure defense against abuse.

Feeling Parts

Just like adults who have dissociative symptoms, children learn to wall off parts of themselves that carry negative feelings—the ones that feel bad or that are disapproved of by others in their lives. Some DID children have parts that carry just one feeling; others have parts that seem to have a broad range of feelings or feeling behaviors. Anger, which is a powerful (and often forbidden) feeling, is apt to be carried in one or more parts separate from other feelings. Angry and mean parts are often the child's protector parts. Scared feelings are often the youngest parts; they may hide from the child and the therapist longer than other, less vulnerable parts. Figure 6.1 shows Monica's drawing of two feeling parts.

Figure 6.1 "Caroline," a happy part ("so happy she could cry") and "Lisa," a sad part. Caroline takes care of Lisa. Drawing by Monica, age 10.

April had a part she called, "Snobby April." When this part came to session one day, she asked to be called Darbie. Darbie explained that she gets back at people who treat April badly, but other people and other inside parts don't like her.

Although April was ten years old, Little Debbie, a scared part, was only four. Debbie told me that she is usually pretty scared and stays inside most of the time. She played in the dollhouse, keeping one finger in her mouth most of the time. I stopped her from prying the glued pictures off the dollhouse walls—something April's older parts did not have to be told.

Inside Playmates

An imaginary friend is an extension of oneself; many young children under five have one. It may be one of the first personalities created by a child who is lonely, fearful, neglected, or abused.

Some researchers theorize that the imaginary playmate may be the "birthplace," so to speak, of a dissociative disorder when traumatic conditions in the child's life make it necessary (Putnam, 1989). Most children eventually give up imaginary companions, developing better awareness of what is real and not real and more sophisticated ways of coping as they mature. However, an inner fantasy world that is peopled with fun characters can remain an important coping tactic for children who continue to need dissociative defenses.

Peter was severely neglected as an infant by a single mother who was alcohol and drug addicted. At age eight he had two invisible playmates, a boy he called "Stanley" and an older girl (a possible stand-in for the absent mother).

❊ ❊ ❊

By his mother's report, Adam had an imaginary playmate named "Casper the Friendly Ghost" at about age three. This imaginary companion stayed on to become one of Adam's personalities. In a therapy session, Casper stated that he had "jumped out of a comic book."

Personalities with Helper Roles

Children have parts to function in various settings in their lives: some go to school and are able to do the academic work; others go to school and form friendships at recess. Some parts must be available to be with a current or former perpetrator if the child lives in an abusive home or has visitation with an abuser. The child may need to use parts such as "little helper" or "the baby" to be with the perpetrator in a role that works. If there has been a divorce, the child may have different and separate parts to be with one parent or the other. She can then switch to the appropriate part(s) when living with or visiting a particular parent.

Merrie discovered that several of her parts had jobs to do at her natural mother's house. One part used to help mother by being negative to people mother didn't like, or by making dinner, even when she was only four. Another part came out to play with mother. A third part was happy all the time and gave mother compliments; she called herself the "Compliment Queen." A fourth part used to get a tummy ache to get attention from mother; a fifth was able to be angry with mom. Two other parts that most of the personalities disliked were created to be "mean" like mother's family of origin in order to survive; as they put it: "We have to."

Certain personalities may act as protectors for the child. Angry or "tough guy" parts may help the child defend himself or feel less anxious in various situations at home or school. While these parts are often perceived as uncooperative, scary, or "mean" by parents or by the child's other personalities, they represent the child's will to survive and protect himself.

I have noticed that DID children gradually assign a helper role to one or more of their parts to assist the child in therapy. This part may play the role of mediator between parts in working with the therapist, speaking the thoughts of another part who is too shy to come out yet, or getting input from the whole system.

Denial Parts
Denial parts play an important role both in the child's inner world and in the outer world. It may be necessary for a child to believe that things are "fine" in a world where constant abuse or double-bind messages exist and where there is no safe haven except inside one's own head. Being able to *behave* as if things are fine may be important to survival. Figure 6.2 is a child's drawing of one of these adaptive personalities.

Denial also allows a measure of safety and protection *inside* for the vulnerable parts who have been abused and who feel scared, sad, angry, or in pain: denial allows the hurt parts to "hide out" inside and be invisible to the child herself. Therefore, denial parts may or may not know other parts inside and are likely to be defensive with the therapist. They don't want to know about being multiple; they just want to be "normal." However, once their trust is gained, they often turn out to be helpers, who can in turn enlist the aid of other vulnerable parts.

Borderline Parts
As in adults, I have encountered personalities in DID children that have borderline traits. These parts are able to show the child's neediness and wish to be "special" and taken care of. However,

Figure 6.2 A "funny" part that can be silly and make jokes during dark times. Drawn by April, age 11.

their behavior may be manipulative, demanding, angry, whiny, suicidal, and just plain difficult. These parts may expect punishment or abandonment when they express needs. When such feelings and behaviors are directed at the therapist, the therapy will advance if the child learns it's OK to be angry at the therapist and to feel needy. It is important that the therapist establish and maintain behavioral boundaries toward the child without being punitive or judgmental.

April was taken aback upon discovering that other children who come to see me play with some of the same toys she does and also have access to my jar of candy. I commented that it looked like she was feeling a bit jealous and angry with me about that. April agreed, saying "I want to be the only one." Then she asked, "Do other kids want to be the only one too?" I assured her they did, that it's OK to want to be special.

The following week we had two sessions before I was to leave for a vacation. April volunteered that she was angry that I was leaving. She made a picture of me and ripped it through with her pencil. I drew a picture of April next to the one she had made of me, and put a cartoon bubble with the words, "I'm mad at you, Lynda!" Laughing, April added the words "Look what I have to put up with!" She wanted to do more, and decided to hit the bean-bag chairs with a bataca, telling her angry thoughts about all the times she had been left by adults in her life.

Sexual Parts

Sexual parts may be containers for the child's natural sexuality; they may also be parts of the child who endured sexual abuse and/ or were required to respond sexually. Or they may be personalities that identified with the abuser and continue to act out sexually to get something for themselves, whether sexual gratification, a sense of control, or revenge. Often the child is ashamed of these parts and tries to hide them from caregivers, from the therapist, and from herself. The child will need reassurance of their importance, as well as reframing to bring out their positive aspects.

Monica admitted to sexual behavior only after I reassured her that I already knew about it. Her mother had had information from the older sister that Monica had a reputation at school for being "sexy." Monica also had put pictures of scantily clad women on her walls at home, to her mother's dismay. We began to talk about how a sexual part might be good and even helpful to have.

* * *

Kristie, age 14, described a part of herself who was "hyper" or very happy and bubbly—a part that tried to cover up feeling depressed. This part asked to be called Yvonne, and said she had always been 15 years old, even when Kristie was little. Yvonne turned out to be the part of Kristie who was sexual, flirtatious and outgoing; she liked to sing, smoke cigarettes, and show off. Yvonne tended to come out when Kristie went to church camp or to the mall; she flirted with the boys, causing Kristie to lose time and to feel embarrassed when her behavior was reported back to her by friends.

Boy/Girl Personalities

Children with DID may have personalities that they perceive as being of the gender opposite to themselves. For example, a girl child may see a part of herself that identifies with a male abuser as male. Sexual parts may be male or female in a child of either sex, depending on how acceptable the child's own sexuality feels to him or her, the dynamics of the sexual abuse, and the way the child coped. In some cases, particularly during ritual abuse, an abuser may require a child to "be" the opposite sex, or to be both male and female (Bryant et al., 1992).

Children may create personalities of the opposite sex for other reasons as well. Children often perceive males as physically stronger than females, so they may create male protector parts. Nurturing traits may be seen as appropriate to female parts of themselves. Feelings or self-perceptions that seem unacceptable, such as helplessness or "weakness," may be relegated to personalities of the gender opposite to the biological one.

Adam had two girl parts. One was quite young and hated to be outdoors hiking or getting wet feet; a second part was seen as a teenager who "mothered" the younger parts.

* * *

Kristie's angry part was male. She perceived this part as taller than herself and stronger. His thoughts in her head had a male voice. This part of Kristie was strong, protective, and able to be assertive in social situations.

Spiritual Parts

Many children, even at an early age, have a spiritual part. When talking with a child, I may call it "a part who knows God or who feels close to God." When asked about it, some children readily admit to having such a part and may even ask, "How did you know?" Some children profess not to have a spiritual part. Others say "all the parts know God." As with other parts or personalities, there is no best or right way to be.

One of the last parts Merrie told me about was one named Maria. "This part is sad," she said, "and wants the truth to be known. And this part knows God. She tries to help the others."

* * *

Matt had a part named Luke. He described Luke as "the one who stays awake all night watching over me." Luke came to session once and volunteered to make a drawing; taking a yellow pastel crayon, he drew a large star that gave off a soft, yellow light.

* * *

April's spiritual part decided she would meet me one day. April closed her eyes to switch; she opened her eyes, and sat looking at me very quietly and calmly, and surveyed my office with a measuring glance. When she spoke her voice and demeanor were quite unlike that of any other part of April I had met.

Core and Essence Personalities

Some children with DID have a core personality (or "original" personality) from which other parts were created, and which may remain fixated at an early developmental level. For example, a ten-year-old child may refer to a core part as being four or five years old. Some children may have one personality that is the "essence" of the original child, which has continued to age through the child's life (Bryant et al., 1992). The essence is similar to what other authors refer to as the "host" personality in an adult, but may not be the same. "Host" is a term given to the personality that presents for treatment and is the identified patient in adult clients; the host may or may not be a single personality (Putnam, 1989).

Some, but not all, DID children seem to have core and/or essence personalities. I speculate that whether or not a child dissociates (in order to preserve) a core part of herself or an older "essence" of herself might depend on how young the child was when overwhelmingly severe trauma occurred, or on how prolonged the trauma was. It might also depend on how long the child has had a safe home by the time she comes to therapy. Or it may depend simply on the child's individual inner style of dissociative coping.

In any case, when children do have parts that fit the characteristics of a core personality or an essence, those characteristics are similar among the children. For example, an essence personality is always the child's correct chronological age and knows little if anything about trauma the child has suffered. A core personality is always younger than the child's true age and well protected by other parts. Out of all the personalities, the essence personality usually elects to retain the child's given name; the core part is sometimes *also* given this name, so that the child ends up with two parts named Robert or two named Susan. Children may call these parts "Big Rob and Little Robbie" or "Big Susan and Little Susie." While the essence may know little about specific traumatic events in the child's life, this part may be particularly vulnerable to anxiety, needing to switch to other parts to take care of tension and discomfort.

April, who was ten when I first saw her, eventually chose individual names for each of her dissociated parts. However, one part who had originally called herself "Nervous April" did not want a new name for herself. She wished to be called "just April" and gave her age as ten. This part did not know what job or role she played in the inner system or in the outer world; she could think of no particular feelings she had, except "nervous." A different four-year-old part was called "Little April." These two parts may have been the essence and core personalities, respectively.

TECHNIQUES FOR GETTING ACQUAINTED WITH PARTS

There are many ways to help the child get acquainted with her personalities. The Gestalt dialogue described in Chapter Five works well with DID children. Writing, instead of talking, to another part is another somewhat less threatening way to get acquainted. Children may have one part who is especially communicative or more willing than other parts to risk contact; this personality becomes a "connector" for the inside system.

April's connector part, Abby, was not acquainted with the part called Snobby April. So she wrote to Snobby April asking her to be friends. She decided to take the letter home and put it with her private things, and wait to see if Snobby April would write back.

* * *

Adam wrote a letter to his angry parts to help them begin to get acquainted with the other inside parts. The letter went as follows:

> Dear Stuntman, Monsterman, Destroyer, and Angry,
>
> Hi, guys! This is Adam. I wanted to get to know you more and find out why you guys are always mad.
>
> Love, Adam
>
> (P.S. Write back soon.)

Making a Book about the Parts

Some children respond well to making up a "Book of Parts." Multi-colored construction paper works well, so each part can pick a color for his or her page and have room for writing and drawing. The child can then write about each of her parts, using a separate page for each one. I encourage each of the child's parts to come out and create his or her own page for the book. Include information such as favorite foods, what he or she likes to do, "things I don't like," other inside parts she knows or talks to, people she knows in the outside world, etc. Figures 6.3 and 6.4 are examples of pages from two children's "Book of Parts."

Drawing Where the Parts Live Inside

I ask children to draw a picture of their inside world where the parts live. It helps both me and the child to get a better idea of how the child conceptualizes the personalities and their separateness or connectedness. Some even show me their idea of how switching occurs or how one part gets to be "out." Some children will draw all their parts as being in their head; others draw personalities in various parts of their body, such as head, chest, arms and legs. Once the inner world is made metaphorically concrete by a drawing, the drawing becomes a framework for the inner "construction work" of building communication and cooperation. Figures 6.5 and 6.6 are children's drawings of their inner worlds.

Figure 6.3 A page from his "Book of My Parts," by Adam, age 10. Adam made the drawings and dictated sentences for the therapist to write.

Merrie's inside place was "like a big Disneyland." "I can do mind-scope and mindtravel, too," she explained. "Mindscope is three (parts) at a time, and mindtravel is on a bus. On the mind-bus, the parts become invisible. At [a relative's] house last weekend, she wouldn't let me get up at night to go to the bathroom, because it's not mature. So when I wanted to be back home with my foster mom and dad, I took the mind-bus and went home!"

Merrie's inner world had three main "towns," but it also had one

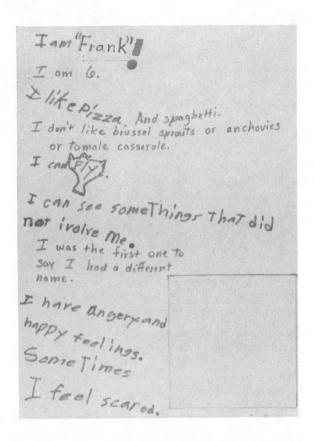

I am "Frank"!

I am 6.

I like pizza. And spaghetti.
I don't like brussel sprouts or anchovies
or tamale casserole.

I can Fly.

I can see something that did
not involve me.
I was the first one to
say I had a different
name.

I have anger and
happy feelings.
Some Times
I feel scared.

Figure 6.4 A page from Jeremy's book of parts. Jeremy and the therapist took turns writing. The square at the lower right is space for a photograph or drawing.

separate place called "Stoneville." Asked about Stoneville, Merrie replied, "That's a place that's not very nice." According to Merrie, Stoneville was surrounded by a high wall, separated from the other three towns. It had only one house and three occupants, one girl and two boy parts. Everybody there dressed in black. Merrie told me sadly that the three parts who lived there used to live in other houses, but now had to live alone in Stoneville.

As you can see, Merrie's inner world was rich in metaphoric descriptors of dissociation, separateness and connectedness, and in clues to her ways of coping in the outer world. It also gave informa-

Figure 6.5 Adam's drawing of the inside house where his parts live. On the left is a "slide to get in to the house;" going down on the right is a "ladder to get out of the house." In the center, an arrow points to a "little ladder for people who can't go the hard way."

Figure 6.6 Merrie's inside world is "like a big Disneyland." Her parts live in separate houses. Note the "Rec house," the "Band room" and the swimming pool.

tion about particular roles and experiences some of her personalities may have had.

Diagramming the Parts
Diagramming is similar to what Virginia Satir used to call "mapping" (Satir, 1983). When it is used with couples or other adult clients, mapping the family of origin and the nuclear family helps illuminate for therapist and client the patterns of relationships down through the generations of the family. The resulting genogram highlights the important data. With DID clients, whether adults or children, mapping or diagramming creates a visual layout of the inner "family" of personalities.

Begin by making a list of the parts that the child herself has identified. As you find out from the child and her parts which personalities know which others, and their various developmental ages and roles, you can add those to the list along with verbal descriptors and connector lines. The child's drawing of her inner world can also be developed into a pictorial map that shows the location of her parts and their relationships to each other.

I am careful not to leave any of the child's parts out of the diagram or to omit any part from the "Book of Parts." The child needs to know that each and every one of her parts is important and necessary. Helper parts, social parts, and the less vulnerable ones will be the first to appear and volunteer to be known by the therapist and the other parts. Parts that contain experiences and memories of abuse and pain or "negative" feelings like anger and fear may watch the others and wait until much later to be known. Some parts whose role is only to contain traumatic memories and feelings may never appear until abreactive work starts.

Even some very young children may have complex inner systems. One child conceptualized each of her personalities as having three parts: one younger, one the correct chronological age, and one "older" than she currently was. Each grouping of parts had a similar role in her life. For example, she spoke of "the Maybels" as being very helpful to her natural mother when they were with her; this grouping consisted of three parts named May, Maybel, and Maybella. This particular child also volunteered that she had three Controllers and three Judges who "decide who does what and who gets to be homecoming queen."

BUILDING COOPERATION
BETWEEN THE PERSONALITIES

Once the child accepts the concept of different inner parts and begins to get acquainted with each of them, the processes of becoming a friend to oneself and learning to be self-nurturing begin in earnest. The therapist helps the child develop these abilities in several ways.

Reframing the Parts

As mentioned in Chapter Four, all children learn early in life which of their feelings and ways of thinking and behaving in the world are acceptable and approved of by others, and which are not. Usually, the child learns to feel about her own parts the way she perceives that others do: she likes those parts of herself that others like or admire; she "hates" or feels ashamed of those parts of herself that others disapprove of or punish. The personalities seen as negative will need to be reframed in a positive light by the therapist to help the child begin to accept those parts as well. Some of the positive personalities can also be reframed as helpers, or mediators, and learn to help the disliked parts be more accepted by other parts.

Negative parts almost *without fail* can be reframed as having a protective role or function. Angry parts are "sticking up for" the child or unhappy about things that aren't fair; mean parts may be strong enough to fight or try for what they want against incredible odds; sexual parts may be reframed as wanting to feel good or trying to get something for themselves after all the times of being used. The child needs to hear the importance of being able to feel angry, scared, mean, sexy, sad, etc. Of course, the best reframing includes how that "negative" part may be uniquely able to help the child.

Sometimes a DID child may have felt shame about being multiple. In that case dissociation itself must be reframed to the child. The following is an example of such reframing in a puppet story I made up for April.

"Once upon a time there was a kitten who was outside playing in the woods. A big, mean bear came along and trapped the little kitten and put her in a cage. The kitten fought back and tried to get out, but she couldn't. She felt sad, and scared and mad at the bear, and her paws hurt terribly. She wished she weren't feeling so bad—in fact, the little kitten wished that the whole thing wasn't happening. She didn't want all the bad feelings so she gave them away to parts of herself and pretended they were other animals. The mad feelings became a skunk, the scared feelings a mouse, and a puppy took the sad and hurt feelings.

"The little kitten had to stay in the cage for a long time, but eventually a fairy godmother came visiting in the woods and noticed the little kitten. The fairy godmother let the kitten out and took her far away from the bear. After she got out of the cage, the kitten still didn't like feeling mad, sad, scared, or hurt, so she left her feelings in the other animals. Trouble was, the skunk and the mouse and the puppy all followed her around and wanted to play with her and live with her in her new home in the city. But the kitten didn't like them—she was ashamed to tell the fairy godmother that the other animals really belonged to her. You see, the kitten thought that since she was a cat, all her parts should look like cats too, and act just like her! The kitten never heard of any cats who actually liked skunks or mice or dogs. But the fairy godmother said, 'Skunks are very useful friends, you know. Your skunk friend here can just SQUIRT anything troublesome that comes around. Dogs can also be useful; they are very loyal—why, that's why they're called Man's Best Friend. And the little mouse? Well, mice are good runners, they're very fast. And they can set the dog barking if anything scary comes near your house at night.

"So the little kitten made friends with the animals. She grew up to be a beautiful tiger. And the tiger was quite fortunate: because of the other animals she knew how to be kind, and smart, and strong. You see, she had made all the animals' feelings her own again. (Here I put the other three puppets inside the tiger puppet to indicate oneness.)

April loved this story and wanted to see it again. The following week, she was ready to tell me about the voices she heard inside that sounded "wimpy," "sexy," "angry" and "snobby." These were parts that she hadn't wanted to accept as hers before.

* * *

Monica picked the shark puppet to represent her mad part. She told me that the shark scared her "mouse part," who then got the bear, the "tough" part, to protect her from the shark. All the puppets said that "Tough" would take care of Monica. They didn't want the shark around. Monica went on to say that God would help her not to be angry, and the shark must die. I asked Monica to talk to her shark part.

"I hate you. I wish you would die," Monica told the shark. I *asked if any of the parts liked the shark at all. Monica said the bear, the "tough" part did; "I like you a little—sometimes," the bear told the shark. It turned out that the shark was mad at Monica's [relative], who had been a perpetrator; the bear wasn't sure it was OK to be mad at him. Monica said, "It's my fault [the perpetrator] went to jail, and now he's mad at me and everybody in my family." Although it had been years since the abuse had ended, Monica didn't know for sure what her mother thought of what she had done in disclosing the abuse. Mother came in at the end of our session and validated Monica's anger and her right to have the abuse stop. Responsibility for putting the perpetrator in jail was placed on the court judge.*

Building Inside Communication

Increasing communication among the child's inner personalities leads to increased co-consciousness. "Co-consciousness" is the ability for personalities to be mutually aware of each other or for several parts to simultaneously take in information from the outside world. To be co-conscious, the inner barriers that separate two personalities have to come down or at least become permeable. Since children with DID may have less rigid amnestic barriers than adults, many of them already have some inner dialoguing.

One of the best ways to help the child begin to increase communication between her parts is to use her own metaphor for her inner world. Children may fantasize that their inside world looks like a house with separate rooms for each part, or a community with separate neighborhoods, or separate houses for many parts, etc. Using the same drawing the child has made earlier, you can encourage the child to draw in telephone lines and roads connecting the towns or houses, walkways within the "neighborhood" so parts can visit with each other in person, group meeting rooms,* telephones in every house, and an intercom system* inside the house with a speaker in every room. (See Figure 6.7.) The possibilities are limited only by the imagination. One child even installed a mail chute.

In the design, it is important to safeguard each part's privacy as

---

*I am grateful to Vick Graham-Costain for this idea.

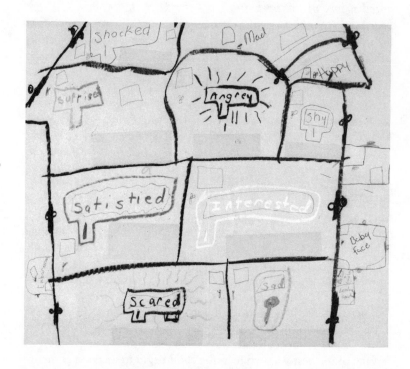

Figure 6.7 Monica's drawing of the place where her parts live inside. She has drawn in windows and doors, as well as on/off swiches for an inside intercom.

well as to provide an opportunity for each part to get to know the others. Some parts may be too overwhelmed by the thought of a physical or visual connection at first, but may be willing to "listen in" through the intercom to what others are saying and doing. Other personalities may be too frightened by the sounds of other parts crying or fighting—or even just the thought of hearing something—but they may be willing to have windows in their rooms to allow them to look into the next room or "down the hallway" of the inside house. I may suggest that they provide curtains they can pull over the windows when they want to stop looking.

A group meeting place may be useful later for gathering to look at old memories or to comfort one another. I find that some children are too anxious to use this meeting place right away; the other methods of "peeking" or "listening in" feel like safer ways of building co-consciousness in the early stages of therapy.

Jeremy decided that the inside communication line should begin at the house where a protector part lived; the cable and all the inner "houses" should be connected to that one.

* * *

Monica decided that when she had to go places or visit people who made her feel anxious, the scared parts could shut their inside windows and doors and switch off the intercom so they didn't have to see and hear. That way, all the parts could feel safe inside, even when the outside environment didn't feel safe. It also allowed Monica to choose to use more or less dissociation as needed.

* * *

Merrie drew connecting telephone lines between her inside houses. I asked her which of her parts could see and hear her while she did this, and Merrie said, "All of them." As she drew, I talked to all of the parts about what we were doing and how they could use the phone line to get acquainted. Lainie, the part who was drawing, told me she was afraid of listening in on what all the other parts said, because she didn't want to know scary things. I told Lainie and all the other parts that it was OK for now to just use the phone line to get acquainted — to say "hi," and find out what the others liked to do. They could wait to tell each other about the scary things when they felt ready.

Checking in with Parts

Once the lines of inner communication have been established, the child can learn to consult other parts when she needs to make decisions or when problems arise. It also becomes easier to pass information around the inner system, which helps all the parts learn important "house rules" of the outside world.

"House rules" are often set by parents or by parent and child together. Some examples might be "Clean up your room on Saturdays" or "Be in bed by nine o'clock." Basic rules also exist in the school setting. The child can use her inner communication system to make sure all the parts know these rules so no one gets in trouble; parts can discuss which of them will take care of the problem if one part forgets the rules.

The child can learn to check inside with all the parts by turning on a master switch to the entire intercom system. This is helpful if the part who is now out missed hearing some important information while another part was out. Instead of being told something again and again by a parent at home or by the therapist in session, the child can retrieve the information herself by "checking in."

One day Merrie came into the office as "Melly." She said she wasn't here with me the previous week and didn't remember any of the last session, except playing with one of the toys at the end. I told Melly which part was at the last session and asked her to check inside and see if that part or someone else would tell her what we did. Melly listened inside and reported back accurately.

Later she told me she was not acquainted with another part who had been here before, a part who was often angry and who had demonstrated her anger with the batacas. I asked her to listen inside for the angry part. Melly closed her eyes and became very quiet. Then her eyes flew open wide and she exclaimed, "She told me the f--- word!" She had discovered inner communication.

* * *

Jeremy needed to have an inside conference. Some of his personalities were leaving their toys outside after dark. His father wanted a rule that all the toys had to be picked up and put away at the end of the day. But what if a little one, age two or three, left the toys out? Jeremy's parts talked together through the intercom line about their choices: the older parts could tell the little ones to pick up the toys (talking to them from the inside); or an older part could come out and pick up the toys for the little one and put them inside. After talking among themselves, Jeremy's parts chose to have an older part come out and take over the clean-up. We told Jeremy's father his decision; the two agreed that it would also help to write down the new rule and put the paper up on the wall over Jeremy's bed, where all the parts could read it.

When Cooperation Isn't Happening
When the DID child is breaking house rules right and left or failing to keep agreements, or when the child is angry and acting out a lot, it may be an indication that inner cooperation isn't working. There may be several reasons for this, some pertaining to the outer environment, and some related to the child's inner world.

Lack of safety in the environment. The child's parts may not be willing to make the effort for unified teamwork either with their parts or their parents if the outside environment is not safe enough to do so. If the caregivers, or school, or visits with relatives, etc., cause too much anxiety or trigger memories of old trauma, the result may be that the child does not feel safe enough to use a co-conscious approach to life. To cope with high levels of anxiety, the child must fall back on the old standby of his dissociative defense—using amnestic barriers to protect vulnerable parts of himself.

Lack of safety inside. Another reason for failed inner cooperation is that the child herself may not be ready to face the thoughts, feelings, and behaviors of some of her other parts. For many children, checking inside and conferring for problem resolution may just be too overwhelming during early stages of therapy and may continue to be difficult when the child is processing traumatic memories.

Monica had one or two quite adaptive parts, who were more than willing to make behavioral contracts with mother or siblings. However, other parts did not agree, and broke those contracts when Monica switched. One day Monica was picked up for shoplifting at the mall. She was distraught, fearing that both God and her mother would punish her. But because of this confrontation with her own behavior, Monica's denial parts opened to the possibility

*that some personalities did things Monica didn't like and didn't
know about until it was too late.*

* * *

*April's grandmother reported that April was not communicating
inside daily or using her intercom system. Her "at home" personalities had no knowledge of school events of the day. April explained
to me in session that it was hard for her to use the intercom system
all the time, "because then everyone feels the pain." At that time
April was doing lots of memory work and needed to have a way to
contain and store the feelings and memories that had surfaced—
otherwise she resorted to using amnestic barriers to separate herself
from them (see Chapter Seven).*

   Old habits are easier. True cooperation among inside parts takes
time. Old ways of coping with anxiety, anger, jealousy, or neediness are familiar and much more easily called into action when
things go wrong at home or at school.

*One day Monica made a list of parts who didn't listen in on the
inside intercom. One was "Louie," a rageful part who rarely
talked—he just acted out; others were Lora, another angry part,
"Bored," who got tired of therapy, "Shy," who didn't like to hear
the others, "Embarrassed," and "Scared." Monica and I talked
about what would enable these parts to listen in. We sent them
messages that it's OK to be mad, bored, embarrassed, shy, or
scared. When the parts began to fill in information, we discovered
that Monica had an inside cycle. When tension started up at home,
the scared ones felt it first, and then passed the tension around to
other parts until it ended up with Louie, the angry one. Louie tried
to help dispel the tension by acting out destructively. I reframed the
scared and angry ones as helpers, and we asked for their help in
finding new ways to get rid of the tension and nervous feelings. A
meeting with Monica's family would also be needed to help her
mother become aware of tension in the home and better ways to
handle it with Monica.*

Working with Very Depressed or Uncooperative Parts
Certain personalities, such as angry or rageful ones, may refuse to
cooperate with others (inside or outside), fail to follow through on

agreements, or resist communicating and getting acquainted with others. Much of their "uncooperativeness" and negative behavior reflects an attempt by those parts to protect the child in some way. However, the depressed and/or angry emotions these "tough guy" parts carry can frighten both child and caregivers.

If these scary parts are validated and accepted by the therapist, as well as the parents or caregivers, the child can learn to love and accept them too. These "negative" parts then turn into strengths and become willing to help and protect the child in better ways—*if they feel safe*. No person, young or old, feels comfortable dropping tried and true defenses unless safety prevails.

Inside "house rules" may be necessary to create safety. One inside house rule, for example, might be that no part is allowed to hurt the body "accidentally" or on purpose (i.e., by cutting, suicide attempts, or daredevil stunts); another might be that no part is to endanger the others by running away from home. As with rules set by parents, consequences need to be built into the plan.

The therapist can make a no-harm pact with the depressed or angry part who actively thinks about or might carry out such plans. But a back-up plan also helps other personalities feel more secure. Parts can team up to protect themselves if they are worried that one personality might break a rule; they may decide on a consequence and inform the others. For example, the protective team can agree that if one part truly threatens to endanger the child, they will tell the parents or the therapist.

April had voiced suicidal thoughts following an attempt to run away from home. After talking about how sad her family would feel if she came to harm, April admitted that her suicidal thoughts scared her, too. She made an agreement with me not to harm herself—but I was not speaking to the part who had wanted to die. So April "went inside" and asked the parts if they would agree to the no-harm contract, too. She reported back, "A couple voices said 'No,' and I told them 'You have to.'" Several personalities who were listening made a pact with me that if any part became scared that another part would hurt her body, one of those parts would call me or ask Grandma to call me. April expressed relief at our solution. Before the session ended, we informed her grandmother of the agreement.

Borderline Parts

When working with children or adolescents who have prominent borderline traits or personalities that act out in borderline ways, you may find that the path to inner cooperation among the parts is long and arduous. These children and teens are more apt to use suicidal gestures of cutting or burning, may be more actively destructive toward property or other people, and may be highly demanding of the therapist's time and energy, much like an adult client with similar symptoms. Family life around these children also tends to be chaotic, as caregivers and siblings add their own fuel to the fire.

If the parent or caregiver can be extremely consistent with firm boundaries for behavior and lavish with time and energy for listening to feelings, the child can settle down. If the parent is showing signs of his or her own disturbance in the form of depression, adult DID, or a personality disorder, that parent may not be able to provide the kind of home climate that will feel safe to this child. Client, parent, and therapist may find themselves living from crisis to crisis. In some families an emotionally abusive (if not physically abusive) cycle may develop in which both child and parent feel battered.

A hospital or residential treatment setting that specializes in treatment of dissociative disorders in children and adolescents is an option under these circumstances. In an out-of-home setting the child and parents get respite from each other, and the child receives the boundaries, consistency, attention, and therapy to do some uninterrupted work. If at all possible, the parents should also be involved in the child's treatment, as well as in therapy *for themselves*. The child's absence may afford the parents an opportunity to evaluate their own problems and get some help while the home is calmer.

INVOLVING THE NONABUSIVE
CAREGIVER IN THE CHILD'S TREATMENT

Working with the nonabusive caregivers of a dissociative disorder child is crucially important. Parents, therapist, and the child's own parts become the therapeutic "team" that will bring healing to the child and to the family. This section discusses assistance to caregivers of a DID child who is in treatment; however, *my points apply only to nonabusive parents and current caregivers who are not perpetrating.* For measures to take when the child is currently at risk for abuse or is currently being traumatized, see Chapter Three.

From the time of diagnosis, it is important to begin validating to the caregivers the fact that the child has parts or personalities. Explaining how dissociation works and how the adults can best support the child's treatment at home is imperative. Parents or caregivers of a DID child need almost as much support as the child client.

It helps to define and describe dissociation to the caregivers in much the same words you use with their child. This gives the parents words to use when talking about DID with the child. Stress safety, structure, and consistency in the home.

Caregivers must be generally accepting, nonthreatening, nonpunitive, and able to maintain firm, clear boundaries (rules and limits) with the child in order to bring about a lifestyle that will be comfortable to everyone in the family. This is a tall order! However, without the atmosphere of acceptance and consistency, chaos will reign inside the child.

Discipline
Discipline that works with other children may not work with the DID child, due to the child's dissociative defenses. Rules and requests made to the DID child may actually be heard only by the one personality who is out—others may not get the information and will swear (honestly) that they were never told the rule, never heard it, etc. Similarly, punishments or consequences doled out to the child may actually be experienced only by one personality; the others, therefore, do not learn from consequences and will repeat the misbehavior.

The failure of many attempts to discipline the child may leave the parent in a state of angry frustration. Parents in such a state are apt to threaten, cajole, cry, or punish the child more severely than they would otherwise, leading to further trauma for the DID child and an increased need to use the dissociative defense. In other words, use of normal discipline without knowledge of the child's dissociative mechanism may result in a vicious cycle of misbehavior, rage, anxiety, and frustration for the whole family. The following may help.

Lower parental expectations. Remind parents that sometimes their child "regresses" to age two, or three, or four, etc., and will think and behave as a child much younger than his real age. Parents can help by lowering their expectations, especially during the initial phases of therapy, before the child has gained and is able to use a lot of cooperation and co-consciousness among his personalities.

When the child is in a ten-year-old part and wants and is able to do ten-year-old things, parents can treat the child as ten. When they see a weepy, confused child behaving like a toddler of two or three, that is when the child needs to be treated *at that level* — not at a ten-year-old level. In other words, parents need to "go with the flow" and not expect the child to always function at his chronological age.

Regressive behavior is a sign that the child is anxious or has been triggered in some way. It is important to stress to parents that regressive behavior is not a conscious attempt on the child's part to manipulate the parent; this switch in personality states is simply something the DID child has learned to do when he feels anxious or threatened.

Set rules and consequences in advance. For a DID child, less anxiety is better than more. Whenever possible, parents must learn to think ahead in their day with the child. They can set rules or plans in advance, set up comfort or security measures in advance, and plan consequences of misbehaviors in advance. That way the child will know what might happen if he does A or B and won't be taken by surprise or feel threatened when a consequence hits.

For example, if a parent knows the child has trouble going to sleep at night, or trouble going to bed, the parent can state the rule clearly early in the day: "Bedtime is at 9:00." She can set up comfort and security in advance: "From now on, you can get pajamas on at 8:30, and I'll read you a story until 9:00," or "You can have a glass of water by your bed, and lights are out at 9:00." Consequences can be planned and stated to the child in advance:

"No getting up after 9:00. If you do, you'll just have to go right back to bed, no visiting in the living room."

Make sure rules get passed around the inner system. Some parents are comfortable asking the child to use the intercom or their inside message system to tell all the parts a new rule or to set up a consequence, etc. Other parents find that it works better to draw or write a sign or poster and tack it up in the child's room where all the parts can see it *over time*. Again, parental expectations for instant changes need to be lowered, particularly in the beginning stages of therapy. If the child's behavior poses a particular problem, she may need to talk it out with the therapist so that all the parts who are involved or are affected by a particular house rule have a chance to voice their fears, concerns, anger, etc.

If all else fails. If the above methods fail, assume that you, the therapist, have missed something important in the child's inner system or in the family dynamics that is contributing to and maintaining a problem. Confess this to the parents. If discipline fails, it does not mean the child is bad or manipulative. It means we— the therapeutic team—have all overlooked something important. I always assume a child has a good reason for doing what he does: a reason that involves survival and coping with the anxiety of living. This applies to parents, too. Reframing difficult problems as opportunities for good detective work by the team can turn down the heat on a situation.

Chapter Seven

DID CHILDREN WORKING THROUGH TRAUMA

> " . . . things are worse than ever," thought [Alice], "for I
> never was so small as this before, never!" . . . As she said
> these words her foot slipped, and in another moment, splash!
> she was up to her chin in salt water. Her first idea was that
> she had somehow fallen into the sea. . . . However, she soon
> made out that she was in the pool of tears which she had wept
> when she was nine feet tall. "I wish I hadn't cried so much!"
> said Alice, as she swam about, trying to find her way out.
>
> From *Alice's Adventures in Wonderland*

Working through the trauma means gradually allowing back into
consciousness the parts of the experience that the child "escaped"
from by dissociation. It means going back into that "ocean" of
physical and emotional feelings and painful memories that she has
tried so hard to forget. DID children in treatment have probably
been letting you know all along about trauma, loss, or abuse they
have suffered. They drop clues in their play and story themes, and
disclose small pieces of larger events.

Processing the trauma begins at the beginning of therapy. The
child's early work will often bring up pieces of memories in fragments rather than chunks, but that is for the best. The child unconsciously paces herself this way, gaining support and permission to
show herself to the therapist and to remember more as she goes
along. As the DID child builds communication and cooperation

with her personalities, processing the trauma gains clarity and depth. This chapter will cover steps four and five of the treatment process with DID children:

4. Abreaction and cognitive processing
5. Sharing memories and feelings throughout the inner system.

PREPARATION

Personal safety in the real world is the best preparation for working through trauma. The child needs her dissociative defenses if she is in an unsafe home, if there is any chance she will return to abusive caregivers, or if her current home situation cannot provide enough safety from perpetrators (i.e., if the child still visits relatives who are abusing or threatening). To complete her work, the child must be in a safe environment, and her family must be willing to commit to the work of therapy along with the child (Dell & Eisenhower, 1990; Hornstein & Tyson, 1991). Chapter Three discusses safety issues involved in the treatment of dissociative children.

In addition to external safety, internal safety and preparedness also facilitate abreactive work. DID children benefit from identifying and meeting their personalities. The personalities need time to learn to trust each other and cooperate with each other in the business of living. School, family life, and friends are just as important as working on the trauma. The child needs time to build inner communication and get used to being more co-conscious if she isn't already. She needs to get used to using that inside communication system for co-consultation and decision-making to solve problems of daily life. As the child gets to know herself, the parts have a chance to form a good relationship with the therapist as well.

The inner safety and support that this kind of preparation gives the DID child makes it easier for her to tolerate memories and feelings as they surface and to reown them. While it has been part of therapy from the beginning, the work of processing painful experiences can progress on a deeper level after the child has accessed her own inner resources.

ABREACTION: REMEMBERING WITH FEELINGS

Abreactive work with children seems to occur in cycles that become more inclusive with each pass. Early in treatment, bits of history and some feelings appear in play therapy. The therapist will often have to express the feelings for the child at this point. As she becomes accustomed to the process and the feelings, the child expresses more of them for herself. The therapist helps the child gather all the memory pieces, the feelings and the personalities involved in major traumatic events that occurred. Then structured sharing of memories, emotions, and physical feelings increases integration of the experience throughout the child's inner system.

Children don't enjoy remembering scary things. If the trauma is several years old or has been chronic, they have spent the better portion of their young lives trying to forget it. In therapy, these children may prefer to avoid remembering and feeling. They need the therapist to structure the work and make it positive.

Play therapy allows dissociated memories and feelings to surface in a way the child can tolerate. As she plays metaphorically about awful events and about fear, rage, sadness and loss, and pain, these dissociated aspects of herself move in closer and closer. Although children may not abreact in a way that is as visible or lengthy as adults do, they do gradually allow themselves to have the feelings, the pain, and the awareness of what happened, some of it in regressive form.

Why is this necessary in therapy? As Braun (1988) notes, dissociation can occur on four levels: behavior, affect, sensation, and knowledge (B-A-S-K). Memory is more than just knowledge of what happened; it has to include awareness of the *experience* of what happened. For example, most of us know from grade school that the Civil War occurred as an event in U.S. history; however, we have no memory of its happening. To have memory of it, we must have psychophysiological components: how it felt emotionally, and in our bodies. We have to have "been there." Therapy must help the child to reassociate all the lost components of her experience.

Abreaction doesn't require the child to become retraumatized. That is not the point. The goal of having the child work through the trauma in therapy is to help her regain her ability to experience life fully—with behavior, emotion, sensation, and thoughts, to renew her ability to stay in contact with herself and her environment so that she knows who she is and where she is and what and why things happen.

> The goal is to have traumatized children reach the point where they can say something like, "Yes, that happened to me. That's how I felt and how I behaved when it happened. This is how I understand it all now. I won't really forget it happened, but I don't always have to think about it either. (James, 1989, p. 49)

To do this kind of work, the child must have safety and support from the therapist. The therapist's job is to provide a safe setting, to validate the child's experience and her feelings, to reframe the traumatic event in such a way that the child's distortions in interpretation of that event can be corrected, and to provide nurturing and comfort (Bryant et al., 1992, p. 158).

Using Play Therapy for Abreaction
Play therapy is the foundation for most of the work of processing dissociated memories and feelings with young children. Abreactive work begins while the child is still getting acquainted with her parts and with the therapist. Play makes this early surfacing of memories and feelings safe. In the dissociative "pretend" mode, the child acts out the behavioral aspects of the trauma: what happened to her and what she did. The child's play, like any other form of communication, has themes and is embedded with meaning. There is a "literal" level and a metaphorical level of play. When the child is playing about the dolls she is holding, you know, as therapist, that she may also be playing about the trauma.

I watch for shifts in the content of the play, in the child's wording, or in the child's affect that signal a change from strictly symbolic play to replaying old trauma. With DID children, this shift may be accompanied by a switch in personalities. For example, the child may be playing in the dollhouse about dinner and homework, and then change to a different tone of voice and mood when playing about the story child taking a bath or getting ready for bed.

This may signal a shift into playing out a traumatic event. Or the child may be narrating the play story in third person ("The man tells the boy to hurry up") and then switch to first person ("I don't want to—I'm going to hide in the corner"). When these changes occur, it is important to quietly follow the child's lead and "shift gears" with him.

Matt was working in the sandtray, recreating a scary scene from a movie he had seen. "The doctor puts the tools in the trunk of his car and takes them to the cemetery."

"And then what happens?" I asked.

"He gets out of the car. There are two kids hiding there because it's dark," Matt replied. He put one doll in a corner, and one behind a wooden "gravestone."

"And what does this boy see from his hiding place?" I asked, touching one of the doll figures.

Matt's voice suddenly became low and excited. "More people are coming. That's the guy's friend—and that's my grandpa!"

I picked up the second child doll figure and continued, "Boy, I'm glad we're hiding. What are they doing over there?"

Matt continued the play story in first person. The shift in story line, in affect, and in narrative style indicated that he was recreating part of a traumatic event.

As dissociated memories come up in play metaphorically, the feelings that were dissociated along with them will also start to surface: fear and terror, anger and rage, sadness and depression, guilt and shame. These will be the very feelings that were too overwhelming or distressing for the child to allow herself to experience their full impact when the trauma was originally occurring. And they are often feelings that adults in her life, including perpetrators, didn't want to see. She will have major internal injunctions against reassociating those feelings. It is important, therefore, to give the child permission to experience and express feelings and even to predict common ones, such as fear or anger. This is best begun early in the therapy. Ways to teach children about feelings and to reframe those the child considers "bad" are presented in Chapters Four and Five, and they work well with DID children.

The best opportunities to give permission for and desensitize the child to feelings occur within the metaphor of play. Sometimes this is best done in several "passes" or over many sessions. For example, in the scenario above in which Matt recreates a traumatic event, I might omit verbalizing the feelings while he is showing me what happened, especially if this is one of his first attempts. Feelings can be encouraged during a second time playing through the scene or during another session in which a different story is depicted but similar feelings are evoked.

DID children need time to gradually become accustomed to uncomfortable feelings. Certain feelings may be too difficult for them to express at all at first, even in metaphorical play. Feelings may also have been dissociated from the context of the trauma. However, the *therapist* can express the feelings that would normally be felt in that situation if it were real life. When the therapist voices the feelings of the play figures, the child experiences the feelings vicariously, which is much more powerful than just talking "about" how the characters in the story feel (Gould & Graham-Costain, 1994a).

Acting as the voice of the doll, or the kitty, or the boat, or the car, the therapist can express what the child cannot at first. It is important to use expressions that convey the feelings well without overstating them, and to keep the level of verbalization simple. Start with mild feeling statements and move to more intense feeling statements (Gould & Graham-Costain, 1994a). For example, to express scared feelings I might use comments such as, "I don't like that!" to start with, and as the child gets used to it, I can use more direct comments of "I'm scared! I feel like crying." Or for angry feelings I might say, "I don't want to do that! I wish you'd stop," and in later sessions, "You're mean—I hate you!" Creating dialogues between the doll characters in the child's story is also helpful in making feelings explicit and relating them to the situational context. The child and the therapist can each play one of the story characters or objects.

Children will show differing comfort levels for various feelings; for example, anger may be easier to allow themselves to feel than fear or helplessness. In play therapy, start with the feelings that are easiest for the child and move gradually to more difficult ones

(Gould & Graham-Costain, 1994a). *Eventually*, as he desensitizes to seeing and hearing the therapist express difficult emotions such as fear, sadness, anger, rage, and helplessness, the child should be able to take over verbalizing these feelings himself during the play.

I try to keep in mind that any character or role depicted in the child's metaphorical story may portray one of the child's inner personalities. Any behavior, thought, or feeling—whether negative or positive—may represent a dissociated aspect of herself. The child's inner parts will be listening to the messages I am sending through the play therapy. Accordingly, it is important not to minimize any aspect of a metaphorical event the child brings up, or to bypass a difficult belief or feeling with reassurance, or to label a particular character or situation as negative before exploring how the child perceives it. As she watches and listens to the story being created in play, the DID child has a chance to metaphorically experience the interacting of her own dissociated parts. For the therapist, this process may also illustrate the roles that each personality played during trauma and may continue to play as part of the child's inside system.

Merrie created a scenario in the dollhouse. In her story, the mother and her boyfriend were at work. Grandpa had rearranged all the furniture in the house, throwing out the nice things and replacing them with tacky furniture. Afterward, grandpa was watching TV and drinking beer. Marilyn, the mother's oldest child, retrieved all the good furniture that grandpa had thrown in the garbage and locked him in the cellar. As Marilyn's voice, I offered: "I don't like it when grandpa gets out all the yucky stuff. I'm mad at him." Mother and boyfriend came home and were surprised and pleased with the furniture exchange that Marilyn had completed. Then Marilyn and her brother Tommy went to sleep together on the roof, because "it's safe up there." Again I played the voice of Marilyn, the little girl. "I'm nervous about what mother will say when she finds out I put grandpa and grandma in the cellar. I'm glad we're sleeping up here where it's safe." Merrie, playing Tommy, then laughed at the sister in a rather malicious way. Continuing as Marilyn, I said, "I don't like it when you laugh at me. You're scaring me." Merrie made the mother and boyfriend appear again

and say they loved what Marilyn did with the furniture. Then
suddenly the mother was angry at Marilyn and went to unlock the
grandparents from the cellar. As Marilyn, I said, "I'm confused!
Mother was happy and now she's mad at me all of a sudden. I don't
understand." Merrie then decided Tommy shouldn't have laughed
and been mean to his sister. To Tommy I said, "I wish I could tell
you things that scare me, but sometimes you scare me, too. I don't
know if I can trust you." Again as Tommy's voice, Merrie replied,
"Tell me or I'll take your TV away!" I made Marilyn run away and
hide from him, saying she felt scared.

The child characters in her story represented parts of Merrie.
This interchange with Merrie and I both playing parts gave me a
chance to validate her angry and scared feelings. However, in this
instance, Merrie was not yet able to voice those feelings herself.

Anger

Anger is a complicated emotion to which many other feelings may
be attached. A traumatized child may find it difficult to own and
express anger, especially toward a perpetrator who is also someone
she loves. Shame and self-blame may get in the way, and need to be
approached and expressed gently in play therapy. For some children, fear of punishment may block angry feelings from being conscious. Others have parts who are fearful of behaving "out of control" if anger is expressed. The therapist's comments during play
can help the child distinguish feeling from behaving, or wanting
from doing, and can show the child choices for expressing anger.
For example, in the play scenario Merrie created above in which I
voiced the doll's angry feelings, I might have added, "I'm so mad, I
wish I could hit grandpa. Or yell at him. Let's see, I wonder what
else I could do with my mad feelings?" Metaphorical puppet stories
can also help clarify these issues, allowing the child to see and hear
how the story characters feel and think without necessarily having
to interact in the dialogue herself.

Once it is allowed, anger is quite empowering. After playing in
the sandtray about what some bad guys did and verbalizing how
scared the play figures felt, "stomping" the bad guys into the sand
feels very good. Commenting that it is OK to be mad, that the bad
guys can't punish or hurt the child anymore, emboldens the more

timid personalities to speak up as well. This points out how critical it is for the child to truly be safe in real life. Some children are able to get to the really vulnerable feelings only after they have tested out this reality: that the bad stuff will not happen anymore.

Vulnerable Feelings

Some of the last feelings to come out will be physical pain and terror. Those make the child feel the most vulnerable and helpless. It is important to uncover and express fear and helplessness, so that the child can let go of the sense of guilt for things he might have done or not done, as well as the dissociative fantasies or reenactments he may have used to feel powerful. Gradual desensitization and support through play therapy make it possible for the child to allow the helpless feelings to be. Some children who have identified with a perpetrator or who have been forced during abusive events to perpetrate on others may have particular difficulty allowing themselves to experience vulnerable feelings (Burgess, Hartman, & McCormack, 1987). However, the child's "stuck" places can also be explored through the metaphor of play.

> For example, if the hypothetical child . . . perseveres in playing out angry, aggressive characters and cannot, even with encouragement from the therapist, play out the roles of the characters who are the victims of this aggression or even come to appreciate the feelings of sadness and vulnerability attributed to them by the therapist, the therapist needs to comment on the difficulty the aggressive character has in empathizing with the victim. Then the therapist can, within the metaphor of the play, search for reasons for the character's lack of compassion for the victim, in an attempt to elucidate for the child why he cannot forgive himself for his own utter helplessness at the hands of his perpetrators, and why he cannot move into his own feelings of grief and sadness over how badly he was hurt. (Gould & Graham-Costain, 1994a, pp. 8–9)

Reconnecting with feelings of powerlessness allows the child to leave off empty enactments of power and aggression and helps the child move into true feelings of anger, strength, and mastery.

Physical Sensations

Physical or sexual trauma is often accompanied by uncomfortable body sensations or pain; like fear, sadness, and anger, these are feelings that children don't like to have or remember. The body may act as a separate container for trauma memory in the same way a personality does. "Body memory," can appear in the form of physiological arousal, bruise spots, aching joints or muscles, headaches, and other pain. In play therapy, the child learns to give the body a "voice," in much the same way that she learns to tolerate and express emotional feelings (Gould & Graham-Costain, 1994b).

PROCESSING RITUAL ABUSE

Ritual abuse memories initially begin to show themselves in much the same way any other memory of trauma surfaces. Children give clues to the existence of ritual abuse in their history, in their play, in drawings showing themes of magic, occult images, or unusual symbols, and in their behaviors. The experiences of ritual abuse are so terrifiying that they may be among the last ones the child is willing to talk about. But the play, the drawings, and even dreams will be starting points. As mentioned earlier, play therapy allows the child to recreate and reenact the abuse and to reassociate all the aspects of the experience without having to say, "This is what happened to me." Playing about it happening to a doll character feels infinitely safer than playing about what happened to *me*.

Children who have been ritually abused by a group that dabbles in the occult or by an organized group with a structured belief system will be particularly triggered by some fairly common things in the environment. Not only are these clues to what happened, but they can be used to help the child release the dissociated experiences. For example, if birthdays are especially hard, you can make a list of scary things that could happen on birthdays and then play them out in great detail, letting the child improvise. Scary movies that trigger fear and nightmares can be used therapeutically. I ask the child to tell me the scenes that are the scariest, and I write them down. Then we recreate them in the sandtray. However, instead of replaying the movie story, I ask the child to improvise a story around that scene.

As with other types of trauma, play therapy helps the child process what happened during the ritual abuse. However, there are some additional cautions for working with ritually abused chidlren. The therapist needs to be alert for signs of purposeful programming and indoctrination, as well as to the possibility that ritual abuse perpetrators may still be active in the child's life. For example, if the child has been programmed to report back to abusers whenever one personality discloses anything at all — and the child is still in contact with those abusers — the child may indeed reveal to the perpetrators what he has told the therapist, and be punished for any information he may have given. There may be programs for recontacting the group, for being available for contact, or for resisting therapy, among many others (Neswald, Gould, & Graham-Costain, 1991).

Gould and Graham-Costain (1994a, b) give step-by-step information on play therapy with the ritually abused child. They include guidelines for helping the child access feelings that don't begin to surface on their own, a list of cognitive misperceptions and beliefs that ritually abused children need to work through and correct, and ways to access and detoxify cult programming that keeps the child stuck at various points in therapy.

How do you know when the child is done processing ritual abuse memories? Gould and Graham-Costain list certain criteria:

> Termination of the child's therapy can be considered when the therapist feels that most or all of the trauma has surfaced and been dealt with cognitively, emotionally, sensorially, and in terms of the attitudes and beliefs engendered by it. The therapist who is considering terminating the child's treatment needs to feel confident that the child's internal dissociative structure has been explored and treated and the associated programming has been adequately neutralized as well. . . . Though the child's improved functioning is not sufficient reason to terminate the therapy, evidence that the child's play has become normal is a sufficient indicator that much healing from the abuse has been achieved. (1994b, p. 19)

Treatment of children who have been ritually abused demands an educated awareness and an organized plan for therapy, as well as a good therapeutic relationship. The emotional and intellectual challenges to the therapist can be intense. Consultation and support may be necessary, as well as advisable, in order to fill informational gaps and help the therapist deal with his or her own internal responses (Golston, 1992; Gould, 1992).

COGNITIVE PROCESSING

DID children and adults often have inner hidden observers (Hilgard, 1986) who may record and store in memory the knowledge of the trauma that they have experienced. However, every trauma victim displays at least behavioral memory of traumatic events and experiences (Terr, 1990, 1994). While the child may not consciously remember context and details, he may still play it out or reenact it in therapy quite accurately (Hollingsworth, 1986; Terr, 1990). Play therapy media allow the child to behaviorally release the information about what happened. Much healing can occur by reassociating feelings with events portrayed in symbolic form.

The child's thoughts and beliefs about what happened are also part of the "knowledge" aspect of the trauma memory. Because young children are developmentally egocentric, they tend to blame themselves when bad things happen and often believe that they do or should have control over those things, even when they are truly powerless. Perpetrators may reinforce these beliefs covertly or overtly. Erroneous beliefs and misperceptions cause children to make mistakes in the *meaning* they take away from the traumatic experience.

In situations of complete helplessness, children may also turn to fantasy as a way to feel and believe they are in control. When the child is playing out a traumatic event, you may see some sudden shifts in perspective or "fantasy material," such as, "Then the kid turns into Superman and kills the bad guy!" These shifts may indicate how the child dissociated and the "story" he created inside to cope with what was happening, or they may indicate the child's switching mechanisms, showing where other personalities had to come in to take over so he could get through the abuse. He may indeed have pretended he was Superman at one point during the abuse; if that maneuver helped enough, and if the trauma occurred often enough that the "Superman" idea was needed often, then a "Superman" part may have split off and become encapsulated from the consciousness of the child, assuming a separate identity and becoming a separate personality (Braun & Sachs, 1985). These fantasies may have strengthened the child's dissociation from what really happened and from overwhelming feelings of helplessness. They may also mask the child's painful beliefs that he is weak, stupid, or responsible for what happened.

As you get to know the child, her play will show patterns in themes or events—patterns that indicate the meaning she has made of the events she is showing you, even if those events are "made up." These themes, although they may be metaphors rather than literal depictions of actual events, will tell you how the child felt, how she experienced important events and people in her world, and what sense she was able to make of them.

In a later session, Merrie again created a scenario in the dollhouse, playing all the roles herself. The grandpa was drinking beer and getting rid of all the good furniture again. The little girl in the story complained to her mother that "grandpa is mean when he drinks, and scares me." The mother replied that Grandpa was OK. The little girl persisted, "He hits me with a belt." Mother replied, "You deserved it." The little girl got mad, and mother sent her to her room. Then the mom sent grandpa in to whip her. The little girl told the grandma, but the grandma only stated, "Grandpa is the boss, you have to do what he says." Merrie concluded her story: "The girl gets an idea! She gets a rifle and gets the grandma to take her target shooting. Then while grandpa is asleep and drunk, the girl shoots his bed to scare him and get even."

Here Merrie was able to express both fear and anger and validate her own feelings much more in her play. The story also indicated the messages Merrie was given about physical punishment ("You deserved it") and about authority figures (grandpa is "the boss" and whatever he does is "OK"). These messages would need to be explored and challenged, again within the context of play therapy.

Some common beliefs that children carry as a result of trauma may include the following:

- "Bad things happen to me because I am a bad child."
- "I should have (and could have) stopped the abuse."
- "Girls are weak and helpless and stupid."
- "Boys have to be strong/mean/aggressive."
- "People who love you hurt you."

The list is endless. Erroneous beliefs can be checked out as they come up in the metaphor of the child's play. Once you know the messages that the perpetrators "taught" the child, or the faulty interpretations the child told herself in order to make sense of the situation, you can challenge those in several ways: by expressing an opposite or more realistic belief through one of the story characters; by creating a dialogue between two story figures in which one character questions a belief; by creating a different metaphorical story with puppets or doll figures that exposes and corrects the faulty belief.

For example, in Merrie's story above, I might question the messages being given the child character. "Grandpa gets drunk and hurts the girl. Is it OK for grown-ups to hurt and scare children?" After Merrie makes the little girl doll shoot the grandpa's bed, I might add, "Boy, she's mad at that guy. Nobody in this family will listen to her and believe her. That's not fair." During another session, Merrie and I might play different roles in a similar story. Playing one of the doll figures, I might voice the hidden belief ("I deserved to be hit") and start a dialogue about it with another story character. The child begins to understand the event from a different perspective, e.g., that "Grandpa was wrong to hit," or "There were too many big people around—there was no way the little child could stop them."

When the beliefs begin to change, other dissociated feelings also start to surface. Often, the processing a child does in therapy just keeps itself going. One piece of work triggers or jiggles loose another piece of information, or a feeling, or a picture, and so on.

OTHER WAYS TO RELEASE MEMORIES AND FEELINGS

Something that has worked well for me is to make lists with the child of scary things or things that make kids mad, etc. To create a list of "scary things that can happen to kids," I start with something that I know will be relevant but not too anxiety-loaded for the particular child, such as "losing my homework." Then the child takes a turn. If I know some details of the trauma that has happened to the child, or some things that his parents have informed me that he is scared of, I will gradually add those to the list, saving room for the child to add things I might not already know. Then the child and I can play about some of these scary things. The same technique can be used with other feelings, such as anger, rage, sadness, jealousy, or embarrassment.

One day Monica and I were talking about fear. We took turns doing a row of pictures that said, "I feel scared when . . . " She was able to say that she felt scared of being in the bathroom. With my examples of "things kids and other people sometimes feel scared of" she was amazed to find that others sometimes have a feeling of "not knowing where I am." She admitted that this was something that happened to her and scared her. Following this, Monica drew her own set of "Scared Pictures" and brought it in to show me (Figure 7.1).

* * *

One of the things Jeremy was most afraid of was "accidents." So we made up stories about all kinds of accidents—car accidents, falling off of things like bicycles or jungle gyms, etc. Using the baby doll figurine, I asked Jeremy to show me what accidents could happen to a baby (knowing Jeremy had been traumatized when he was younger than three). Jeremy got out a female doll and said, "We need a crib." He made the adult doll take the baby from the crib and drop it. Jeremy's affect changed significantly as he created this particular scenario, compared to any of the others he had previously imagined. After making this scene, he made the baby attack the woman furiously; I voiced the feelings and thoughts: "I'm mad at you—you shouldn't have done that!"

The following session, I continued the story of the baby and the

Figure 7.1 A series of pictures drawn by Monica showing progressive levels of feeling scared: "Oh, boy," Biting lip, Screaming, Yelling, Chattering, Trying to scream but nothing will come out, and Going crazy.

accident with another of Jeremy's parts. This time the woman in the story was drunk. She dropped the baby, picked it up, and then put it roughly back in its crib. In his story the baby had an older brother and sister who got even by overturning all the furniture in the house; they tied up the woman and then tied up two other adults, who were downstairs. The brother found a bottle of alcohol in the house and smashed it.

Following that, I drew a picture of Jeremy's story as he told it. This time Jeremy switched again. This personality told me that the baby's name was "Bobby," a little boy who lived across the street. He said he had seen the incident happen to the neighbor boy: "I was looking out of my window and saw it all happen inside the house across the street. It was sad." The following week however, Jeremy told his parents about it, stating "It happened to me."

Jeremy had begun to reconnect with fear, rage, sadness, and knowledge of an earlier event, as well as showing me how he had dissociated the trauma. Making the incident seem like it was happening "across the street" to another child and only seeing it "from the window of my room" are apt descriptions of dissociative coping by a resourceful child. While it is unclear just what occurred or exactly how old Jeremy might have been, working through trauma in a metaphorical approximation is very healing. The physical pain, as well as the meaning Jeremy had made of this event (e.g., belief that he was a "bad baby"), also need to be processed.

Art and Journaling

Children may be open to painting, drawing, or using clay for abreactive work. Drawing "scary things" or "things that make me mad" are good starts. Actually, any drawing or sculpture a child produces may lead into a Gestalt dialogue between the child and a part of the artwork, or between the therapist and an object in the picture, or between two parts of the picture or sculpture. Feelings and beliefs surface in this way, and can be handled within the metaphor just as in play therapy.

Older children, in particular, may find art or journaling helpful. Angry or sad personalities may be willing to write letters to the perpetrator, or to someone they may have hurt. In most cases letters are better left unposted; this makes the activity safe and healing for the child.

Kristie, age 14, had a part named "Little Kristie." One day Little Kristie drew a picture about abuse. As she drew, she commented that she was making the picture from a "top" view. "I can fly," she said, "so I went up above and looked down." Her picture showed scared feelings, wanting mother, feeling alone, and finally feeling safe (see Figure 7.2). Little Kristie was able to verbalize these feelings as she told me about the picture. We talked about the fact that the abuse was over and that she was safe now from the perpetrator. This younger personality had been able to hear Kristie's voice from the inside for some time; she told me that she knew Big Kristie was now able to take care of her.

During a separate session, a different part of Kristie expressed angry feelings about the abuse. Designating a big mound of clay as the old abuser, Kristie bashed him with a rubber mallet. As she pounded the clay, Kristie voiced her thoughts and feelings: "You were supposed to care about me. You took my innocence and betrayed me. You make me so mad!"

Drama Role-plays

For some children, role-playing or creating a drama is a way to begin talking about abuse. A caution: I don't think it's a good idea

Figure 7.2 Abreaction drawing showing fear of the perpetrator ("like being in a cage with a lion"), and other events and feelings as the trauma progresses: "I want Mommie," "I'm all alone," and finally "Safe." Drawing by a younger part of Kristie, age 14.

for a child or her therapist to role play or "take on" the part of an abuser. Pillows and chairs can be stand-ins for abusers. A child may want to "show me" what she did to cope. And since she has dissociated parts inside, she may role-play one of her other inside parts, or switch into that part and show me what she did.

Merrie's talent for storytelling and playing roles was not only her way of coping with trauma but also a strong personality trait. Drama felt safe to her because she insisted on being in charge, giving orders about what came first, second, and third, and directing what I should do in the drama. One of her stories began with a mother coming to take a child for visitation. This child had a secret: unbeknownst to her mother, the little girl had three of each of her parts. So when one part had to go with mother, the other two stayed inside and comforted each other. As the drama continued, these two "sister" parts began to gather other parts to help the girl, including a boy protector part, so the other parts wouldn't be so scared.

Another day, Merrie again created a role-play about three parts: a "baby" part, an older girl, and an even older "sister." These were analogous to Merrie's conception of her own parts; each part was triplicate, with one Merrie's correct age, one younger, and one older. She directed me in playing one of the "sisters" as they talked to each other. In this dialogue information came out that Merrie had to do housework, even as a preschooler, and had to do it right or she would be given more work. One of Merrie's older triplet-parts taught herself to sort laundry correctly by promising herself she could "go to the ball like Cinderella" if she could do it right. If she goofed, only one of the three triplet-parts got punished—"the other two weren't around."

It would be easy to take off from either of these two drama scenes to verbalize the feelings associated with each part. Therapist and child can exchange roles during the play, so that the therapist can express some of the feelings the child is unable to. An alternative is for the therapist to hold a puppet or stuffed animal to express the child's hidden feelings and thoughts and to dialogue about those with the child, so the therapist herself doesn't have to "get out of role."

Use of Dream Content or Themes

The dissociative child's dreams may be metaphorical references to trauma. This is common to children who have suffered trauma and the post-traumatic stress that follows (Terr, 1990). Dreams are another altered state of consciousness; as such they are similar to other dissociative states, and can be helpful to therapy (Franklin, 1990). Using the child's dream (or nightmare) as a base, you can jointly draw the dream scenario or reconstruct it in the sandtray or dollhouse (see Chapter Five). Sometimes, if the dream is extremely frightening, I will draw it as the child tells it to me. Being chased by a terrifying figure from a movie or television seems to be a common theme for children who are being "chased" by the life trauma they are trying to escape, both externally and internally. The therapist's asking for help in getting the placement of figures or the perspective right engages the child in the process while allowing her to maintain some distance.

Monica took out her drawings of scared feelings and told me of a dream she'd had that fit the picture "Trying to scream but nothing will come out." I drew a picture of the dream as she told it to me, and we noted her feelings at each point in the dream. It was a dream of a Frankenstein man chasing her; she kept running, barely out of his reach, scaling high walls to elude him. Finally, when she had to stop running, a policeman who "just happened to be there" helped her and put the man in jail. Monica acknowledged that she felt very frightened of the monster in the dream, angry at the monster for chasing her, and relieved that the policeman put him in jail. Monica's biggest fear at this point in her life was that the man who molested her would get out of jail and come after her. Asked if this dream reminded her of feeling scared and mad about someone or something in her life now, Monica thought of the perpetrator. We drew a courtroom scene and discussed some historical details, noting that the judge had decided that the perpetrator would not be allowed to see her. Following that, Monica wanted to draw a picture of the man. She drew him as a devil, then scribbled over the drawing with crayon and ripped it up.

When Monica was able to express some of her old fears and her current fears about the perpetrator metaphorically, and to feel safe while doing so, her anger bubbled right up and demanded expression. Monica's knowledge of the perpetrator's imminent release from prison now triggered the old helplessness as well. Her anger was a natural result of forced helplessness, and expressing the anger relieved some of that powerless feeling.

Hypnosis

DID children are already adept at entering trance states, and in switching from state to state. They have perfected the arts of fantasy and dissociative defense that are common to most children. Some may have been taught to use self-hypnosis, e.g., in a context of ritual abuse; most DID children learn it unconsciously. Any therapy intervention that makes use of the child's facility in entering altered (dissociative) states might be considered mildly hypnotic. Such "hypnotic" techniques as visual imagery, storytelling, and imaginary role-playing can be used without formal hypnosis (Gardner, G., 1977; Gruenewald, 1971). Various therapeutic requests and suggestions also make use of the DID child's dissociative flexibility. For example, I may say, "I want everyone inside to turn on your intercoms so you all can listen right now," or "Everybody listen up!", which then allows me to "talk through" whichever part is out to all the other parts inside (Kluft, 1982; Putnam, 1989, pp. 197–198). I often ask the child to "go inside and listen," or "go inside and ask [a part] how he feels about that," to encourage the child to increase communication and cooperation.

Creating an inner safe place is a hypnotic technique; imagining a container inside for storing newly uncovered memories or feelings is another (see section on "Containment of Memories and Feelings" later in this chapter). More highly structured hypnotic techniques may also be helpful with children, not only in getting acquainted with personalities and in learning about their various roles, but also in facilitating abreaction and integration (Kluft, 1985a, c). However, I find that play therapy, storytelling, and art, which allow the child to make use of her own dissociative mode, are usually sufficient when working with children.

Physical Symptoms

Somatic complaints are common with dissociative children. The body may carry anxiety and it may contain some of the memories of trauma. Children may experience discomfort or pain in their bodies that seems "unattached" to emotions or to any knowledge of what might have caused it. When the child gives the physical feelings a voice, emotions and awareness may surface as well.

Jeremy came in one day with a stomachache and a headache. I asked him to draw. He drew a picture of a jack-in-the-box I had in the playroom. It was an elephant that could be pushed down inside the box and then released by pressing a button. I asked him to "be" the elephant and talk about what it was like to be inside the box.

Jeremy said, "I'm scrunched and uncomfortable. My stomach is in a knot, my head hurts, and my legs are uncomfortable. I'm mad because I can't get out of this box, and I'm sad and mad because someone else controls my life. I can hear from inside the box, but I'm still mad I'm in there and can't get out. What I need is an anvil—I need a helper to crack open the box so I can get out." I asked whether this might be the way Jeremy felt, and he agreed. This led to a talk about how to help an inside part that feels anxious or angry, or one that may need to "get out" to do something or tell Jeremy something important.

CONTAINMENT OF MEMORIES AND FEELINGS

Remembering and processing trauma are not always comfortable and may arouse anxiety at various stages. Sometimes the child can even trigger herself in her work, bringing up more anxiety. Children need some time and some outlets within the therapy space to regain their balance, reorient to the safe present, and back away from painful work a bit. This helps to make the therapy itself safe enough so that the work can continue.

Creating an Inner Safe Place

I think it is important for a dissociative child to have a "safe place" inside where any of the parts can go to rest or to feel secure when scary feelings or memories come up. To help them create one, I use Violet Oaklander's (1988) technique, which goes something like this: "Close your eyes and imagine a place where you feel very, very safe—a place where no danger is and no harm can come to you. It might be an indoor place or an outdoor place, it might be a place you know about, a place in your life now that feels safe, or it might be an imaginary place that you would like to be able to have or go to. (Did you pick an inside or an outside place?)" If the child picked an indoor place, I continue: "Look around your inside safe place and see what you would like to have there. Is there furniture, or not? Are there things on the floor, or the walls? Is there a door to go in or out? See if you want to have any other people or animals in your inside safe place, or if you want to be by yourself there.

You can put anything you want in your safe place." If the child picked an outside place, I continue: "Look around your outdoor safe place and see what kind of a place it is. Does it have hills and mountains, or is it flat? Are there trees, or flowers, or water nearby? Or rocks and sand? See if you want to have any other people or animals in your safe place, or if you want to be by yourself there. You can put anything you want in your safe place."

When the child has made up mental imagery of a safe place, I ask her to open her eyes and draw it. This makes it more concrete and easily visualized as well; sometimes children will embellish the mental picture in the drawing, which is fine. Figure 7.3 shows April's indoor safe place, which was a room for herself.

Jeremy's safe place was a bit different. Jeremy had great difficulty allowing himself to express any negative feelings toward an adult. I made a puppet show for Jeremy in which a beaver told a kitten that

Figure 7.3 April's drawing of her safe place, showing a room for herself.

its feelings were important and that he could come and talk to him
and stay safe with him any time he wanted. Following the story,
Jeremy and I talked about where he might feel safe to talk and have
feelings. Figure 7.4 is the outdoor safe place Jeremy created. Tak-
ing off from the story I had told, he drew a mountainside on half of
the page, with a waterfall down the middle. The top of the beaver's
dam (the safe place) is just visible at the bottom of the waterfall;
this is where the kitten goes to stay with the beaver when he wants
to feel safe. A fish is visible in the waterfall; in Jeremy's story, the

Figure 7.4 Jeremy's safe place. Shows a waterfall splashing down onto the top of a log house where a beaver lives. The beaver's home is safe. The encapsulated fish in the center carries messages up the waterfall to an unseen kitten. The kitten stays with the beaver in the house under the water when he receives a warning message: "Danger—the parents are coming."

fish travels up and down the waterfall and brings messages to the kitten to let him know, "Danger—the parents are coming."

Once the child has a good picture, I ask him to close his eyes and know that he can have a safe place just like that inside for any or all of his parts to go to when they feel scared, or mad, or sad, or even just tired. They can play or rest, or share their feelings with another part that can listen.

It is important for the DID child to have this special place of safety inside once the work of reowning memories and feelings begins. Some of the child's inside world may be scary, since it contains scary memories and pictures or scared and angry voices. The safe place is different; it is meant to be a haven. After hard work in therapy, one or more parts may want to go to their inside safe place for respite and comfort.

Creating Containers for Memories and Feelings

No matter how safe your therapy room is, and how safe you are as a therapist, if the environment outside your office isn't safe, the child won't feel safe enough to do the work. This includes taking therapy home. If he brings up "scary stuff" in the form of memories and feelings he has formerly kept locked and guarded in separate compartments in his head—and then those memories and feelings, now "on the loose," invade his home space—the child won't feel safe enough to do the work either. The DID child, and sometimes the child with PTSD, needs a good place to "put away" those thoughts and feelings while he is away from therapy.

So it's important to have a container of some kind for storing newly surfaced memories and feelings—but in a different way from the child's usual method. In the past, these things were unconsciously dissociated, and just as unconsciously "popped up" again in the form of flashbacks, nightmares, and fears. Now the child can consciously put them away safely inside, in a place of his choosing, where he can reaccess them when he is ready, i.e., during a future therapy session.

I give the child some ideas for containers to start him off, such as a heavy box with a lock on it, or a special room inside just for storage, which he can lock and unlock himself. Figure 7.5 shows

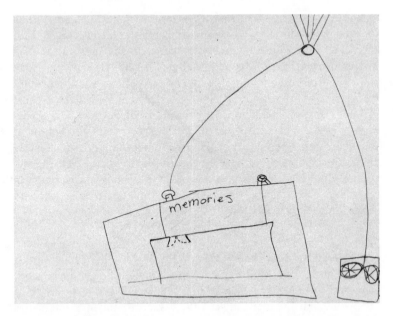

Figure 7.5 Jeremy's picture of a container for storing memories and feelings that come up during therapy. He has drawn a pulley system for raising the concrete lid.

one child's concept of a container for "therapy stuff": a huge concrete storage tank, with a lid so heavy it has to be lifted by a crane. No chance that stuff is going to leak out during the week at home or school!

Another way to contain the therapy material within the therapy session is symbolically to leave it in the therapy room. You might designate a special bag that can be sealed, or a box with a lid, as a repository for "Things I Remember" and "Hard Feelings." Or, you can have the child draw a box, and draw inside it the memory and the feelings, and write in the words that go with them—all that he is "putting away" inside it. The drawing, along with the images and thoughts the child deposited in it, is left in the therapist's file in the office.

Of course, this doesn't always work. If the child is faced with a situation at home or school that is a major trigger, i.e., something that resembles the traumatic event or stimulates feelings just uncovered in therapy, not even imaginary concrete will prevent the rush of feeling or memory that results. But it certainly helps. You may ask, "Isn't this just encouraging the child to use dissociation again?" Yes and no. Dissociation in and of itself is not bad; only when it prevents adaptive behavior is it a hindrance. Dissociation is something we all do; psychological defenses are necessary and helpful at times to normal people. Learning to contain the work consciously and allowing himself, with the therapist's help, to consciously reaccess traumatic material and process it with safety and support in the therapy setting are much healthier and feel much safer and more controlled than before.

"Time Off" in Therapy

Following intense work, especially if the play has been fairly realistic, it helps for the child to have some "down time" in the session. Save time at the end of each session for the child to just play or to choose a game or other fun activity. Make sure the material he has just worked on is safely contained, and that any inside parts who were scared or saddened by the therapy work have had a chance to be comforted. This helps make a safe space around the therapy work and cushions the child's reentry into "real life." Caregivers at home may also need to be alerted that the child needs extra rest or an easy evening to readjust.

Worries Children Have During Abreactive Work

Many DID children worry that if they allow a certain personality out, or allow it to meet you, the therapist, that part might do something bad. For example, April worried that her mad parts might say mean things to me, and then I wouldn't like her anymore. Kristie's younger parts got scared when the mad parts spoke, interpreting anger as "being mean." Adam, too, was first scared when he heard his own "mad voice" inside. I assure them that using their mad voice is OK and tell all the parts that it is all right for the mad parts to do some things when they are mad (e.g., draw mad pictures, pound on clay, use the batacas). I also tell little parts that if it is too scary to listen in while mad parts are out, they can close their own windows or curtains and turn off the intercom in their room for a while. Since safety is allowed, these little parts often choose to watch and listen in after all—finding out afterward that nothing terrible happened this time when they were vulnerable.

Sexual parts or personalities that act out sexually need to be reframed, encouraged to get acquainted, and validated as important before they will risk meeting you and telling what they did and how they felt during memory work. Anger, revenge, shame, and confusion are big feelings that these courageous and necessary parts carry, along with their behaviors. Once their feelings and positive intentions come out and are validated, these parts, like others, find better ways to help take care of the child.

Parents of the children I work with have often wished the child would just "leave on" the internal intercom system all day, so that any information the parent puts in, such as "always pick up your toys," or "here's a good way to get going on your homework," would be available to all the personalities at once; it saves the parent repeating herself with switching personalities that appear and know nothing of what just went on. But DID children may not be able to leave the inner communication line open all day, every day. Many children have told me they are afraid that if they "all" listen in all the time to everyone—become completely co-conscious—they will know all the "bad stuff" or hear other parts crying or in pain. To some extent, that *can* happen. And early in therapy, that may be too hard for the child to tolerate. It's not necessary for all the personalities to know all the feelings and all the bad memories all at once. I let children know that the scared parts can turn off their intercom switches or shut the curtains in their rooms, and those parts that feel able to watch and listen and help can do that.

SHARING MEMORIES AROUND THE INSIDE SYSTEM

At some point during this processing of trauma, the child's abreactive work and her growing acquaintance with her inner personalities begin to overlap. It is important to find out which personalities carried which feelings, thoughts, or behaviors, and to acknowledge the role of each part who helped the child cope with major traumatic events.

Sometimes the child can find out which personalities participated in a traumatic event simply by "asking inside." I might then ask each personality to talk with me in turn about his or her role and thoughts and feelings. By asking all the personalities to keep their intercoms open or to meet in the common conference room while we discuss the traumatic event, all the parts can listen in or contribute to the discussion.

April became aware of several traumatic events that had happened to her prior to age five. Because April and I had already become acquainted with each of her personalities, I could ask, "Who knows about this event?" That part then told what he or she knew. In some cases, one part pretty much knew the whole story. But it might not have the feelings or the physical pain that April experienced. Those might be stored in other parts. Then I asked, "Who knows about XYZ part of the story? And this (other) part? Who knows about the scared feelings we played about?"

Each personality may need some individual therapy to fully own her feelings or to appreciate her "job" during a traumatic event. It is important to allow each of the splits or parts that functioned during the abuse to express what they experienced. The therapist then can reframe their activities so the child can own that part of the experience as something that helped her get through it. Each dissociative coping mechanism the child used — whether it was to "melt into the wall" or "become a ghost who was invisible" or pretend she could "turn into Spiderman and scale the wall to escape" — needs to be discussed. The feelings each part experienced need to be expressed and validated. Individual personalities may have negative beliefs about their feelings or what they did to cope.

Once you get the whole story of a particular event, write it down, with the child's help. Some older children may want to write it down themselves; younger ones may prefer to just tell it while the therapist writes. The story of the traumatic event should be as complete as possible, with what happened first, second, third, and so on. As the story progresses, write down which of the inside personalities was present for each part of the event, and how that personality felt at the time (V. Graham-Costain, personal communication, 1991). The result will be a record of what the child went through, each switch in personality she made during that event, and each different feeling and thought and behavior the child made during the event, as well as what the perpetrator(s) did and said.

When the child is ready, this story of the traumatic event can be shared around the inside system. Each personality takes a turn to share his or her individual experiences, thoughts, feelings, or behaviors with the others in sequence as the story of the event unfolds (V. Graham-Costain, personal communication, 1991). The child may show by body language and facial expressions that she is reexperiencing the old feelings. However, because she is doing it with support, nurturance, and safety—and with the dissociating under her own control—it is healing.

Body memory may return while the child is doing this. For example, April shared with all her inside parts a memory of sexual abuse during which she had to kneel on a hard surface. Bruise spots appeared on both knees, even though she was seated in a beanbag chair with her legs out in front of her during the abreaction.

The child may be very tired after a shared abreaction of this kind. Immediately afterward, it is important to ask how the child and all his or her parts are feeling. Those that are sad or hurting need to be comforted; those that are scared by what was told or what they heard need to be asked about their worry, and reassured and comforted as well. Some children may have concerns about letting themselves know or letting others know about what happened, especially if they were threatened. Usually, however, these fears will have been discussed earlier or dealt with when the memory first surfaced in the context of play therapy.

More feelings may come up following this kind of sharing around the inner system. The essence or "main" personality may feel anger she has not experienced before about the incident. (While angry personalities may have stored and felt and acted on anger, other parts may not have before.) Some children like to "get" the perpetrator by smashing a clay figure as they tell it how they feel; others like to write a letter to the perpetrator, even if he or she is no longer alive, spilling all the angry feelings they have not been allowed to own until now.

Sad feelings, too, may bubble up throughout the whole inner system. Another result of the inner sharing of each major traumatic experience may be a significant reduction in specific post-traumatic fears. Following one of April's systemic sharing experiences, for example, she reported that for the first time she was no longer afraid of being in the bathroom.

As he progresses in therapy, the DID child's play often shows him getting better in many ways. He is more able to express feelings in play or art and connect them to what has happened in his life. The child's individual personalities may show a broader range of emotion and more inclusive roles within the inner system. His play themes show his awareness of events and of how and why they happened. His stories may also show the child getting help, feeling strong, and making active choices to solve problems.

Because abreaction allows the child to regain her capacity to experience fully—with safety and support—healing can happen. She can then integrate the trauma into her conscious collection of life experiences so that it "takes its place as one of many events in an evolving life" (Monahon, 1993, p. 126). This allows the child not only perspective, but also freedom from the tyranny of a fragmented life that feels out of her control.

Chapter Eight

THE DID CHILD: INTEGRATION AND FOLLOW-UP

Integration is a joyful experience for most DID children, although it has its bittersweet moments along the way, for integration, like all the other work the child does, is a process. From the moment a child begins a journey of discovering herself, she begins to integrate. And it's a process, once begun, in which she joins the rest of us already on the road; we keep growing and developing right up to the end of our lives.

The DID children I have worked with have let me know when they were ready for integration. Some children catch on early in the process as to where the therapy could lead them—and they are eager to know about it. Others are slower to want information and take their time mulling it over. Children can be given a choice about integrating; I truly believe children will do what takes care of them best. Children who do not complete integration may not have a home environment safe enough to allow them to dispense with dissociative defenses. This chapter will cover the last two steps of the treatment process with DID children: integration of personalities and post-integration work.

WHAT IS INTEGRATION?

"Fusion" is a term commonly used to refer to two personalities becoming one. "Integration" is a more global term, often referring not only to the rejoining of personalities to the child, but also to

Figure 8.1 April's conceptualization of integration. Flower petals and leaves (parts) come together into a whole flower.

the overall process of reassociating knowledge, feelings, sensations, behaviors, and parts of oneself back into consciousness. Some DID children may benefit from fusing two personalities into one (still separate) personality; others may simply integrate each separate personality into the whole. If the child has an essence personality (see Chapter Six), that part becomes the receptacle for the other personalities.

I provide the child with a way to conceptualize the personalities as separate parts of a whole, explaining separateness as a way the child protected himself during trauma or loss and leaving open the possibility of the parts' reuniting into one whole child at some point. DID children, often being exceptionally quick and creative, may have their own concepts of separateness and wholeness and how integration works. April's attempt to visualize the concept appears in Figure 8.1; Adam's is in Figure 8.2.

Figure 8.2 Adam's picture of integration showing individual fish (parts) entering a big wave to become part of the ocean. The arrow points to the part about to integrate.

Merrie's idea was a bit more dramatic, as befit her character. One day early in treatment (without any previous information that her family or I knew of), she informed her foster mother that one of her parts, named Little Merrie, was "the one who was here before all the others." Later, Merrie wanted to talk with me about how all the parts could go "back into the stump." Explaining her idea to me, she drew a picture of a tree on the blackboard. "Once," she said, "I was one healthy tree, and then it got chopped down, branch by branch. We could graft the parts back onto the stump!"

The following week, Merrie continued defining the process for herself. She redrew a picture of the "stump," then wanted to create a scene in the sandtray. The story that evolved was about "Star Hill and Windshield Wiper Lake." A storm came that hit the hill and the lake, burying both of them and everything else in the scene. But two children in the story dug themselves out, replanted all the trees

*on the hill, and restored the lake. In all the digging the chil-
dren did, they also found buried treasure they could keep. Merrie
had created a beautiful metaphor for the entire therapy/inte-
gration process, one that illustrated her own inner strength and
resilience.*

As Kluft notes (1985a), children are not as invested in separateness as adults with dissociative identity disorder. The younger parts
who have gotten "stuck" being five years old while the child grew
up are often envious of the older child, much as a younger sibling
would be; they may eagerly anticipate being "big."

TIMING

Integration in the broad sense occurs gradually and spontaneously
during the course of therapy. As the child's personalities become
more fully acquainted with one another, each seems to expand in
ways that allow them all to experience more from each other (because they are increasingly co-conscious) and to widen the range of
feelings and behaviors they have in their still separate repertoires.
Many parts reach the point where they are more alike than different. For example, Kristie noted that her parts seemed to be "getting
closer together and more alike." When there is no longer any need
or reason to remain separate, and the child is conscious of all the
information and/or feelings that one part holds, fusion or integration is a natural outcome (Dell & Eisenhower, 1990; Kluft, 1985a,
c). It is possible that in some cases of very young children, integration can even resume unconsciously, according to the original developmental process that nature began but which was interrupted
by trauma (Albini & Pease, 1989).

Whenever possible, I have found it wisest to let the child be in
charge of timing and which personalities fuse or integrate first. As
memory work and abreaction progress, some of the child's parts
may want to fuse fairly quickly. This can happen especially if one
part's work is finished, if the role that part played or the service it
performed for the child no longer needs to be kept separate (Dell

& Eisenhower, 1990). Sometimes a split-off part may have stored a particular memory or feeling involved in a certain traumatic event; when that memory or those feelings are processed and shared with the child, that part's job is finished in the sense of keeping the material separate from the child. The personality may then be ready to integrate, along with the once dissociated information. This may not always be true, however; some parts do stick around to help out in other ways, especially if their role is to be protective.

The fusion of two personalities can often have immediate positive effects. April's first fusion was judiciously chosen as to timing and parts involved. One part carried a lot of feelings; the other part could verbalize the feelings and ask to get her needs met. The fusion of these two parts produced one who could do all of these functions without switching. The choice of which parts to fuse first was made by April herself; I couldn't have made a better one.

CHILDREN'S FEARS

Children may have some worries about integration. "Will I make more parts if something bad happens to me again? Like if my cat dies?" One cannot predict the occurrence of new events that are inadvertently traumatizing, such as a car accident or death of a relative; but generally speaking, if the child is not purposely retraumatized, and if he has support, comforting, and a chance to make sense of the event, splitting off new parts is no longer needed. However, if a new event occurs that is sufficiently traumatic, especially if it is abusive, or if the child is thrown back into an environment of danger, severe dissociation may again be used as a defense (Kluft, 1985a, c).

It is also possible for two parts that have fused to reseparate. This can happen if the two parts were not really willing and prepared to join, or if an overwhelmingly stressful event (such as being reabused) occurs shortly after the fusion, requiring the child to resplit in order to cope. Usually, if the fusion lasts several weeks, it will continue to hold.

Sometimes a child is astute enough to realize that there may be advantages to being multiple, even when physical safety is not currently an issue. Adam, for example, wanted to know if all his parts could integrate into a younger part so he could stay little instead of being eleven years old. This question indicated to me that Adam had some fears about "being big" that needed to be addressed. We made a list of the things he might not like about being older. It turned out that "the worst part about being big" was going to school. His fears revolved mainly around being with other children; he particularly worried about knowing what to do when he felt angry either at home or at school. Adam needed to talk about and experiment with behaviors for expressing anger. He had quite correctly deduced that being integrated meant he would be expected by others—and himself—to behave like an eleven-year-old, rather than a younger child. By asking the question ahead of time, Adam was preparing himself to be able to cope adequately with anger without having to keep his angry parts (many of which were "younger") separate.

*   *   *

April pushed herself to integrate a part that accomplished most of the academic work at school. Shortly after the fusion, this part reseparated. In therapy, I talked with April and with the other part, named Angie. It turned out that April had felt unprepared to do all the schoolwork that might be required of her. Together they decided that April needed to know Angie better and have Angie teach her the school information gradually before integration, as Angie put it, "so April won't be worried about doing all that work." One month later, a few weeks before school started again in the fall, April was ready to invite Angie to join her again, and that integration was successful.

Dialogue is the easiest way to get fears out in the open so they can be resolved. Below are two letters written between April and a part named Sarah, sharing their fears in preparation for integration. Sarah was a social part of April; she made friends with other kids at recess during school hours, but did not do classwork as Angie had.

To April,

I am eleven and I like soccer. I guess you could
say I'm outgoing sometimes. I like to shop for
clothes and gifts. I like going to parties with my
friends. I have a sense of humor and I love school.
Most people say I'm weird. But they sort of like
my humor. I'm not shy, that much. I could probably give you the ability to make friends and not
always do the school work. You'll have more fun.
When I go together with you I could come out
more as the fun part of you. I hope this helps you.

Sarah

Dear Sarah,

I'm a little worried that you will power me over
and never let me out! I don't really want that many
friends because people might envy me and be
mean. Most of the people who think they're popular are snotty and I don't want to be that way.

April

April's fears of being taken over by this part, of being undeserving
of admiration from peers, of being visible and being disapproved
of by peers all got in the way of her accepting Sarah as part of
herself. These fears were greatly allayed when April discovered that
she did not have to be a "social butterfly" when she integrated
Sarah; rather, she would have choices: she would have her shyness
and her awareness of vulnerability, as well as her ability to make
friends and be liked. She could choose when to be friendly and with
whom—choosing to be open with kids who felt safe. About being
"powered over," April was recalling what it felt like to switch, as
Sarah came "out" and did things with friends that April felt too shy
and awkward to do herself. With the knowledge that Sarah could
not overwhelm her like she used to before they had a cooperative
inner system, April felt much more comfortable.

Children have some of the same fears of integration that are common in adult DID clients. If they are old enough, children may be aware of their lack of certain skills and prepare for the integration with an uneasy expectation of having to "do it all" themselves now. And truly, the child has every right to experience some performance anxiety; these misgivings have a measure of reality. Until now, her abilities, whether to do schoolwork, make friends, be funny, or be assertive, have been dissociated from her—she's been doing all these things but has not *experienced* herself doing them, so she has little confidence in her abilities. "I've never done math—how am I going to know how to do it all of a sudden? What if I fail? People scare me; what if I laugh, and nobody else does? What if other kids don't like me? Maybe they liked *her*, but they won't like *me*." Sometimes these fears can best be allayed by slowing the joining process, as April did with her "Angie" part above—taking time for the child to "learn" all the skills a specific personality has preserved and developed for her *before* they fuse. That way the child has more confidence in her ability to continue to function without using dissociation.

STRUCTURING THE INTEGRATION

I usually encourage the child to integrate one personality at a time, but some children have wanted to integrate several at once and have done so successfully. Trusting the child's wisdom has worked for me; children do take care of themselves by asking the questions they need to if the relationship with the therapist is a safe one.

Sometimes children may consciously fuse a personality without the therapist's help. For example, Adam came into session one day and announced that one personality had integrated with him. This part had in the previous session voiced a desire to integrate. Adam had devised his own imagery for the fusion, and it was successful. However, in my experience, most children generally seem to want and need some guidance from the therapist in integrating.

Involving Caregivers

I usually let caregivers know when the child is ready to begin integration of parts. This is an exciting time, for both the child and the parents. The child will need rest immediately after each fusion/ integration process. A couple of relatively stress-free days afterward are also helpful, as the child gets used to feeling different inside and adjusts to the feelings and memories that are now "hers," brought to her by the part that integrated. Some children like to have time for a personality to say "good-bye" to a parent if it is a part the parent knows well. Some like to say "good-bye" to me also. About the actual integration process itself that follows, I leave it up to the child as to whether she wants to share what happened with a caregiver. Some children prefer to keep it private; others don't mind letting caregivers in on how it was done.

Integration Imagery

Before we begin the fusion, I ask the child to pick an imaginary place for the two parts to join into one. Some children like to pick a different place for each fusion. Images of standing in a meadow full of flowers, or walking on a sandy beach, or floating up on a fluffy pink cloud are among the pictures that children have chosen. Others choose to be in their inner meeting place or just in the therapy room. Having choice and allowing comforting and pleasurable pictures make the process relaxed. At the beginning of the planned fusion, I also like to give the child a chance to thank each part for helping or for being "brave" or for keeping the child's feelings or abilities safe until she could reclaim them.

Let's say the child picks the beach on a sunny day for her imaginary place in which to join. My narration might begin something like this: "Now imagine that you and [the personality] are at the beach together. Look around and enjoy the warm sand, and the feel of the water. It's such a beautiful place. And while you are there together, see if there is anything you'd like to say to one another before you join. [Personality's name] is that wonderful part of you that can _____. She's been keeping those abilities safe for you—abilities that have always belonged to you, since you were a little baby. And now she's willing for you to have them back, and to be part of you, just the way you were meant to be."

I continue with a visualization exercise for joining, one that provides the child with mental imagery for making two parts become one. As Kluft (1982) notes, it is better to use imagery of joining rather than images of one part going away or dying. It is important for children to know that they will never lose any part of themselves by integrating; rather, something is gained. I tell children that after integration they will have all of their parts—just as they always *have* had all their parts—but now their parts will be with them in a new way. It is not possible or desirable to get rid of parts. Everyone needs *all* their parts, and each is important to have in order to be whole.

There are many types of imagery that will work. Kluft (1982) offers one in which each part that is joining stands close together, being "bathed in a radiant glowing light"; the separate glowing balls then merge into one light "in which all memories, feelings, strengths, and knowledge flow together. All settle together, the glow fades, and a single strong individual stands forward, unified now and forever" (pp. 236–237).

Another one that children seem to like is an image of "hugging" another part into themselves. The visualization seems to work best by imagining the two parts close together, the child standing behind the part she is integrating, putting her arms around it in a big hug. She hugs the part closer and closer until she pulls the part right into herself and ends up with her arms around herself in a hug. Sometimes I bolster the imagery by verbalizing the joining, from the feet up to the head and "from the tummy all the way to the backbone."

I follow up by commenting again that "now all those wonderful abilities, feelings, and knowledge that [the personality] had belong to you and are yours, forever." Then I usually close by allowing the child to rest within the imagery of her chosen place, letting the new feelings, and sensations, and awarenesses settle in, getting used to having that part with her in the new way.

The metaphors you use in the visualizations, your voice, and the process itself put the child into trance, which facilitates the integration. The words themselves are meant to nurture and to allow the child to experience the integration as nurturing and enriching. It is an opportunity to model loving and accepting internal self-talk that the child can remember and use later for himself.

Merrie's first fusion joined one singleton part and one set of "triplets." She wanted to do a fusion based on her own idea of going "back into the stump." Being the storyteller she was, Merrie also created a story of how the four parts went into the tree stump to become one. It began with each part surfing in the ocean on their surfboards; when they landed on the beach, each had to climb up into the tree, where they found a hidden door. Inside the tree stump was a radiant light; as the four parts went down inside the tree into the light, they became one. This child, who was only nine years old at the time, created this symbolic picture entirely on her own. The spirituality and universality of her metaphors were striking. After she had told me the story she wanted to use, she sat down on a beanbag chair facing away from me, visualizing the story as I narrated it back to her. She gave the one resultant part of herself a new name, which was a combination of the original names.

THE CHILD'S EXPERIENCE OF INTEGRATION

When the child comes out of the visualization or trance and back to the present, he or she will often report feeling "different." Most feel very tired afterward. The first integrations often take longer than later ones, and the children report that they get easier to do with practice.

After her first fusion, April was a little anxious about moving her body. Cautiously, she touched her own hand first, and then looked around the room. She commented that the traffic noise outside the office window sounded louder than usual and that she "never noticed before how far the lamp light goes" across the room. April said that inside she felt happy, sad, scared, excited, weird, and tired. "I'm so tired I can't hold my head up. My heart feels funny." When she finally stood up, she exclaimed, "Boy, I even feel taller!"

When Kristie integrated a male protector part, she reported, "This sounds silly, but it felt as if my arms got bigger and stronger!" Adam, too, thought sure he had gotten taller. Whatever occurs inside during integration, there seem to be perceptible physical or sensational differences for the child who is experiencing it. We know from some initial research that certain changes do occur in the brain following integration (Braun, 1983). Just *how* it occurs neurophysiologically may be a mystery for some time to come.

With a little time to get used to the fusion, children report noticing other interesting changes in themselves. After integrating two parts into herself, Kristie noted, "It's been easier to think." She found herself thinking more about how her behavior affected others; she was also less willing to put up with negligent or mean behavior from friends. The empathy and assertiveness were traits that had previously been stored in those two parts.

The last one of April's parts to integrate had been my co-therapist all along and had periodically played quite a prominent role in April's life, much as "dominant" personalities do for adult clients. Just before she completed the final fusion of this last remaining separate personality, April and "Carol" wrote about what it was like inside with all the changes happening.

"Being a multiple is hard. I always felt different. It feels like everyone else can tell I'm a multiple because I'm different. One minute I'd act all happy, and another minute be mad, and I'd worry that people could see the changes. But after a while I realized most people can't really tell. Now that I only have one part left, I'm looking forward to not being a multiple because I'll feel normal—I won't feel like I stick out. I also like integrating because it's much quieter inside, and you don't have all those noises and voices going on!"—April, age 13

"I'm the last one of April's parts. I'm lonely in here, but at the same time it's peaceful. I'm scared and happy because I'm going to be the one to finish being a multiple. I'm worried about what it'll be like for April when there's nobody inside except her, but she says she'll be OK. It's not like we're leaving forever—we'll still be a part of her. It's very hard to be a multiple, but after you integrate you'll have a lot to look forward to."—Carol, age 11

After the final fusion takes place, more changes are noticeable. Adam's mother stated that "right away he seemed less unpredictable, calmer. As each day goes by, he becomes more and more solidly whole, and all the once well-defined behaviors blend together and are no longer so distinct." The children themselves comment that they definitely feel better in some ways. April noted, "I get to be me—I get to do what I want to do." Kristie stated that she had much more energy and found it easier to focus on tasks and to get things done. So there is an increased sense of control over one's life that was lacking before. In both girls, previously the essence personality was depleted of energy and pizzazz—the "juiciness" had been relegated to dissociated parts, while the child was kept busy holding scary feelings and memories at arm's length. When she was reunited with "herself" and the inner barriers were removed, the life energy was free to flow into the child.

Adam summed up the child's experience of the integration process:

Integration
Warm, tiring, exciting, scary, energetic, wonderful, happy,
sad, curious, strange, good, sleepy, odd, different, depressing,
THE GREATEST THING THAT'S HAPPENING TO ME!

POST-INTEGRATION ISSUES

Children who have few dissociated parts to begin with, or who are able to dissolve dissociative barriers while they are still quite young, may have few problems afterward. With many latency years ahead of them, children may have time to develop social skills and learn earlier concepts they may have missed due to dissociation. Those with few split-off parts may have developed more aspects of their personality as well; following integration of the few dissociated parts, these children or teens may find life more manageable and feelings easier to handle right from the start. However, children who have many personalities or fragments, and/or who are in puberty or teen years by the time they integrate, may expect some rocky times ahead.

For the child who has been living with a fractured self for many years prior to integration, being whole will seem unfamiliar at first, even though he or she has looked forward to it eagerly. The child may be uncomfortable with all the feelings she now experiences.

This may be true especially if integration was rapid or done early in treatment, as opposed to fusing personalities gradually and over an extended period of time to allow the child to "grow into" the feelings. This doesn't mean that the latter is the best treatment method, however. Some children are able and ready to integrate early in therapy and would rather deal with the feelings afterward. Adam, for instance, had lots and lots of different feelings following completion of integration. He had wanted to finish integrating all his parts quickly before he entered junior high school. This agenda required that he continue his work on becoming more comfortable having and expressing his feelings *after* integration.

The integrated child may still have some processing of old memories and feelings to do. Old needs that were unmet when the child was younger will still be present after the child integrates. Now that the whole child can feel their force, those old needs seem bigger and stronger. Behaviors aimed at getting those needs met may increase. And if the needs can't be met right away in the child's current life situation, milder dissociative behaviors may appear to decrease the child's discomfort with those needy feelings.

What kind of behaviors may show up? We might expect the same kind of dissociative behaviors that non-DID children show to avoid feeling difficult feelings or letting in painful awareness. About the time April finished integrating her parts, she had to move temporarily to a new home with different caregivers. As the stability in her life plummeted, she did not split again or create new parts, but she did dissociate hurt feelings, which resulted in several episodes of acting-out behaviors.

It may be that if a DID child is puberty age by the time she integrates (and if she also had several personalities), the sense of newness that integration brings, combined with the stresses of life, may be difficult to cope with for a while. Using some dissociation as a defense would be natural for such a child. The adolescent who integrates is faced with several challenges besides her own "newness." She is trying to be a teenager, to cope with hormones coursing through her body, to figure out developmentally "who she is" in relation to everybody else she knows, to fit in and be accepted. Besides coping with new anxieties about daily life, she is trying to deal with old memories that may creep into her mind, to fill up old needs for trust, love, acceptance, and nurturing, while she also works around the clock to sketch in lost developmental skills such as taking risks, making friends and balancing a daily schedule. That's a pretty tall order!

Puberty is a full-time task for normal teens who have already had eleven or twelve years to get ready; for a child who has only recently put himself together, the task can be a bit overwhelming. I would expect that many older children and teens who integrate fall back on dissociation as the defense with which they are most familiar and comfortable. *This does not mean they will create new parts*—but they may disown their intense feelings or resort to some problem behaviors to mask those feelings from themselves and others (see Chapter Four).

Working with Caregivers
In some ways, parents now have a brand-new child; it helps to put it just this way for them. Parents may find themselves feeling ambivalent in some cases about their new child. They may miss some of the younger personalities who were so cute, or the uncomplicated simplicity of the loving, affectionate parts. This new child is more complex, a mixture of feelings and behaviors, rather than a sequence of different "children." Parents may have some adjusting to do. And they will find that their child has *lots* of adjusting to do. Caregivers need to be told that integration will not be the panacea for all the child's problems. They will continue to see some old problems, perhaps expressed in slightly different ways, and they will see some new problems.

Parents need to know that the child may revert to milder forms of dissociation to cope with the newness of feelings, with stresses in the family, and with various developmental problems. As the child begins to work on developmental skills she may have missed earlier, some of her emotional needs may still seem rather big for a child that age. The integrated child once coped with all those old needs by dissociating them into separate parts; now those wants, needs, and feelings may loom up with great intensity. Sometimes the child may relegate them to the unconscious and play them out in problem behaviors; sometimes the child may express them in direct confrontations with parents. Caregivers can learn to expect some testing.

The post-integration child may also need to relearn things she used to be able to do as a "part" of herself. As a multiple the child may have made friends easily; now she has to discover how to make friends for herself. For some newly integrated children, making friends may be especially difficult. Because having peer friendships is so important developmentally for older children and teens, this skill is crucial. Parents may have to help, even to the point of *requiring* that the child spend some time with peers. Other children go to the other extreme and take care of peers too much or engage in hazardous relationships. These are issues that the child can work through in therapy if needed.

Previously, the child may have switched into a compliant part to get her chores and her homework done; now she may have fears about her abilities. Or she may show new feelings of rebellion: "Hey, I want to do what I want, now that I can!" Parents must not expect their "new" child to be able to function in a completely age-appropriate manner, as if he or she had never been multiple; children require time to grow into their new abilities and roles in the world. These are the challenges they once let other personalities manage. The post-integration child needs to hear that she can take her time learning to do things, and that parents will help.

With the child who occasionally uses dissociative behaviors of lying or stealing, the parent can be reassured that this too will pass, if they can continue to help the child increase awareness and expression of needs. The newly integrated child needs lots of mirroring that she is lovable, acceptable, and valued. With the child who gets stuck awhile in expressing negativity or neediness, the parent must doggedly maintain active listening and consistent limits for behavior (see Chapter Four). Sometimes the parent may perceive this child, with needs typical of a younger child, as "childish," but this must be reframed. The integrated child has to process her feelings, her experiences, and her pain in her own time.

Many of the new problems caregivers encounter will be those that most parents have with developing children in a developing family. The problems the therapist sees after integration may be more typical of those encountered with other families in therapy, including discipline and delegation of family tasks (Fagan & McMahon, 1984).

POST-INTEGRATION THERAPY

Children continue after integration to learn how to have and express feelings, to ask for what they want, to protect themselves and be protected, and to comfort and care for themselves as they grow up. Gradually, they replace dissociation with empowerment and self-nurturing.

Dealing with Feelings and Needs

In order to give up dissociation at an unhealthy level, even after integration, the child must have a safe, nurturing environment, and she must be empowered gradually to take care of her own needs as she grows older. Empowerment includes equipping the child to have and express feelings, to ask for what she wants and needs. It also means that the child learns to allow herself to become aware of new dangers and to protect herself from them. She must discover that dissociation no longer protects her from danger; rather, it lets her fall back into it.

Children who have had to use dissociation in order to survive trauma have often learned to either discount or overreact to signals from the physiological "early warning system" we all come with at birth. Feelings of anxiety and fear are meant to be attended to in order to mobilize the organism to protect itself. Conscious validation of internal feeling signals of anxiety, discomfort, or danger is the first step toward self-protection. Increasing cognitive skills helps with decision-making (see next section). The child can role play with the therapist various ways to respond to situations that arouse her discomfort, situations such as confrontation with adults, pressure from peers, and unwanted sexual advances.

Once integration is secure, the child can begin to find out what she wants for herself, from food to fun to friends. Knowing what you want comes before asking for it. The integrated DID child has already been acquainted with her protector parts, which were often parts that were able to be angry. Sad, scared, and angry parts contained clues to things the child needed. The therapist can ask the child, "What do you think _____ part would have done to help you get this need met?" or "What would she have tried in that situation?" The integrated DID child can come to view her previous experiences with parts as a continuing resource for ideas and behavioral options.

Integration doesn't erase the old needs that didn't get met during times of trauma, loss, or abuse. Hearing "no" from friends or caregivers when the child wants something now may be especially disappointing for the newly integrated child. Anger, disappointment, and hurt may feel especially intense in the first several months after integration, before the child has found new ways to store or express such feelings, now that she is no longer dissociating them into personalities.

For this child, many experiences, although they are not new, will *seem* new. Just because her parts were able to be angry or sad or silly with peers doesn't mean that after integration the child herself is instantly able to be so. To the child, it's as if it wasn't "me" having those feelings before but such-and-such a personality. So doing it *herself* feels new and risky. She may need to talk about feelings again as herself, and to experiment with behavioral ways to express them, especially anger.

Most likely, the integrated child will continue to use some milder forms of dissociation to lower the intensity of certain difficult feelings for a while. She needs time to get used to them and to try out ways of having them. Over time, and in a safe and accepting home environment, dissociative behaviors will decrease as the child learns to allow herself to feel anxious or angry and learns ways to express feelings directly or to take care of herself so that she feels safe. Then she is able to move on.

Much of post-integration work involves self-nurturing. The child has learned (hopefully) something about nurturing from caring adults in her life and from becoming acquainted with her parts as self-protectors. After integration she can learn ways to nurture and take care of herself consciously so that she doesn't leave herself feeling uncomfortable, angry, or scared.

After integration Adam was worried about his anger, saying that when he felt angry he wanted to break something. I asked him to draw a picture of his anger. Adam drew a container shaped like a bottle inside a picture of his chest. He said, "It's full of old anger along with new anger, and it needs to break itself." We made a list of things Adam does sometimes when he is angry. These included: "I squeeze my hand tight; I yell; sometimes I break things; listen to loud music; lay on my bed; go outside." We talked about which of those things felt good, and which of those behaviors he felt good about after doing them. Next we made a list of things that used to make him angry, things that he was still mad about, and things that made him angry now. It came out that Adam sometimes didn't feel loved when others were angry with him, which affected how he felt about his own anger. We talked about being able to be angry and being loved and lovable at the same time.

Then Adam was ready to try an experiment. He chose one item from his list of things he was still angry about from the past. He drew a picture about the person he was angry with, and wrote out all his angry thoughts and feelings. He read his angry thoughts and feelings out loud to the picture, then tore it up and put it in a bottle I had provided. We wrapped the bottle in several layers of newspaper and took it outside; Adam hit it with a hammer and stomped on it. He said that he felt a great sense of relief and that he was "breaking up" some of the anger he held inside. He redrew the picture of the bottle in his chest—this time with less anger in it. Following this exercise, Adam decided he didn't need to do it again—he was learning to express and dissipate the inside feelings in other ways at home.

Building Cognitive Skills

Post-DID children may also benefit from cognitive work. Some chronically traumatized children have learned to short-circuit their reasoning as well as their feelings, and have conditioned themselves to react to the demand characteristics of a situation. This kind of conditioning has taught them to rely on dissociative behaviors or inner responses that sidestep awareness temporarily, but which lead to more discomfort, danger, or regrets later. So integrated children need to learn to sort out what they think as well as how they feel about current life situations and problems.

Planning, role-playing, or drawing responses for various problem situations can be helpful. Children also learn problem solving by questions that help them focus cognitively: When that happened, what did you say to yourself inside your head? How did you feel? So when so-and-so did X, what did that mean to you? And what did you do? How did you feel about doing it? The child can plan how she would like to respond in a similar situation next time, and practice her plan.

Cognitive skills also include positive self-talk. Parents can help by liberally doling out affirmations as often as they do requirements for responsibility. Newly integrated children especially need to learn such nurturing self-statements as: "I can take my time deciding what to do," "I don't have to know right this minute," "I can ask for help if I need it," "I can make a good decision," "If it doesn't work out, I'll try something different next time," and "I did good! Nice going!" Journaling and letters to oneself are ways to practice these.

Planning and organizing time may also be difficult at first for the integrated child. Success in junior high or high school may require the focused attention of both the child and helping adults on developing a daily schedule and a "plan of attack" for obtaining and completing homework assignments. The newly integrated child may find the task of overseeing her many life functions a bit overwhelming at first. After all, these various roles and jobs used to be compartmentalized and accomplished by dissociated parts. The child is now learning not only to conceptualize herself *internally* in a newly organized way, but also to organize and conceptualize her *outer* world. As the one task progresses and becomes easier, so will the other.

When things are going better at home and school, a break from treatment lets the child consolidate his learnings. But it is important to plan for follow-ups and be available for check-ins at later developmental stages, just as you would for non-DID children who have been in treatment for trauma (James, 1989). It may also be wise to schedule periodic check-ins to make sure that no dissociated personalities or fragments were missed in the treatment process (Dell & Eisenhower, 1990; Kluft, 1985a, c).

Integration, while not the very end of the child's journey to wholeness, is a big milestone. For the child, the experience is healing in and of itself, and allows for more and more healing and wholeness as the child grows older. For those of us who are privileged to be a part of that experience, integration is a touching affirmation of the child's spirit, of the will to exist and to be fully human.

Appendix

RESOURCES

Believe the Children
P.O. Box 797
Cary, IL 60013
(708) 515-5432 (Staff will return messages left on this voice-mail number.)
Offers information on ritual abuse, resource listings, newsletters for members, and conferences.

International Society for the Study of Dissociation
5700 Old Orchard Road, First Floor
Skokie, IL 60077-1057
(708) 966-4322
Members receive quarterly newsletters and journals; offers local chapter meetings for interested professionals.

Office for Victims of Crime
633 Indiana Av., N.W.
Washington, D.C. 20531
(202) 514-6444
Information on state offices for victim compensation and assistance.

Mothers Against Sexual Abuse (MASA)
Claire Reeves, President/Founder
503 1/2 S. Myrtle Avenue, Suite 4
Monrovia, CA 91016
(818) 305-1986
Offers support for non-offending parents of sexually abused children and a referral network of legal, medical and psychological professionals who specialize in child sexual abuse.

REFERENCES

Albini, T., & Pease, T. (1989). Normal and pathological dissociations of early childhood. *Dissociation, 2* (3), 144–150.

American Psychiatric Association (1994). *Diagnostic and statistical manual of mental disorders (Fourth edition)*. Washington, DC: Author.

Bornstein, B. (1946). Hysterical twilight states in an eight-year-old child. *Psychoanalytic Study of the Child, 2,* 229–240.

Bower, G. (1981). Mood and memory. *American Psychologist, 36* (2), 129–148.

Bowlby, J. (1969). *Attachment and loss.* New York: Basic Books.

Bowman, E., Blix, S., & Coons, P. (1985). Multiple personality in adolescence: Relationship to incestual experiences. *Journal of the American Academy of Child Psychiatry, 24* (1), 109–114.

Braun, B. (1983). Neurophysiologic changes in multiple personality due to integration: A preliminary report. *American Journal of Clinical Hypnosis, 26* (2), 84–92.

Braun, B. (1984). Towards a theory of multiple personality and other dissociative phenomena. In B. Braun (Ed.), *Symposium on Multiple Personality. Psychiatric Clinics of North America, 7,* 171–194.

Braun, B. (1985). The transgenerational incidence of dissociation and multiple personality disorder: A preliminary report. In R. Kluft (Ed.), *Childhood antecedents of multiple personality* (pp. 127–150). Washington, DC: American Psychiatric Press.

Braun, B. (1986). Issues in the psychotherapy of multiple personality disorder. In B. Braun (Ed.), *Treatment of multiple personality disorder* (pp. 1–28). Washington, DC: American Psychiatric Press.

Braun, B. (1988). The BASK model of dissociation. *Dissociation, 1* (1), 4–23.

Braun, B., & Sachs, R. (1985). The development of multiple personality disorder: Predisposing, precipitating, and perpetuating factors. In R. Kluft (Ed.), *Childhood antecedents of multiple personality* (pp. 37–64). Washington, DC: American Psychiatric Press.

Brick, S., & Chu, J. (1991). The simulation of multiple personalities: A case report. *Psychotherapy, 28* (2), 267–272.

Briggs, D. (1970). *Your child's self-esteem: The key to life.* Garden City, NY: Doubleday.

Bryant, D., Kessler, J., & Shirar, L. (1992). *The family inside: Working with the multiple.* New York: Norton.

Burgess, A., Hartman, C., & McCormack, A. (1987). Abused to abuser: Antecedents of socially deviant behaviors. *American Journal of Psychiatry, 144* (11), 1431–1436.

Burgess, A., & Hartman, C. (1993). Children's Drawings. *Child Abuse & Neglect, 17,* 161–168.

Burns, R. (1982). *Self-growth in families: Kinetic family drawings (K-F-D), research and application.* New York: Brunner/Mazel.

Burns, R., & Kaufman, S. (1972). *Actions, styles and symbols in kinetic family drawings (K-F-D).* New York: Brunner/Mazel.

Carroll, L. (1960). *The annotated alice: Alice's adventures in wonderland & through the looking glass.* New York: Clarkson N. Potter.

Coons, P. (1985). Children of parents with multiple personality disorder. In R. Kluft (Ed.), *Childhood antecedents of multiple personality* (pp. 151–166). Washington, DC: American Psychiatric Press.

Deblinger, E., McLeer, S., Atkins, M., Ralphe, D., & Foa, E. (1989). Post-traumatic stress in sexually abused, physically abused, and non-abused children. *Child Abuse & Neglect, 13,* 403–408.

Dell, P., & Eisenhower, J. (1990). Adolescent multiple personality disorder: A preliminary study of eleven cases. *Journal of the American Adademy of Child & Adolescent Psychiatry, 29* (3), 359–366.

Dinkmeyer, D., & McKay, G. (1989). *The parent's handbook: (STEP) Systematic training for effective parenting.* Circle Pines, MN: American Guidance Service.

Donovan, D., & McIntyre, D. (1990). *Healing the hurt child: A developmental-contextual approach.* New York: Norton.

Elliott, D. (1982). State intervention and childhood multiple personality disorder. *Journal of Psychiatry and Law, 10,* 441–456.

Erikson, E. (1950). *Childhood and society.* New York: Norton.

Evers-Szostak, M., & Sanders, S. (1992). The Children's Perceptual Alteration Scale (CPAS): A measure of children's dissociation. *Dissociation, 5* (2), 91–97.

Fagan, J., & McMahon, P. (1984). Incipient multiple personality in children. *Journal of Nervous and Mental Disease, 172* (1), 26–36.

Franklin, J. (1990). Dreamlike thought and dream mode processes in the formation of personalities in MPD. *Dissociation, 3* (2), 70–80.

Gardner, G. (1977). Hypnosis with infants and preschool children. *American Journal of Clinical Hypnosis, 19* (3), 158–162.

Gardner, R. (1977). Mutual storytelling with a compulsive boy. In C. Shaefer & H. Millman (Eds.), *Therapies for children: A handbook of effective treatments for problem behaviors* (pp. 38–40). San Francisco: Jossey-Bass.

Gil, E. (1990). *United we stand: A book for people with multiple personalities*. Walnut Creek, CA: Launch Press.

Gil, E. (1991). *The healing power of play: Working with abused children*. New York: Guilford.

Ginot, H. (1965). *Between parent and child: New solutions to old problems*. New York: Avon Books.

Golston, J. (1992). Ritual abuse: Raising hell in psychotherapy. *Treating Abuse Today, 2* (4), 4–12.

Goodwin, J. (1985). Credibility problems in multiple personality disorder patients and abused children. In R. Kluft (Ed.), *Childhood antecedents of multiple personality* (pp. 1–20). Washington, DC: American Psychiatric Press.

Gordon, T. (1970). *Parent effectiveness training*. New York: P. W. Wyden.

Gould, C. (1992). Diagnosis and treatment of ritually abused children. In D. Sakheim & S. Devine (Eds.), *Out of darkness: Exploring satanism and ritual abuse* (pp. 207–248). New York: Lexington Books.

Gould, C., & Graham-Costain, V. (1994a). Play therapy with ritually abused chidren, Part I. *Treating Abuse Today, 4* (2), 4–10.

Gould, C., & Graham-Costain, V. (1994b). Play therapy with ritually abused childen, Part II. *Treating Abuse Today, 4* (3), 14–19.

Gruenewald, D. (1971). Hypnotic techniques without hypnosis in the treatment of dual personality: A case report. *Journal of Nervous and Mental Disease, 153* (1), 41–46.

Heffron, W., Martin, C., Welsh, R., Perry, P., & Moore, C. (1987). Hyperactivity and child abuse. *Canadian Journal of Psychiatry, 32*, 384–386.

Herman, J. (1992). *Trauma and recovery*. New York: Basic Books.

Hicks, R. (1985). Discussion: A clinician's perspective. In R. Kluft (Ed.), *Childhood antecedents of multiple personality* (pp. 239–258). Washington, DC: American Psychiatric Press.

Hilgard, E. (1986). *Divided consciousness: Multiple controls in human thought and action*. New York: Wiley.

Hollingsworth, J. (1986). *Unspeakable acts*. New York: Congdon & Weed.

Hornstein, N. (Speaker). (1994). *Dissociative disorders in children and adolescents* (Cassette Recording No. 17-929-94A,B). Alexandria, VA: Audio Transcripts Ltd.

Hornstein, N., & Tyson, S. (1991). Inpatient treatment of children with multiple personality/dissociative disorders and their families. *Psychiatric Clinics of North America, 14* (3), 631–648.

Hudson, P. (1991). *Ritual child abuse: Discovery, diagnosis and treatment*. Saratoga, CA: R & E Publishers.

Izard, C., & Malatesta, C. (1987). Perspectives on emotional development I: Differential emotions theory of early emotional development. In J. Osofsky (Ed.), *Handbook of infant development (2nd ed.)*. New York: Wiley.

James, B. (1989). *Treating traumatized children: New insights and creative interventions.* Lexington, MA: Lexington Books.

James, B. (1994). *Handbook for treatment of attachment-trauma problems in children.* New York: Lexington Books.

Jolles, I. (1971). *A catalog for the qualitative interpretation of the house-tree-person (H-T-P).* Los Angeles: Western Psychological Services.

Kahaner, L. (1988). *Cults that kill: Probing the underworld of occult crime.* New York: Warner Books.

Kluft, R. (1982). Varieties of hypnotic interventions in the treatment of multiple personality. *American Journal of Clinical Hypnosis, 24* (4), 230–240.

Kluft, R. (1984). Multiple personality in childhood. *Psychiatric Clinics of North America, 7,* 121–134.

Kluft, R. (1985a). Childhood multiple personality disorder: Predictors, clinical findings, and treatment results. In R. Kluft (Ed.), *Childhood antecedents of multiple personality* (pp. 167–196). Washington, DC: American Psychiatric Press.

Kluft, R. (1985b). The natural history of multiple personality disorder. In R. Kluft (Ed.), *Childhood antecedents of multiple personality* (pp. 197–238). Washington, DC: American Psychiatric Press.

Kluft, R. (1985c). Hypnotherapy of childhood multiple personality disorder. *American Journal of Clinical Hypnosis, 27* (4), 201–210.

Kluft, R. (1986). Treating children who have multiple personality disorder. In B. Braun (Ed.), *Treatment of multiple personality disorder* (pp. 79–105). Washington, DC: American Psychiatric Press.

Langone, M. (1993). *Recovery from cults.* New York: Norton.

LaPorta, L. (1992). Childhood trauma and multiple personality disorder: The case of a nine-year-old girl. *Child Abuse & Neglect, 16,* 615–620.

Lewis, D. (1991). Multiple personality. In M. Lewis (Ed.), *Child and adolescent psychiatry: A comprehensive textbook* (pp. 707–715). Baltimore, MD: Williams & Wilkins.

Los Angeles County Commission for Women (1991). *Ritual abuse: Definitions, glossary, the use of mind control.* Report of the Ritual Abuse Task Force.

Ludwig, A. (1983). The psychobiological functions of dissociation. *American Journal of Clinical Hypnosis, 26* (2), 93–99.

Malenbaum, R., & Russell, A. (1987). Multiple personality disorder in an 11-year-old boy and his mother. *Journal of the American Academy of Child and Adolescent Psychiatry, 26* (3), 436–439.

Malinosky-Rummell, R., & Hoier, T. (1991). Validating measures of dissociation in sexually abused and nonabused children. *Behavioral Assessment, 13,* 341–357.

McElroy, L. (1992). Early indicators of pathological dissociation in sexually abused children. *Child Abuse & Neglect, 16,* 833–846.

Miller, A. (1981). *The drama of the gifted child: The search for the true self.* New York: Basic Books.

Mills, J., & Crowley, R., with Ryan, M. (1986). *Therapeutic metaphors for children and the child within*. New York: Brunner/Mazel.

Monahon, C. (1993). *Children and trauma: A parent's guide to helping children heal*. New York: Lexington Books.

Nathanson, D. (1992). *Shame and pride: Affect, sex, and the birth of the self*. New York: Norton.

Neswald, D., with Gould, C., & Graham-Costain, V. (1991, Sep/Oct). Common "programs" observed in survivors of satanic ritualistic abuse. *The California Therapist*, 47–50.

Oaklander, V. (1988). *Windows to our children: A Gestalt therapy approach to children and adolescents*. Highland, NY: The Gestalt Journal Press.

O'Regan, B. (Ed.). (1985). *Investigations, 1* (3/4), 1–23.

Perls, F. (1971). Four lectures. In J. Fagan & I. Shepherd (Eds.), *Gestalt therapy now*. New York: Harper & Row.

Peterson, G. (1990). Diagnosis of childhood multiple personality disorder. *Dissociation, 3* (1), 3–9.

Piaget, J. (1963). *The child's conception of the world* (J. and A. Tomlinson, Trans.). Paterson, NJ: Littlefield, Adams & Co. (Original work published 1923).

Pruyser, P. (1981). *The psychological examination: A guide for clinicians*. New York: International Universities Press.

Putnam, F. (1985). Dissociation as a response to extreme trauma. In R. Kluft (Ed.), *Childhood antecedents of multiple personality* (pp. 65–97). Washington, DC: American Psychiatric Press.

Putnam, F. (1989). *Diagnosis and treatment of multiple personality disorder*. New York: Guilford.

Putnam, F. (1991a). Dissociative disorders in children and adolescents: A developmental perspective. *Psychiatric Clinics of North America, 14* (3), 519–531.

Putnam, F. (1991b). Dissociative phenomena. In A. Tasman & S. Goldfinger (Eds.), *Review of psychiatry* (Vol. 10, pp. 145–160). Washington, DC: American Psychiatric Press.

Putnam, F. (1993). Dissociative disorders in children: Behavioral profiles and problems. *Child Abuse & Neglect, 17*, 39–45.

Putnam, F., Guroff, J., Silberman, E., Barban, L., & Post, R. (1986). The clinical phenomenology of multiple personality disorder: Review of 100 recent cases. *Journal of Clinical Psychiatry, 47*, 285–293.

Reagor, P., Kasten, J., & Morelli, N. (1992). A checklist for screening dissociative disorders in chiden and adolescents. *Dissociation, 5* (1), 4–19.

Rila, B. (Speaker). (1992). *Real moms and dads: Promoting attachment in foster care and adoption*. (Cassette recording of presentation to San Luis Obispo County Dept. of Social Services, San Luis Obispo, CA).

Ross, C. (1991). Epidemiology of multiple personality disorder and dissociation. *Psychiatric Clinics of North America, 14* (3), 503–517.

Ross, C. (1992). Childhood sexual abuse and psychobiology. *Journal of Child Sexual Abuse, 1* (2), 95–102.

Ross, C., & Anderson, G. (1988). Phenomenological overlap of multiple personality disorder and obsessive-compulsive disorder. *Journal of Nervous and Mental Disease, 176,* 295–299.

Ross, C., Anderson, G., Fraser, G., Reagor, P., Bjornson, L., & Miller, S. (1992). Differentiating multiple personality disorder and dissociative disorder not otherwise specified. *Dissociation, 5* (2), 87–90.

Ross, C., & Clark, P. (1992). Assessment of childhood trauma and dissociation in an emergency department. *Dissociation, 5* (3), 163–165.

Ross, C., Ryan, L., Anderson, G., Ross, D., & Hardy, L. (1989). Dissociative experiences in adolescents and college students. *Dissociation, 2* (4), 239–242.

Sachs, R. (1986). The adjunctive role of social support systems in the treatment of multiple personality disorder. In B. Braun (Ed.), *Treatment of multiple personality disorder* (pp. 157–174). Washington, DC: American Psychiatric Press.

Sanders, B., & Giolas, M. (1991). Dissociation and childhood trauma in psychologically disturbed adolescents. *American Journal of Psychiatry, 148* (1), 50–54.

Sanford, D. (1990). *Don't make me go back, mommy.* Portland, OR: Multnomah Press.

Satir, V. (1983). *Conjoint family therapy (3d ed.).* Palo Alto, CA: Science and Behavior Books.

Satir, V. (1988). *The new peoplemaking.* Mountain View, CA: Science and Behavior Books.

Smith, M. (1993). *Ritual abuse: What it is, why it happens, how to help.* New York: HarperCollins.

Smith, M., & Pazder, L. (1980). *Michelle remembers.* New York: Congdon & Lattes.

Spencer, J. (1989). *Suffer the child.* New York: Pocket Books.

Spiegel, D. (1986). Dissociation, double binds, and posttraumatic stress in multiple personality disorder. In B. Braun (Ed.), *Treatment of multiple personality disorder* (pp. 61–78). Washington, DC: American Psychiatric Press.

Spiegel, D. (1991). Dissociation and trauma. In A. Tasman & S. Goldfinger (Eds.), *Review of psychiatry* (Vol. 10, pp. 261–275). Washington, DC: American Psychiatric Press.

Summit, R. (1983). The child sexual abuse accommodation syndrome. *Child Abuse & Neglect, 7,* 177–193.

Terr, L. (1989). Treating psychic trauma in children: A preliminary discussion. *Journal of Traumatic Stress, 2* (1), 3–20.

Terr, L. (1990). *Too scared to cry: Psychic trauma in childhood.* New York: Harper & Row.

Terr, L. (1991). Childhood traumas: An outline and overview. *American Journal of Psychiatry, 148* (1), 10–20.

Terr, L. (1994). *Unchained memories: True stories of traumatic memories, lost and found.* New York: Basic Books.

Torem, M. (1990). Covert multiple personality underlying eating disorders. *American Journal of Psychotherapy, 44* (3), 357–368.

Tyson, G. (1992). Childhood MPD/dissociative identity disorder: Applying and extending current diagnositic checklists. *Dissociation, 5* (1), 20–27.

van der Kolk, B. (1988). The trauma spectrum: The interaction of biological and social events in the genesis of the trauma response. *Journal of Traumatic Stress, 1* (3), 273–290.

van der Kolk, B. (1994). The body keeps the score: Memory and the evolving psychobiology of posttraumatic stress. *Harvard Review of Psychiatry, 1* (5), 253–265.

van der Kolk, B., & Greenberg, M. (1987). The psychobiology of the trauma response: Hyperarousal, constriction, and addiction to traumatic reexposure. In B. van der Kolk (Ed.), *Psychological trauma.* Washington, DC: American Psychiatric Press.

van der Kolk, B., Perry, J., & Herman, J. (1991). Childhood origins of self-destructive behavior. *American Journal of Psychiatry, 148* (12), 1665–1671.

Weiss, M., Sutton, P., & Utecht, A. (1985). Multiple personality in a 10-year-old girl. *Journal of the American Academy of Child Psychiatry, 24* (4), 495–501.

Whitman, B., & Munkel, W. (1991). Multiple personality disorder: A risk indicator, diagnostic marker and psychiatric outcome for severe child abuse. *Clinical Pediatrics, 30* (7), 422–428.

Wilbur, C. (1985). The effect of child abuse on the psyche. In R. Kluft (Ed.), *Childhood antecedents of multiple personality* (pp. 21–35). Washington, DC: American Psychiatric Press.

Williams, L. M. (1992). Adult memories of childhood abuse: Preliminary findings from a longitudinal study. *The Advisor,* Summer, 19–21.

Wohl, A., & Kaufman, B. (1985). *Silent screams and hidden cries: An interpretation of artwork by children from violent homes.* New York: Brunner/Mazel.

Wolff, P. H. (1987). *The development of behavioral states and the expression of emotions in early infancy.* Chicago: University of Chicago Press.

Wolff, P. H. (1989, May). *The development of behavioral states: A dynamic perspective.* Paper presented at the annual meeting of the American Psychiatric Association, Los Angeles, CA.

Young, W., Sachs, R., Braun, B., & Watkins, R. (1991). Patients reporting ritual abuse in childhood: A clinical syndrome. Report of 37 cases. *Child Abuse & Neglect, 15,* 181–189.

INDEX